# *Love, Your Mother — Like it or not*

A Memoir
J. W. SUTHERLAND

Jim Sutherland, Publisher
Bellingham, Washington

Names of the individuals mentioned in *Love, Your Mother* have been changed to protect their privacy.

Library of Congress Control Number: 2011910841

ISBN: 978-0-692-01447-9

Cover Design by Kathleen Weisel: weiselcreative.com

Book Design and layout by Rod Burton: rcburton.com

Author may be contacted at:
loveyourmotherlikeitornot@ymail.com

Jim Sutherland, Publisher, Bellingham, Washington
Printed in the United States of America

*In memory of my brother, David*
*1944–2007*

# Prologue

David and I emerged from his modest house. I pushed the wheel-chair where my brother sat with a three-ring binder in his lap. We slowly crossed the wide lawn and headed toward the footpath at the edge of the grass. The path was one of several that gave access to the fourteen acres of southeastern Connecticut woods where he lived.

"Where would you like to go today?" I asked as I maneuvered the chair from the thick grass to the uneven dirt of the path.

"I don't know. As far as we can or until you get tired. Can you last until we get to the foundation?" answered David.

"What do you mean? You think I'm too feeble to make it that far?"

His remark annoyed me.

David turned in the chair and looked up. "No, but it might not be easy for someone your age to go that far," he said. Then he laughed, enjoying the jab he had thrown at me. We were both in our sixties. I was the elder brother by two and half years.

Luke, David's aging Australian Shepherd dog, ran ahead of us. He stayed on the path for a short distance before he dashed off to explore a movement off-road that caught his eye, and continued crisscrossing the path as he led the way into the woods. Periodically he stopped on the path, his head up and nose twitching. Luke sensed the presence of deer. If he were lucky, this meant a chase until David yelled at him to come back.

Three cats brought up the rear and kept their distance from the wheelchair. Like the dog, the cats did not travel in a straight line. They explored the edges of the path but they were quite content not to venture off. Every so often, the cats stopped abruptly and sat down on the path. Deciding the adventure was still worth their interest, they rose and continued to follow behind. The cats had followed David on walks like this one many times in the past. I had also accompanied my brother down this path before, but this was the first time behind a wheelchair.

The procession continued quietly, both of us caught up in our own thoughts. My gaze went back and forth between the pathway ahead and the back of David's head. I pushed the chair and tried to avoid the small rocks that jutted out of the hard ground. David had forgotten his hat again. Looking down at his baldness, I remembered how I had always envied my brother's shock of thick, dark brown hair. My own hair was very thin and mostly gone by the time I was 50.

How ironic, I thought. I have more hair than he has now.

The chemotherapy sessions had extracted a high price from David, and this included his beautiful hair.

Until I learned of David's cancer, we had lived most of our lives at opposite ends of the country. The family "fat genes" had by-passed my brother and he had always been thin. Now his body looked frail. All muscular definition was gone and he resembled a skeleton. I was not sure which was worse—the disease or the cure. David had aged to the point that he now looked older than I did.

David never complained about the treatments that made him nauseated and tired. He remained positive despite his illness. He was more concerned about Luke and the three cats than his own welfare. He had always been like that. Nothing had changed, even as he fought for his life.

We continued through the tall deciduous trees. The early morning sun in late April was very warm. Sunlight reflected off the young leaves of the mature trees and softened as it fell on the moss-covered rotted logs that lined the path. A pale green shower of brightness bathed the woods.

The air was quiet. We heard only the creaking of the wheelchair and the sound of birds. They sang as they flew unseen overhead from branch to branch.

We reached the small pond and the path changed from its straight line to a semi-circle that hugged the water's edge. On the bank, turtles basked on flat rocks and frogs lay in wait for bugs. At the sound of the wheelchair, the turtles and frogs hit the water like tossed pebbles. We heard many splashing sounds and we stopped to watch the rings spread and then vanish from the surface of the pond.

Our destination was the remains of a stone foundation, once the base of an eighteenth century colonial house. Not far from the foundation, what might be mistaken for a dry riverbed ran from north to south. Over the years a blanket of undergrowth and small trees had covered this gouge in the earth, but its shape and the size of the indentation were still visible. The riverbed was actually what remained of a forgotten road.

In the woods behind the foundation were fragments of the stone walls that once divided the now abandoned fields. Whatever house had stood on the foundation had disappeared. Trees, living and dead, and thick vegetation covered most of what had been a small farm over 200 years ago.

I suggested contacting the local historical society to see if they would be interested in excavating the house foundation. David had a fit. He was very protective of his land, especially from outsiders.

David insisted that nothing be disturbed. He would not even pull the weeds that grew in the flower garden near his house. "Leave them alone. They were here before anyone else." The few flowers he planted had to share their space with weeds most people would have pulled. I was annoyed whenever I saw the puny flowers struggling to survive amid the tall weeds. Why did he even bother?

But the land was his and he had lived there happily with the weeds and fallen trees for over 25 years. There was no point discussing it. David wouldn't listen anyway.

We reached the foundation and stopped at a large flat rock. I walked to the front of the wheelchair and set the brake, and offered David my arm. He slowly rose from the chair. David placed the binder on the seat and we walked to the flat rock.

Luke was far into the woods searching for the deer. The cats caught up with us and seeing that we were no longer moving stopped as well. They stretched out across the path, enjoying the warm sun in the way cats do. One cat batted at the buzzing insects flying low among the wild flowers growing near the path.

"I love coming out here. It's like another world where I can forget about chemo, radiation, the pills, and that wheelchair." His voice trailed off until he gathered the strength to continue.

"Sometimes I feel that if I sit here long enough, these woods will cure me. Owning this land is better than winning any lottery. I can come out anytime I want and no one bothers me. I've walked the woods every day for years. I know everyone thinks I'm crazy for living this far out in the country. I don't care. I love it here."

In the last six months, David had endured a series of doctors and radiation and chemo treatments at three different hospitals.

The worst part was waiting for the test results, then more waiting for the next treatment. At the same time, the woods lifted his spirits in a way that no treatment ever could.

David looked at me and said, "So you wrote a book about our mother."

"I wrote something. I hope it's a book."

"And no one knows about it except me?"

"Just you. I'll tell our sister later. I wanted you to be the first to know."

David repositioned himself to a shadier spot on the rock. "I'm surprised you did this. When did you have time? I didn't even know that you could write."

"I didn't know either," I said. I leaned back and stared up at the sky through the branches of the trees. "I'm not working any more, and what else do I have to do every day? If I'm not here, I'm home. Being retired has given me too much free time. I guess I needed something to keep me busy."

"Still, that's amazing stuff. My brother writing a book," he said in mocked amazement.

"I just started writing and somehow it took off and turned into a book. Does it bother you that I wrote about her?"

"No," he said laughing. "I think it's great. I just wonder what she would have said. I can hear her now: *What da hell you talking about, writin' my life story. You gotta be crazy! Who da hell wants to hear about an old lady?*"

"This is more than the story of her life. It's about me, and you and our sister. It's about a lot of things, stuff that I've thought about for the last 30 years."

David said nothing. Our mother had passed away eight years earlier.

"I'd like you to read it. That's why I brought you a copy. I really want your opinion."

"You know I don't like to read," he said. "Besides I don't have time. I want to know what you've written about her but I want you to read it to me. If it's about her, then it's going to be a great book. She certainly had an interesting life. Maybe your next book will be about me."

The last comment made us both laugh.

4

"I just thought you would enjoy reading it yourself when you are in a quiet mood."

David became annoyed. "Since you have so much time on your hands, why can't you read it to me? That way when I hear something I don't understand, you can explain it."

I saw no point of pressing the issue; David had a stubborn streak inherited from our mother. If he was ever going to know what I had written, I had little choice but to read it to him.

"Well, are you going to read your masterpiece or not?" David asked.

I got up from the rock, retrieved the binder from the wheelchair and opened it, and began to read.

# Chapter One

I turned 16 in the summer of 1958. David was fourteen. But at that time neither of us was aware of the other's existence. I lived with my father Hollis, my stepmother Ruth and my stepsister, Bev. Hollis had divorced my mother, Cecilia, eight years earlier. We lived in an unincorporated area of Arapahoe County in Colorado south of the Denver city limits. This wedge of land was known as College View because it was located in the eastern shadow of Loretto Heights College, then a private Catholic women's school. Despite its grand name, College View was a lower working class neighborhood. Most of its residents had never attended college.

The unpaved streets were lined with unassuming homes built in the 1920s and 1930s. Many had additions that didn't match the original architecture or paint color. Newer houses were scattered among the older homes and gave College View its rag tag appearance.

Despite being adjacent to wealthier suburban developments, College View maintained a rural flavor. Many people living there had large gardens and raised chickens, ducks, and goats. A working irrigation ditch ran across our backyard, a relic from a time when the area had been covered with truck farms.

Our house was close to the college grounds in the "nicer" end of the neighborhood. We could see the bell tower of Loretto Heights from our yard—a view not available to most residents. While our home was small, it was palatial compared to Depression era shacks still standing further east near the Platte River.

Of the three neighborhoods surrounding the college, ours was the poorest. The heavily trafficked Federal Boulevard separated College View from the neighborhoods of Harvey Park and Brentwood. Harvey Park with its brick ranch style homes sat to the west; Brentwood on the north was less affluent than Harvey Park, but further up the economic ladder than College View.

While Harvey Park had the biggest houses and spectacular outdoor decorations at Christmas, Brentwood boasted its own shopping center. There was no shopping center in College View and any outdoor Christmas decorations were meager. Brentwood's shopping center was newly opened and it was a fascinating place to go when I was 16. But each time I crossed Federal Boulevard, I became more conscience of my family's lower economic status.

Like most teenagers, I had an obsession about getting a driver's license before my birthday in June. That May I went to my father with a request.

"Dad, I'm going to turn 16 next month."

"Yeah, so?"

"Maybe you could teach me how to drive so I can get my license. Rich got his in March and Billy Norton's mom is teaching him."

"Rich's grandparents can afford to buy him a car and Billy's family has two cars. Why do you need a driver's license? You don't even have a car. You plan on buying one any time soon?"

Even though I had a part time job after school and during the summer, I did not earn enough to buy a car.

"Look, Jimmy, I've thought about you learning to drive. You're too young. Driving is an adult responsibility and it isn't cheap to run a car. There's gas and insurance, oil changes and tires, and batteries and stuff like that."

"I know. It's just that all the kids at school are learning to drive."

"I don't care what the kids at school are doing. As far as I can see, you don't need to be driving until 21. That's the way it is, so just drop it."

My father was approaching 60 and had a lot of out-dated ideas about raising children. There was no question that he was an honest and hard-working man. Most of the time he held down two jobs in order to provide his family with the modest means we needed. But he had always been distant. He was from a generation of men who had been raised not to be in touch with their feelings. Being a man meant keeping his emotional side in check at all times. Talking with my father was never easy. As a result we were never close and there is much about the man that I still don't know.

I retreated but I did not give up. I telephoned a local driving school. I had worked for two years at a neighborhood veterinary hospital as a kennel boy before and after school. During the summers, I worked full time bathing and grooming dogs. I earned a $1.00 an hour and had enough money stashed in a cigar box under my bed to pay for the driving lessons.

To avoid having my parents find out, the driving instructor picked me up at the animal hospital. She was an older woman, probably in her early thirties, with long flowing, bright red hair. I don't remember her name but I never forgot the car. At the appointed time and place, she drove up in a new 1958, red and white Chevy Impala convertible. The lessons began early that summer and continued once a week.

One day the instructor said I was ready to take the driving test. She set up an appointment with the Department of Motor Vehicles in Littleton so that I could take the test the next week. As I got out of the car on my last lesson, she told me to be sure to have my birth certificate in hand. I needed it to prove my age.

I asked my father about the certificate that night after dinner. His answer was short. He said, "You don't have one. It burned in a fire years ago," and went back to reading his newspaper.

My best friend, John Elgin, lived in the house across the street from ours. His family had moved from England a few years before and they operated a corner grocery store adjacent to their house. We went to the same high school, although John was two grades ahead of me. He knew about my pursuit of a driver's license. I rushed over to his house and told him of this latest crisis.

"You know, I don't remember our house ever catching fire," I said.

"Maybe it happened before your family moved to Colorado. Besides, you don't need a birth certificate to prove how old you are. A baptismal certificate is just as good. Write to the church where you were baptized and ask them to send you a copy."

"Are you sure you can do that?"

"Don't be daft. Of course you can." John being older was proud of his knowledge of the adult world, knowledge I did not have.

I did not want to arouse my father's suspicion by asking questions. He was not sentimental, and rarely talked of the past when I was very young. I had to rely on my memory of what he had said about the years we lived in Connecticut.

My father once mentioned the St. Phillip and St. James Episcopal Church, and that Reverend Cunningham had baptized me. "Now there was a good man, a very honest, salt of the earth kind of man." Reverend Cunningham and my father may have been good friends, but despite his high regard for the minister, I do not re-member my father ever going to church.

I took the city bus to the main library in Denver, and looked up the address of St. Phillip and St. James Episcopal Church in a Hartford telephone book. I returned home, wrote the letter with my request, and mailed it off. For days I kept a vigil for the mail. As soon as I saw the post office truck, I raced across the lawn to the mailbox that sat on a post in front of our house. I had to get the let-ter before my stepmother got her hands on it.

The letter finally arrived. I grabbed it, threw the rest of the day's mail on the kitchen table, and rushed downstairs to my bed-room. There was a cover letter from the church secretary and an official church copy of the baptismal certificate.

"In the Name of the Father, and of the Son and of the Holy Ghost, Amen" was printed across the top in bright red script. I was giddy as I held the thin piece of paper in my hand. I scanned the document and saw that it had the correct birth date and Manchester, Connecticut as place of birth. It went on to say "James Wiley Suther-land has been received into the congregation of Christ's flock by Holy Baptism on October 1, 1944." I was a little over two years old at the time. Reverend Cunningham had indeed officiated at the ceremony and signed the certificate. David and Marie Wiley were named as godparents. I had no idea who they were.

When my eyes reached the bottom lines of the document, I received the biggest shock in my 16-year-old life. On the line stat-ing the father of the child was typed "James J. Zaldonapolous." The spelling was so strange that I could not pronounce it.

Typed on the next line was the name of the mother of the child, "Frances Postiglione." The implication of the names being dif-ferent did not hit me immediately. Under the two stranger's names, someone had typed "Hollis and Cecilia Sutherland" followed with the words, "foster parents."

Once the shock wore off, I headed across the street to John's house, and showed him what his great idea had produced.

"I don't believe this. Who are these people?" I asked.

John's first idea was that I was adopted. "Maybe even better, what if your father stole you away from gypsies? Those names are certainly strange enough."

Then he said, "If these people are your parents and don't have the same last name, you must be illegitimate. You know what that means, don't you?" He drew close and in a whisper said, "You're a bastard."

Getting a driver's license lost its importance. I talked to the instructor and told her that I could not find my birth certificate, and promised to call when I did.

For the next few days I could only think about what I had read on the certificate. In the privacy of my bedroom, I retrieved the document from its hiding place and examined it again and again, hoping that I had misread the words, but they did not change.

I could not get the strange names out of my mind, and yet I knew that I was part of them. A very unwilling part, but still connected to them in a way that I did not want to think about. Was I really a bastard? I only knew that word as a profanity my father used when angry. I did not want to be associated with it and yet the word had attached itself to me.

I became quiet, withdrawn, and more sullen than usual around my father and stepmother. I spent more time at work and with my friends so I would not have to be around my parents. As the summer passed, my shock turned to shame until anger took its place. The strange names would not leave me alone. I tried hard to imagine who they were and what they were doing on my baptismal certificate, but no answers came to me. All I knew for sure was that my father had lied to me. He must have known these people, yet he had never mentioned them.

I was hurt and scared and I wanted my father to feel the same. I wanted to hit him as hard as those names had hit me. Slowly a plan took shape.

I waited until after dinner one night. He had gone into the living room with the evening *Denver Post* and his cigarettes. He settled down in his recliner to read. Once he was relaxed, I walked over to where he sat, said nothing, and dropped the certificate onto his newspaper. He glanced at the document and looked at me.

"Where did you get this?" he demanded.

I shouted at him, something I had never done. "Never mind where I got it. What does it mean?"

My stepmother rushed in from the kitchen but she stopped in the doorway and made no attempt to come into the room.

My father put out his cigarette and pushed the newspaper aside. He stood up and quietly said, "Let's go to your room. We need to talk." There was a troubled look on his face.

I shouted at him again, this time swearing. "Yes, you're god-damn right we need to talk."

We went to my bedroom. He sat at the desk and I sat on the bed. He looked at me for a long time before he spoke.

"Jimmy, where did you get this?"

When I started high school, I took a strong dislike to being called "Jimmy" and I announced to everyone that I was to be called "Jim." But as far as my father was concerned, I remained "Jimmy" until the day he died.

"It doesn't matter where I got it. Who are those people? Why does it say, 'foster parents?' Tell me."

"I don't know exactly what to say."

"Why don't you start with the truth?"

"It was a long time ago when we lived in Connecticut. One day I came home from work and you were there, a newborn baby. Cecilia told me that your mother was unable to care for you."

"Then Cecilia wasn't my mother?"

"No, she wasn't." My father sat with his head in his hands, looking down at the floor. "Your mother gave you to Cecilia and disappeared."

Hearing that my mother had handed me over to a stranger hurt.

"I never met her. She was someone that Cecilia knew. I don't know from where or how. Your mother told Cecilia when your birth-day was and that you were born in Manchester. That's all she told us."

He started talking about Cecilia. Until now, he had never mentioned her name after they had divorced when I was seven years old. He married my stepmother, Ruth, a few years later. Typi-cal of children in this situation, I was not especially fond of my stepmother or stepsister. Cecilia was a distant memory for me. Even though she had been gone for eight years I still considered her my mother. It was many years after she left before I could think about her without crying.

"I'm sorry I never told you all this before. I know I should have."

There was a long pause before he continued. He looked at the floor and not at me. I watched him intently. I had never seen him so sad.

"Cecilia was never able to have children of her own. About five years before you came to us, we had cared for a boy named Leslie. Like you, Leslie's mother could not take care of him. But we raised Leslie as our own son. We loved him very much.

"When Leslie was about three years old, his mother returned. She came to our door and said that she wanted her son back. Cecilia went to pieces and started screaming and saying terrible things. I came home in the middle of this and I made the woman leave our house immediately. But she came back the next day with two policemen. What could we do? Leslie was her son. We had no proof that she had given the baby to us. Cecilia would not give up the boy despite my pleading. She became hysterical and held him tightly. He screamed and clung to her, the only mother he had known. The policemen had to forcibly take Leslie from Cecilia's arms. It was terrible. Then they left. We never saw Leslie again. You can't believe the pain we both felt after he was gone.

"Cecilia started drinking and never stopped. It was hard to live with her. Booze was her only way to deal with the pain. Then you showed up and she was happy again. I thought that she would stop drinking if she had another baby. I didn't ask any questions. You were there and she was happy and that was all that mattered," he paused and looked at me.

"Eventually she went back to hitting the bottle. You were too little to know about her drinking. Sometimes I'd come home and you'd be asleep in your crib while Cecilia was passed out on the floor. Her drinking was the reason that I divorced her. We were married for 16 years and most of that time she was drunk. I couldn't stand it anymore, so I left.

"Of course, I felt guilty leaving you behind. I've always considered you my son. In the divorce, the court gave her custody because she was your mother. Despite her drinking, I know she loved you. I figured eventually she would not be able to take care of you and that you would become my responsibility again. And that's what happened."

The issue of my real parents was forgotten for a moment. I could not believe how open he had been discussing the past.

"Jimmy, I've raised you as my son and I'm sorry that you found out like this. I never thought there was any reason for you to know. I didn't want to hurt you. Maybe I made a mistake. Ruth always said that I should tell you about this stuff."

"Ruth knows you're not my father? How could you tell her and not tell me?" Whatever compassion I had for him quickly dissipated. I wondered if he really had told me everything he knew. For years he had withheld the truth from me. Why should I believe him now?

Memories of Cecilia rushed back as he talked. I hadn't thought about her after I recovered from the shock of her sudden disappearance. Much of what I did remember was incomplete. However, as he talked about her drinking, my memories changed from faded to vivid.

Shortly after arriving in Colorado in 1947, my father found work as foreman on a large spread called the Mountain View Ranch. The ranch was located on a ridge with a spectacular view of the front range of the Rocky Mountains. Mountain View was a real ranch with ranch hands, barns, horses, and a bunkhouse. However, the ranch hands did not wrangle cattle, they wrangled turkeys—thousands and thousands of turkeys. We lived in the cookhouse adjacent to the bunkhouse. The ranch hands would come to the large dining room for breakfast, lunch, and dinner, cooked by my mother, Cecilia.

After dinner the men retired to the bunkhouse to listen to the radio and get ready for work the next day. I remember how Cecilia spent her days cooking their meals on a woodstove. Early each morning I woke up to sounds of my father loading large chunks of wood into the stove and firing it up for the day's cooking.

When I was five years old and ready to start school, Cecilia told me I had to do well and be smart so that some day I would become a doctor. "Then you'll be able to make Mommy's sickness go away." I can remember how frightened I was of her when she became "sick." Children learn very quickly how to become invisible during the "sick" times. I was no exception.

As a child, I did not know the term "alcoholic." I only knew that she could suddenly become unpredictable and violent. When she was sober, she was a loving mother. I loved her but at times I was also afraid of her. Cecilia was a part of my life for a very short time and I have forgotten much about her, but not the frequent screaming arguments she had with my father.

Cecilia gained custody of me as a result of the divorce, but about six months later things changed. The last memory I have of her is late one afternoon when I was seven. She called me from outside and told me that I had to get dressed up. When she finished getting me ready, we left the motel where we were living and walked along the highway to a 24-hour truck stop café. Cecilia had worked at the café as a waitress after we had moved from the Mountain View Ranch. The job hadn't lasted long due to her drinking.

I carried the small suitcase she had packed and had no idea what was happening. She was very quiet as we walked and I knew that I should be quiet too. We went into the café and my future step-mother, Ruth, stood behind the cash register.

"Have you seen Hollis?" Cecilia asked.

"Not for awhile. He found work in Oregon and left a few weeks ago."

"When's he coming back?"

"I don't know for sure. He said the job could last six months."

"Are you sure? God, what am I going to do?"

"What's wrong, Cecilia?

Her voice broke and she began to speak very fast. "I can't care for Jimmy anymore and I don't know what to do. When he comes back, tell Hollis that he can have Jimmy. It's impossible for me. Things are falling to pieces. Nothing is working out. I can't explain it all right now. I'm really sorry but I don't know what else I can do. Ruth, please take care of Jimmy until Hollis returns. He's a good boy and I know he won't be any trouble. Just tell Hollis what I said. He can try to get a hold of me when he gets back but I don't know where I'll be by then."

I did not understand what was going on or why. Cecilia knelt down and I saw that she was crying. I got very scared and started to cry. She kissed me on the cheek and pushed back my hair. She told me to be good and not to give Ruth any trouble. She stood up, turned, and quickly walked out the café door.

I screamed and ran after her. Ruth came from behind the

counter and grabbed me to keep me from getting out the door. She tried to comfort me as I struggled to get away from her. She was a large woman and I was just a little kid. There was no way I could get back to my mother. I never saw Cecilia again.

Her drinking must have gotten worse. Whatever her problems were, they had become insurmountable in her own mind. She probably did not anticipate our parting would be so painful. Being left alone in the café with a woman I did not know was very frightening. Cecilia must have realized that the best she could do was to give me back to my father.

I have one snapshot of Cecilia. She is standing at the back door of the café. I recognize the face but not the pose. She is laughing and looks happy.

My father's story provided me with nothing new. His confirmation that my parents weren't married was not what I wanted to hear. I was emotionally drained when he left the room. I can't imagine how he must have felt.

The next day I told John what my father had said. While I was upset about the circumstances of my birth, I was also curious. John was far enough removed from my experience that he could look at it objectively. After all, he had two real parents. John saw my situation as a great mystery. He soon had a plan.

"First you need to get your birth certificate," he announced.

"What? Are you crazy? What for?"

"Listen to me. Do you want to get to the bottom of all this and find out who you really are? Or do you want to be a bushel basket baby the rest of your life?"

"I guess ..."

"Write to the hospital where you were born," he said. "Ask for a copy of your birth certificate. I bet there's only one hospital in Manchester."

"How is that going to help?"

"A birth certificate has lots of information, like the address of your parents and how old they were when you were born. Your mother and father's names are on the baptismal certificate. Write the letter and use the last name of the gypsy man on the baptismal certificate and your first name. I bet you'll get back a real birth certificate."

I wasn't sure if John's idea would work. What would I do with my birth certificate if I did manage to get it? I started to regret ever writing for the baptismal certificate in the first place.

But fired by John's enthusiasm for solving the mystery and my own curiosity, I wrote the letter. In a few weeks I received a copy of my birth certificate. It is hard to believe how easy it was in 1958 for me to get this document. I simply wrote a letter and requested it and didn't even use my real name.

When the document came in the mail, I showed it to John. My first name, James, was there but my last name was replaced with Zaldonapolous. The certificate stated that my mother had three previous births and listed her address at the time I was born. It gave my father's birthplace, her birthplace, and their ages: she was 29 and he was 30. It also gave the correct spelling of my mother's last name, and it was slightly different from how it appeared on the baptismal certificate.

John was sure that she was of Italian decent; the man's birthplace was listed as Greece. I was brought up believing that as Hollis and Cecilia's child, I was Scotch and English. In an instant my heritage had changed to Greek and Italian.

As a small child, strangers would look at me and then at my blue-eyed father and say, "He doesn't look like you. He looks Jewish." At least the question of why I didn't look like Hollis was answered.

After repeated examinations of the birth certificate, I figured those few lines were likely all that I would ever find about the truth of my birth. My father claimed that he had told me all he knew. I couldn't ask Cecilia. My father told me that he heard she died drunk on an Indian reservation in Utah a few years after she left me in the café.

I spent the remainder of the summer confused about my identity. I was illegitimate. More painful was the thought that I was unwanted by my birth mother. I was unable to look at my father without feeling angry. His talk with me had destroyed much of what I believed to be true about myself. Now only unanswered questions remained. However, there was a greater turmoil going on in my mind that had nothing to do with the strange names on my birth certificate.

Like a lot of teenage boys trying to find their place in the adult world, my developing sexuality was a source of confusion. I had many questions and no place to go for the answers. What I was feeling was different from my peers, and I did not dare share my thoughts with them.

There was no "gay" in those days, only "queer." It was a brutal word of condemnation. I was so afraid of being labeled "queer" that even telling my friend John the truth was out of the question. While I trusted him with the secret of my illegitimate birth, I was afraid to share my bigger secret with him.

I had friends in high school but none of them knew who I really was. I was afraid of being condemned by my family and friends if anyone discovered my secret. For a time, I thought that I might be mentally ill. The thought that I could be taken to a mental hospital or even jail haunted me. I lived most of my teenage years with these fears. I might be able to hide the secret of my birth, but it was not that simple with my other secret.

Months went by and I continued to wonder about my unknown past. I was ashamed that my birth parents were not married, and was deeply hurt thinking that I had been unwanted by my mother. I had no explanations and nowhere to go for answers. The frustration wore me down. Eventually, I decided that all I could do was to try to forget about it.

# *Chapter Two*

For the next five and half years I hid the circumstances of my birth and my sexuality from everyone I knew. I didn't date in high school because I was not interested in girls in the same way as my male classmates. But I was popular with girls in my class and many became close friends, maybe because I treated them with respect. I overheard my stepmother tell a neighbor, "Jim doesn't have time for dating girls. He's too busy studying." I embraced that role.

I wasn't an athlete or one of the rowdy kids. My place was with the smart kids who took Latin and college prep classes, and made good grades. Otherwise, I was a typical teenager. Or maybe not. While I loved rock and roll, I was among the very few of my peers who didn't like Elvis.

In the early fall, John's parents bought him a used car. He took me to the county courthouse and I finally got my driver's license, without my father's knowledge. To prove my age, I used the baptismal certificate. Since it listed my father and Cecilia as foster parents, the clerk must have assumed that I was adopted and no questions were asked.

John and I never talked about my birth circumstances after that summer. I didn't bring it up and perhaps he was uncomfortable about asking me more questions. The secret of the mother and father with the foreign names felt safe with him. I just hoped that the secret would disappear if I stopped thinking about it.

I graduated from high school in the spring of 1960 and started college the next fall. Although I wanted go away to school, I did not have the money. So I attended a small college in Denver and continued to live at home. In college, I continued to feel isolated by my "other world," which I still didn't understand. Just as in high school, there was no one that I could talk to about my sexual bewilderment. If there were other young men at my college who had the same questions, I didn't have a clue who they were. Even if I had, how would I connect with them? Despite attending an institution of higher learning, there were no sources of useful information on sexuality available. The irony that escaped me then amuses me now.

I was distracted by the turmoil going on inside me. I just wanted to run, but I had no idea where I would go. I dropped out of college at the end of the second semester of my junior year. I told myself that I would return someday.

California was a possible destination. That idea came from Iris, my friend since grade school who is still a friend today. She headed for the Golden State immediately after high school graduation. A year later she returned for a short visit with her parents. I hardly recognized Iris. California had changed her appearance, her attitude, and her outlook. She was very happy in her new life and urged me to move to the west coast right away. Iris probably knew I was gay before I did. She planted that destination in my mind and it grew.

In March 1963, I set out on my big adventure. I purchased road maps and packed up my 1954 Buick. I said good-bye to Hollis, Ruth, and my stepsister, Bev. I was heading west to California. I didn't have a plan. I just wanted to be on my way and on my own.

My decision to leave home was more about my emerging sexuality than about my birth parents. I buried the secrets of my birth deep and became adept at keeping them suppressed. I left Colorado on blind faith, feeling that the answers to my questions about my sexuality would come to me once I left my familiar life behind. Paramount in my thoughts was the need to be on my own. I was not "out" when I got behind the wheel, just very confused.

Prior to the road trip, visiting Ruth's relatives on a Nebraska farm was as far as I had been from College View. Looking at a map I realized there were a lot of roads leading to California. I wanted to see as much of the country as I could. Since I had never seen the ocean, I thought the best way to get to California was to start in Washington and drive down the Pacific Coast. I changed course from due west to northwest.

My Buick broke down in Spokane, Washington. The breakdown was major and I did not have enough money to fix the car. I was too proud to call my father for help. A used car lot took the Buick for $150, and I found a room for $20 a week in a drab hotel on the edge of downtown. Once settled in, I answered an ad for a waiter position at the Golden Hour Restaurant.

My financial situation caused me to exaggerate what I knew

about waiting tables, which was nothing. Despite this, I convinced the manager that he should hire me. I did learn to wait tables and soon came to enjoy my new job very much. The experience was similar to being on a stage. You have everyone's attention as they watch you act your part. It didn't take long to figure out that the better the act, the better the tips.

The people who worked at the Golden Hour were an extended family. They took me in as part of their circle. Soon I was able to afford an apartment and another second-hand car—a blue 1951 Mercury. As I grew comfortable in my new life, getting to California didn't seem as important.

One Saturday night I wandered into a bar downtown and it wasn't long before I figured out that I had something in common with the other men I met. The bar was one of two gay bars in Spokane. I don't remember the name of the bar, but I continued going back, mostly on weekends. It was such a relief to find other men my age who accepted me and helped me understand I was not alone. While I did not fit the straight male role that society assigned to me, it was okay. They didn't either.

But Spokane was a conservative city in equally conservative eastern Washington. The John Birch Society had a large billboard downtown inviting people to join. While waiting tables, I sometimes overheard racist remarks about Native Americans, and about the few African Americans who lived there.

There was certainly no acceptance of a gay lifestyle in Spokane. The gay world was strictly after dark, underground and invisible to most residents. Still I was free enough to begin living on my own terms. I was not out of the closet yet, but I was much closer to the door.

Snow came down early that November. Not a heavy snow, but one that lightly coated leafless trees and dead lawns, and melted by noon. This preview of a harsh winter came at the same time that my routine in my adopted home was becoming stale. I was restless.

I never liked winter and often imagined living somewhere it did not snow. Finding out that I was not English and Scotch but really Greek and Italian gave rise to the thought that my roots were really Mediterranean. No wonder I hated the Colorado winters.

Hawaii called to me, and two weeks later I boarded a Greyhound bus to San Francisco. I could not afford the fare on the passenger liners *Lurline* or *Matsonia*. A one-way ticket on a freighter, *The Hawaiian Rancher* was the alternative. The ship carried a large cargo of fat pigs bound for Hawaiian luaus. Traveling with the pigs didn't bother me. All I cared about was reaching the Aloha State—no winter, no cold, and no snow.

I was 21. It's hard for me to imagine being that spontaneous now. Hawaii was over 3,000 miles away from anything familiar and I didn't know anyone there. I gave little thought about how I would survive. It was all just another big adventure.

When the ship docked in Honolulu, the country was still in shock from the assassination of President John F. Kennedy. His funeral was playing on every television station as I disembarked.

The beauty of Hawaii hypnotized me. It was one of the Union's newest states, having been admitted a few years earlier in 1959. The blue green water and white sands at Waikiki Beach almost blinded me. I never wanted to leave.

The cheapest place to live in Waikiki was the Ala Moana YMCA, and I rented a room for $15 a week. I lay on the beach, played in the water, and watched the parade of visitors from all over the world pass by.

Shortly before Christmas, most of my money was gone. I felt lucky when I found a job at Chez Marc as a dishwasher. Despite the name, Chez Marc was a dive. There was no real dishwasher, only a pair of rubber gloves, a worn-out brush, and a metal sink of greasy hot water. The eatery was located across from Kuhio beach, on the Diamond Head end of Kalakaua Avenue. Chez Marc was a gathering place for locals who stopped in for the cheap breakfasts in the morning. Tourists happened in for lunch, thinking they had finally found authentic local color.

At night, drunken sailors and Marines stumbled into Chez Marc's to sober up on black coffee before returning to their bases at Pearl Harbor and Kaneohe. Most of them frequented the bar next door called "Da Swamp." A more appropriate name would have been "Da Boxing Ring" for the fistfights between the patrons that spilled out to the sidewalk in front. The Shore Patrol often arrived with sirens blaring from their white paddy wagons to pick up the drunken combatants.

Thomas was the owner of Chez Marc. He was a 40-year-old loud, quick-to-anger gay man who weighed around 300 pounds. Thomas had a reputation for tossing customers who complained about his cooking into the street. Employees he fired for real or imaginary offenses were treated likewise.

The "Marc" in Chez Marc was Thomas's young, pampered boyfriend. I never saw Marc do any work, nor did I hear Thomas ask him to help out. Marc was my age, but since I was just hired help, he mostly ignored me. He sat at the counter, looking very bored, chain smoking, drinking coffee, and reading movie magazines. Marc was the first man I saw file and buff his fingernails.

Rats scurried across the floor as I worked in the small kitchen in the back. The first time this happened, I ran out front to tell Thomas. He grabbed me and I had visions of being booted into the street. Instead he hustled me back into the kitchen.

"Shut up about seeing rats and don't ever come up front to tell me the next time you see one. Customers don't need to know that kind of stuff. Don't bother the rats and they won't bother you."

Eventually I moved to a one-room studio apartment not far from Chez Marc, one block off Waikiki Beach near Kapiolani Park and the Zoo. People living in the Waikiki neighborhood were young and transient. In addition, tourists from the hotels, airline crews on layover, soldiers and sailors from the military bases, and crews from the ocean liners calling at the port also frequented the residential streets running off Kalakaua back to the Ala Wai Canal. Waikiki offered a colorful variety of people, cultures, and lifestyles, including many gay men. This jumble added to the already relaxed atmosphere that Hawaii was known for.

I finally came out of the closet in Hawaii and began living openly as a gay man. I had found what I was looking for: men my age who understood the feelings I had suppressed for years. I made friends and became part of a community. My feelings were not wrong, just different. I wasn't a freak. I was okay. In a strange way, the shame I felt about my birth origin made my acceptance of being gay much easier. I already felt like an outsider. Why should I care what anyone thought about my being queer?

After a few months working at Chez Marc, a tip from one of the regular customers led me to a hotel job. Soon I was working as a dining room waiter again. Thomas had a tantrum when I told him I was quitting. Later on I found an even better position as a room service waiter at a newly opened beach hotel. In that job, I saw quite a few Hollywood and TV celebrities up close, and tips were much better.

After two and a half years of living in a paradise, I was bored. I needed a change again. In the spring of 1965, I moved back to Spokane. However, gay life in Spokane was now too underground and confining for me. I felt like I had taken a big step backward into the closet.

One of my friends in Waikiki was Dean, a fellow waiter at one of the hotels where I worked. He moved to San Francisco a few months before I left for Spokane. Dean wrote me continually about his adventures in the big city. The then unknown intersection of Haight and Ashbury was about to become famous. More importantly, Dean's letters made it clear there were no closets in San Francisco. I arrived on June 26, 1966, my 24th birthday.

That I ended up in San Francisco was not surprising, given the City's reputation as a Mecca for gay men and women. I was part of a large migration of gays from other parts of the country. Arriving at the same time were thousands of young men and women, ready to become flower children or hippies.

I met Rolland a year later. He was an older man, a talented artist and gentle soul who was well liked by everyone. Rolland was 6' 2" with square-jawed handsome face and muscular body. He could have been a model for J. C. Leyendecker in an Arrow shirt advertisement from the 1920s. Although we were physically different, we found that we had a lot of similarities. He was from Denver and like me had grown up in Colorado. He too, was a recent arrival and had moved to San Francisco for the same reason I had. We were both looking for a place where we could live openly without fear.

We met while working at the Army Post Office south of Market Street. Rolland's sense of humor complemented my own. Within a year we became involved in a relationship and spent the next 14 years living together.

In late 1975, Rolland and I were living in a two bedroom flat near 14th and Noe, close to Duboce Park. Because the area adjoined the Castro District, it soon became a fashionable gay neighborhood as well. But when we lived there, the Victorian houses and flats on

14th Street were run-down and the rents were low. We were just one of hundreds of working class couples—gay and straight—enjoying our lives in what was then a much different city. That San Francisco no longer exists.

One Sunday morning, I came across a feature story in the *San Francisco Chronicle* about a psychologist in Berkeley. Susan Hamilton was a local advocate and activist in a national organization known as the Adoptees Liberation Movement Association, or ALMA. The goal of ALMA was to open sealed records to mothers who had given up their children for adoption. Some of the mothers had let their children go unwillingly and now wanted to know what had become of them. ALMA also offered to help adopted children search for their unknown parents. Susan herself gave up a baby boy for adoption 20 years earlier. The guilt that haunted her was a driving force behind her work.

As I read the *Chronicle* article, unhappy memories surfaced. For years I suppressed thoughts about my birth circumstances. I read the article again. I wanted to know what my father could not tell me the night I confronted him seventeen years earlier.

For the next week, I could not get the ALMA article out of my mind. Finally I telephoned Susan Hamilton's office. I wasn't sure what to say but I knew I needed to talk to her.

She answered, "Hello, Adoptees Liberation Movement Association. This is Susan."

"Ah, yes... I read the article about you... in the paper last week."

"Thank you. Are you supportive of our mission to open these records, or do you have objections?"

I hadn't given much thought to the opening of the records. I was more focused on my own situation.

"Well, I read the story and it was interesting. And now I would like to talk to you."

"What's your name? You sound a bit nervous."

"I guess I am, sort of. My name is Jim. I want to find my real parents." I had just opened a door with a sign that read, "Keep Out! This Means You."

"How old are you and how long have you known you were adopted?"

"I'm 33. There is so much I don't know and I haven't thought about it for a long time and I don't know where to start." My eyes were starting to burn. "I wasn't adopted and I found out when I was 16."

"I don't quite understand."

"My parents raised me after they got me from my mother, who they didn't know. She never came back and they got divorced. My father remarried and I found out that I wasn't his son but he didn't know who my parents were."

"Jim, slow down. I'm not following you. This sounds complicated. Why do you want to find your parents?"

I had not given any thought to what finding them would really mean. All I wanted to know was who they were, and why my birth mother had abandoned me. Worried that Susan might lose interest, I said, "For medical reasons, just in case there are hereditary diseases that I should know about."

"Are you sure that's all?"

Thoughts that had been buried for years resurfaced and my mind was reeling. How could I share them with a stranger? Still I didn't want Susan to hang up.

"You sound pretty upset right now. Maybe we could talk another time," she said.

"No, please don't hang up. I want to talk."

"I won't hang up. But this might be easier for you if we were not on the phone. Jim, would you be willing to come see me at my office?"

"I don't know. I've never talked to anyone about this stuff. I don't even like to think about it."

"I understand how you feel. Not knowing who your parents are is an awful thing for anyone. It must be terrible not letting yourself think about your past and not being able to talk about it for years. Once I had a painful burden that I kept hidden. But when I faced it, the pain eventually went away. So did the questions that had no answers. It isn't easy but it can be done."

For the first time since I was 16, I allowed myself to think beyond the shame. Susan's calm demeanor relaxed me. I thought about her suggestion to come by her office.

"I don't know what more I can tell you in person. I get mixed up and ashamed, then I get mad and I don't want to think about it anymore."

"I'm a psychologist. One of the things I do is help people come to terms with their past. Are you tired of the unanswered questions about who you are? Maybe you're ready to find the answers. I can set up an appointment for a free consultation. Afterward, I can see you for therapy."

I was put off by her suggestion that I see her for therapy. I didn't need therapy. All I needed to know was who my parents were. Nevertheless, I knew that I had just started down the road to satisfying my curiosity. There was no turning back.

"I could come by after work some night."

"Good. How about 6:30 next Thursday? My office is in Berkeley on Eleventh Street."

For the next few days, I was consumed by what I had started and thought of nothing else. I wasn't sure digging back into my past was a good idea. What if all I uncovered was more shameful information? Poor Rolland listened patiently while I debated about whether or not to keep my appointment.

In the end I showed up at Susan's office. I stood scared on the front porch of a small white house in the Berkeley flatlands. I had never been to a therapist before. She answered the doorbell and led me through the house to her office, a room in the rear decorated in hippie chic. Susan motioned me to sit on the sofa. It was comfortable and offered the security I needed.

Susan sat with a notepad and pen. She was in her mid to late thirties, not much older than me. She was dressed in the same fashion that matched the surroundings. Her attire and her office might have been laidback Berkeley but her manner and intensity were New York.

Not long after I sat down, I poured out the thoughts I had been hiding for years. I talked about my childhood growing up with an alcoholic mother who also disappeared. I told her about my shame when I found out my emotionally distant father was not my real father. I did not know how much I hurt inside until I started talking. Susan gently pried the lid off my feelings. There was a flood of tears. The only part that did not elicit tears was about the life I had created for myself once I left College View.

Two hours later I was exhausted. Every part of my past was in Susan's possession and much of it on her notepad.

I was taken aback when she said, "I don't think you are ready to search for your birth parents yet."

"What do you mean, 'not ready'? I don't want to find them. All I want to know is what happened and why."

"In order to find that out, you'll have to contact them. They are the only two people who have the answers. You need to find out their side of the story. How will you get at the truth if you don't make contact?"

"I hate both of them and I don't know where to start. It was over 30 years ago."

Susan looked at me. "If you don't come to terms with this anger, you may never get the answers. It isn't necessary to feel ashamed about what happened. You were an innocent baby. The fact that they weren't married has nothing to do with you. Your anger and shame will get in your way of finding out the truth."

I knew she was right, but the thought that I would have to make contact with my birth parents in order to find the truth upset me.

"I am angry alright. I'm still angry at my father for not telling me that I wasn't his real son. I'm angry because I don't know who I am. And I'm angry sitting here and telling someone I don't even know how goddamn angry I am."

Susan waited until I composed myself. "I'm sorry. I know you are trying to help. I do appreciate you taking the time to see me. There is no way that I can go back to hiding this stuff again. I just want all of it to go away. So what do I do now?"

"Jim, let's begin a series of weekly sessions. We'll work on these issues of anger and shame. It won't be easy and some things will be more painful than what you felt tonight. You need to prepare yourself before you start your search and you have a lot of homework to do."

The two hours left me weak. I stood up, regained my balance, thanked her for her time and left. I headed down the street to catch a bus back to San Francisco.

The following week Susan and I began with the obvious—the growing anger I had bottled up since 1958. Once I was able to talk freely, I realized just how much anger I carried.

After seeing Susan for a month, I was startled when she said,

"Jim, I think we've reached an end to our one-on-one meetings."

"Are you going to stop seeing me?"

"No, but what I'd like is for you to join a special group of people who meet every Saturday."

"Group? What kind of group?"

"The participants are mothers searching for children they gave up. There are also men and women looking for their real parents."

"Why do you think I need to join a group?"

"In these sessions everyone gets to share their feelings. They talk about how their searches are going and how good or bad they feel about what is going on in their lives. We are open with each other but what we share is kept very confidential. We promise each other not to repeat anything we hear in the group."

The thought of joining a group made me uncomfortable. Susan continued, "Mothers can better understand what they might face in a reunion with a lost child by talking to someone like you. In turn, hearing what the mothers have to say will help you gain insight to what your mother went through. Such knowledge is invaluable. Think about it, Jim. Who better to understand how you feel than the people you'll meet in this support group?"

I did not want to leave the comfort and security of my private sessions with Susan. I tried to imagine standing in front of a group of strangers telling them my deepest secrets. I couldn't.

"Talking openly with others who know the same pain can help dissipate the anger you harbor against your parents. It's still too early for you to begin your search. Even if you found your birth parents tomorrow, do you think they would meet with you as mad as you are?"

I understood what she said but I couldn't see myself sharing my fears and my shame with strangers. Our session ended and I told Susan, "I'll think about it and let you know."

I thought about the group and decided I was finished with Susan and her therapy nonsense. Still, as hard as I tried to rationalize stopping what I had started, it was clear there was no way to go back. And there was no way to stand still either. A few weeks later, I called Susan to tell her I would be at the next group meeting.

The group consisted of 10 to 12 men and women. I spent eight weeks going to the Saturday morning meetings. We talked and shared our thoughts and stories. The similarities that I heard from the other "children" were revelatory. Much to my surprise, I was more comfortable with these strangers than I anticipated.

The men and women looking for parents knew that they had been adopted at birth, while my illegitimacy had been a shameful secret. If I was to become a real member of this group, I had to tell my story.

One Saturday morning, I stood up in front of everyone and let these strangers know why I was there. The telling was a liberating experience. Once I revealed what I had kept hidden, the secret no longer hurt me. It was similar to my coming out as a gay man. Once I acknowledged my secret, the fear and the shame were gone. I ended my story by telling the group that I was also gay.

At these meetings we often participated in role-playing exercises. In one session, Susan paired me with Jean, who had given up a baby boy for adoption twenty-five years before. She asked me to imagine that Jean was my birth mother and I was meeting her for the first time. "What would you say to her?" Susan asked.

I felt self-conscious with the group watching us intently and anticipating what might happen. The game was stupid. Jean was not my mother and I couldn't pretend that she was. I just sat there, unable to say anything.

When nothing happened, Jean asked Susan, "Can I start this? Let me talk to Jim as if he were my lost son."

Her first question was, "Are you angry at me for giving you up when you were born?"

I uttered a feeble "yes."

"I understand why you must hate me. I did a terrible thing."

Suddenly this was no longer a game. My self-consciousness disappeared and Jean became the mother I never knew. I cried and then I yelled at her. The exercise may have been pretend, but it became real for me.

"Yes, I hate you," I screamed.

Startled by what I had said, she wept. "You have every right to hate me. You can't imagine how much I hate myself for what I did. I'm so, so sorry."

"I don't care. I hate you. For years I've had to live knowing that you didn't want me. You gave me away to strangers and made my life a lie."

She took out a handkerchief to wipe her eyes. "The last thing I wanted to do was to hurt you. I loved you so much. It killed me but I had no choice. I had to give you up."

"How can you say you love me after what you did? I can never forgive you or my father, whoever he was. Why shouldn't I hate you?"

Jean started to cry again but her voice came through stronger this time. It was as if she had rehearsed for the day when she might meet her own son.

"You have every right. I can't deny that my decision caused you so much pain. Try to understand that I only wanted to do the best I could for you but I didn't have many choices. In the end, I wanted you to have a future. The only way I could give you a future was to give you up. Can you understand that?

"You can never know what I went through when my baby was taken from me. Yes, I know you've suffered. I've suffered too. I know what it's like to carry a secret. For all of these years, I've wondered what happened to my son, if he ended up with the future that I tried to give him. I don't even know if he is alive. This is the pain that I have lived with for over 25 years."

Had my mother experienced the same pain? I became calmer as I thought of my mother. What had forced her to give me up?

Jean resumed. "I want you to know that a little bit of me died when they took you from me. I never forgot you. Please understand and forgive me."

The room was very still. I asked, "Did you love me, and my father?"

"Of course I loved you. I never stopped loving you. And I did love your father very much. We were human. We were young and in love."

She dropped her pretend role. "I didn't know what to do when my baby was born. Neither did his father. We were too young to handle the situation. In those days, it was a disgrace for a woman not to be married to the father of her baby. When my parents found out, they were furious. They forbid my baby's father to see me and threatened him with arrest if he tried to contact me. I never saw him again. I left school and moved in with an aunt in another state. My baby was born and I only held him once before they took him away. Just before they took my boy from me, I signed papers agreeing to the adoption my parents had arranged.

"I wanted my baby to have a chance. If you are ever so lucky as to find your mother, remember that she probably wanted the same thing for you."

Like my first meeting with Susan, I was emotionally drained. I barely got out of my chair when the session ended, but I had made a breakthrough. I called Susan the following Monday.

"I'm not mad anymore and ready to start my search."

"Are you sure? This is a complete reversal of how you were feeling a few days ago. Do you feel like talking?"

"Susan, the 'mother and son' game that Jean and I acted out was not easy. She had to hear how much her newfound son hated her. The game became real. I meant every word I said, most of which I can't remember now. But I also listened to what Jean was saying.

"Thanks to her, my mother became a real human being. She was no longer just a name on my birth certificate. One thing Jean said I can't get out of my mind was that my mother had done the best she could. That is what Jean had done for her son. Susan, I understand so much more now. Really, I'm no longer angry."

"That is some breakthrough. It does sound like you're ready to start searching for your parents. I hope that you'll continue with the group."

"I was going to ask if you were going to throw me out now that I'm not carrying the anger baggage anymore."

"Of course not. The group can still help. In turn you have a lot to offer the group as you progress through your search. It's a support group, you know."

Letting go of the anger was a freeing experience. I was ready. The only information I had was their names, and that they lived in Hartford in the early 1940s. I was about to look for two people on the other side the country that had been missing for 34 years. Nevertheless, I was ready to put my energy into a serious search for my birth parents. I hoped to learn about the events in their lives that had so dramatically affected my own.

# *Chapter Three*

The few lines of information gleaned from the baptismal and birth certificates became a wealth of data. In Susan's group, several people hoping to find their parents did not even have names. For the mothers, searching was easier because in most cases they knew the social agency involved when they gave up their child.

I continued to attend Susan's Saturday morning meetings. Several people in the group were involved with their own searches. Time was reserved for us to report on our progress. I heard their stories of struggles with bureaucracies. During the mid-1970s most state agencies and religious organizations involved with adoptions refused to help anyone looking for birth parents or children they had given up. The official position was to oppose the release of any information. Even after the children were of legal age, the information was still denied them.

One middle-aged woman in our group approached the state welfare agency that handled her adoption. She wanted to secure information about her real parents. As she sat at the desk of a state official, she was lectured and told she had no business trying to find her birth parents. All the while the official had her adoption file in his hand. He refused to answer any questions.

She returned to the office a few minutes after being dismissed. When she entered, he was not in the room and the adoption file was still on his desk. She took the file, put it under her coat, and walked out. She could have been prosecuted for stealing state property. I understood her drive to find her biological identity.

The birth certificate I received when I was 16 was for James Zaldonapolous, Jr. However, there was never a birth certificate for James Wiley Sutherland. For 33 years I did not legally exist.

The certificate did reveal valuable clues about my birth parents. I was lucky I had obtained a copy in 1958. Laws and attitudes were such that it would never have come into my possession so easily in 1975.

In 1944, Hollis and Cecilia Sutherland had me baptized at St. Phillip and St. James Church in Hartford. At the time, someone in the church office had typed onto my baptismal certificate the names of both birth parents. I am not sure how their names would have been known. Maybe since Cecilia was in a church she felt compelled to be honest with Reverend Cunningham. But without their names on the baptismal certificate, I never would have had a starting point. This chance appearance of my birth parents' names surfacing two years after their disappearance has always fascinated me.

I relied on the library to get started, where I found a current Hartford phone directory. Since it was unlikely that his last name had changed since 1942, I decided to look for my father. James J. Zaldonapolous was listed as living in a suburb of Hartford. I wasn't sure what I should do next. Some caution was in order because I was treading in a sensitive area of someone else's life. I set his information aside and began the search for my mother.

While the Hartford phone directory gave me the location of my birth father, it was not so quick to reveal the whereabouts of my mother. The directory had 14 listings for Postiglione but no Frances. Was she still alive? Had she married? Did she use her real name when she checked into the hospital 33 years ago? If she was alive, had she stayed in Hartford? I had no answers.

Rolland and I spent a great deal of time discussing possible scenarios. If Postiglione was not her real name, then maybe Frances wasn't either. She might be in a mental institution. This was where one of my therapy mate's search for his mother had led him.

Another concern surfaced. How would I make contact once I located them? I did not intend to burst on the scene with "Hi, my name is Jim. I'm that little bundle of joy you abandoned 33 years ago. We need to have a chat."

I wanted to avoid causing havoc in their personal lives. Yet once I made contact, the consequences would be beyond my control. My birth parents knew of my existence, but what about their families? I worried about the impact my appearance might have on their spouses or children.

I intended to move slowly. I was clear on what I expected once I found my birth parents. I wanted to get the answers to all of my questions with a minimum of drama. My idea was to have one telephone conversation with each of them to learn what had happened. No one else would know about our talk or that I existed and their families would be spared any shock. Once the telephone calls were over, I would go away satisfied.

I never wanted to punish my birth parents. I didn't feel vengeful. I was over the anger thanks to my work with Susan. From what I heard from the mothers in the group, it was likely my parents still felt guilty, especially my mother. Knowing my birth parents had lived with their guilt far longer than I had lived with my anger tempered my attitude toward both of them.

Rolland and I ran out of possibilities as to the whereabouts of my birth mother. The Hartford phone book revealed nothing to connect me with her. I had to make a number of assumptions since I did not have many facts.

My first step was to write to each of the fourteen Postigliones listed in the Hartford phonebook. If she had used her real name at the hospital then maybe someone at one of addresses might know Frances Postiglione or be related to her.

I typed each of the fourteen letters on an ancient manual typewriter. It took several evenings to get the typing done on the clunky machine. While it required more time and effort, I wanted each party to receive an original letter. I felt the recipient would not take a photocopied letter seriously.

The antique Woodstock had no delete key and correcting mistakes was tedious and messy. Often it was easier just to start the letter over again. I enclosed with each letter a self-addressed, stamped postcard, and asked everyone to return the card whether or not they had any knowledge of Frances Postiglione.

I mailed the letters and the waiting began. I hoped the replies would soon arrive.

This is the letter I sent.

\*\*\*

*May 20, 1976*

*Dear Mr. Postiglione,*

*Despite the fact that you do not know me, nor I you, I am writing to ask for your help in a matter that is of some urgency to me. I am trying to locate*

*the whereabouts of a woman who lived in the Hartford-Manchester area in*
*the early 1940s. Her maiden name was Frances Postiglione and she was*
*born about 1915 in Hartford. My reason for hoping to locate this woman is*
*that I have reason to believe she is my natural mother. I was separated from*
*her shortly after I was born in June 1942. I need to contact her for biologi-*
*cal and medical information that I am in need of at the present time.*

*I have been searching for several months, but as it is very probable that*
*she has remarried, I have not had much success in locating her yet. Since*
*her maiden name was Postiglione, I am writing to all the Postigliones in*
*the Hartford area in hopes that some information might turn up. I do*
*know that she had at least three other children, however I do not know their*
*names, ages, or genders.*

*I have enclosed a stamped-self addressed card that I would appreciate*
*your returning to me with (1) any information, no matter how minor you*
*might think it may be, or suggestions to help me locate this woman or (2)*
*letting me know that you do not know her or her whereabouts.*

*I don't have much to go on, just a name and a few vital statistics on*
*my birth certificate, but I am trying everything to locate her and thus this*
*letter to you. I do greatly need the medical and biological information men-*
*tioned above. I would be very grateful for any information you could give*
*me in regards to this matter. Thank you for your time and help.*

***

I was concerned that my letter would not be taken seriously. I hoped
that adding my need for medical information would give the letter
a sense of urgency and thus more consideration.

Days passed, and then one night after work, Rolland was
waiting for me at the top of the stairs to our flat. He was so excited
that before I could even close the door and start up the stairs, he
yelled down, "You got a letter from Connecticut but it's not from any
of the Postigliones. It's from Mrs. F. Roccolini. Who is she? Hurry,
get up here and open it."

He was like a child waiting to open a present. I climbed the
long, narrow stairway, my heart pounding.

I expected one of my postcards, not a letter. We walked to the
kitchen in the rear of the flat. For a few moments I stood transfixed.
The envelope in my hand scared me. The postmark read "Hartford,

CT." My name and our 14th Street address looked as if they had been scribbled in a great hurry. On the reverse side of the envelope, was "F. Roccolini, Rocky Hill."

Rolland broke the spell. "Aren't you going to open it?"

"Yeah, I guess I had better. Can you believe I'm almost afraid to open it?" I answered.

I took a knife from a cabinet drawer and opened the envelope. The letter had jagged edges and looked like it had been cut from a large piece of butcher paper. If my heart was pounding before, it was now ready to jump out of my body.

*** 

*Dear Mr. Sutherland,*

*Yes, I am your natural mother. I remarried and my name is Mrs. F. Roccolini. Please forgive me. I lost two sons, one in 1966 with Hodgkin's disease and another in 1974 with kidney trouble. My husband knows nothing. Neither do my other children so please don't make any trouble for me. I am an old woman now. Maybe I could write a better letter next time.*

*Mrs. F. Roccolini*

***

On the reverse side of the page was: *Please don't write to any more Postigliones.*

I sat down after reading the plea of an old woman asking me not to cause her any trouble. Knowing that I made contact with the woman who gave birth to me was overwhelming.

I handed the letter to Rolland.

"You did it. You really found her. I never thought this would happen so fast. This is the first reply. I just can't believe it."

"Me neither."

I read the letter countless times that evening. I felt surprise, happiness, sadness, relief, fear, and joy. Rolland and I talked about what to do next. Later I called Susan with the news.

Mrs. Roccolini didn't give me much time to recover from the

shock of her first letter. When I came home from work the following afternoon, Rolland was at the top of the stairs with another letter, postmarked May 25, the day after she had written the first one. This time she included "Connecticut" after "Rocky Hill." She also took time to find lined paper.

*** 

Dear James,

*I am so uptight after receiving your letter. I would rather that my family would not know about you. You mailed the letter to my brother, Angelo, and I opened it up because I knew the name Sutherland. I would never open his mail but I never forgot that name. When I saw your first name, Jim, I knew it was you. This is Angelo's home. He lost his wife a few years ago and I am here helping to bring up his children.*

*What is it you want to know? If you send your telephone number, I will call and give you whatever information I can give you. I am shaking so much right now that I can't even write. I am so frightened. Please forgive me if you are not able to read my writing.*

*I would so much like to know about you, but I don't know if I really have any right to say that. I know you must be very bitter about me. I am of Italian descent and your father was born in Greece. I know very little about him now.*

*Please don't call here, only write to me. Please don't write too often. I am very afraid my brother might see one of your letters. If he found out who you are, he might become angry and put me out of here.*

*Mrs. F. Roccolini*

*** 

On the reverse side was: *I will tell you more when I speak to you.*

I wrote back to Mrs. Roccolini and assured her that I did not want to cause any trouble. I thanked her for having the courage to come forward and how much it meant to me. I told her I knew how difficult it must have been to write that first letter, and all I wanted was for her to tell me how we were separated.

As she requested, I added my phone number. She could call me collect on any Saturday afternoon. I concluded my letter by saying that once I knew the truth I would leave her alone. The letter went into the mailbox the next day on my way to work.

# *Chapter Four*

On the following Saturday afternoon, Rolland and I sat in our living room on the art deco burgundy sofa that we had found years earlier in a junk store on McAllister Street. We wondered if this was the Saturday Mrs. Roccolini would call. I worried she might change her mind and that I would not hear from her.

The telephone rang at one o'clock. I jumped. Rolland jumped.

"I'll be in the kitchen. If you need me, give a holler," Rolland said and left the room.

The phone rang again.

"Mrs. Roccolini?

"James? I'm so nervous."

"So am I."

Then she started to cry and said nothing. I was at a loss, too, so I said nothing.

When she recovered her composure, she said in a strong voice, "Don't call me Mrs. Roccolini. My name is Frances. No one calls me Mrs. Roccolini."

"Well then," I replied. "Don't call me James. My name is Jim. No one calls me James."

We laughed. This put us at ease.

"I can't believe that I'm actually talking to you. I also can't tell you how frightened I am."

"There's no reason to be afraid. I don't want to upset you or cause any problems. Please believe me. This isn't why I wanted to find you."

"You can't understand what it's been like for me having this secret for so long. I was always afraid that someone would find out about you. As long as no one did, I didn't have to worry. But here you are. You've found me. I never expected that to happen. You must be a pretty smart guy to have done that. I don't know what to do. I don't know what to say."

"I've thought about this moment for a long time. I thought I knew what I'd say but now that you are on the phone, it isn't easy for me either. I just want to talk to you and find out why we were separated."

"You must hate me."

"No, I don't hate you. I'm glad that you answered my letter. I know that was not easy."

Silence.

"I promise that once I hear what happened when I was born, you won't hear from me again. No one in your family will find out about me."

"God is really punishing me. After years of worrying what happened to you, here you come back for one telephone conversation and then you're going to disappear again," she said crying.

"Well, I'm not sure if God is punishing you or not."

"You don't have any idea how much God has punished me all these years. I was a bad mother and I committed mortal sins. This is why God took my two sons from me when they were young men. They died because I was such a bad mother. He punished me more by taking you away and I never knew what happened to you."

As I listened, I began to wonder if I had done the right thing. I was glad we were talking. At the same time I could not help but think, what have I started here? I wasn't sure what to do next.

"I'm sorry that you've had so much pain. Not being a religious person I don't know how God works. But if I were, I'd think that God answered my prayers. Maybe He had a hand in helping me find you so quickly."

Hearing that I was not religious distracted her momentarily. She sounded angry when she let out with, "What do you mean you are not religious? What are you telling me? That you don't believe in God and you don't go to church?"

"I believe in some kind of God, but I don't believe in churches at all and I don't go," I answered defensively. How had our conversation veered so far off track?

She continued, "I believe in God very much but I don't go to church. I haven't been for years except for weddings or funerals. I can't go to church because I committed mortal sins and when you do that, you can't receive communion. But I made all my children go to church. My family is Roman Catholic and I am too, except I am a very bad one."

"Everyone has to make up their own mind about God and attending church," I replied. "It isn't anyone else's business except your own."

Hearing that I did not judge her made Frances relax and she began to ask me questions. Her first was, how did I find out that she was my mother? I told her what had happened the summer I tried to get my driver's license and about sending away for my baptismal certificate. I told her that I had wondered for 17 years what had happened to her and my father. Then I gave her a short replay of my therapy experiences after I met Susan.

She said, "I'm sorry I did this to you and that you were a sad little boy with no mother and never knew what happened to her. This is my fault. I'm a terrible person and will never forgive myself."

"Wait a minute. I wasn't sad all the time and I did have a mother and I didn't spend my entire childhood feeling bad about you. I didn't even know about you until I was 16. Right now I'm so lucky the stuff I told you about happened, otherwise we wouldn't be talking right now. I wish you wouldn't feel like everything was your fault."

"Easy for you to say. You are innocent. Your father and I did a terrible thing—especially me. I was your mother and I still am your mother." She paused. "I don't have any right to say that, do I?"

"You're my birth mother but I don't feel like you are my real mother because I didn't grow up with you. I don't even know you. That's how it is. We don't have to keep talking about this if it's going to upset you."

"No, I want to tell you everything because you have a right to know. It's just that I don't know where to begin. Maybe I could write it all in a letter and get it in order. You have to remember I'm 62 now and when you get to this age, it's hard to remember what happened years ago. Sometimes I can't even remember what happened this morning. If I can ask some questions for a while, then we can come back to this stuff later. There is so much I want to know."

"Sure. What do you want to know? Ask me anything."

"What do you look like? Where did you go to school? What kind of work do you do? Are you married? Where did you grow up? What do you like to eat? Are you healthy? Do you have any hobbies? Were you good in school?" Her questions came in rapid succession and as soon as I had answered one, she had another ready.

After I answered her questions, I asked mine. "What do you look like? What do you do? Are you retired? What kind of work did you do? What is Connecticut like? What about your other children?"

"Besides the two sons that God took from me, I have a daughter, Janice."

Finding out I had a sibling, a half-sister, was almost as exciting as finding Frances. She was reluctant to say much about her daughter and while I was naturally curious, I didn't press the issue. I did wonder how Janice would react if she knew about me, her mother's 33-year-old secret.

In between our cross examinations, she repeated, "I can't believe that I'm really talking to you. It's like a dream. It just doesn't seem real."

"It's not a dream. I'm also amazed that we're talking to each other. After so many years of wondering, here you are."

"You can't imagine how many times I wondered what became of my baby. Sometimes I'd wake up suddenly in the middle of the night and you would be on my mind and I wouldn't know why. I thought that something bad had happened to you."

We had been on the phone for quite a while, but I still hadn't learned a lot. Frances had relaxed enough that she was laughing. I thought this might be a good time to ask her more about my past.

"Frances, what happened? Why did you give me up?"

There was a long pause.

"Frances, are you still there?"

"Yes, I am here. I wish I wasn't. I'm ashamed because of what I have to tell you."

More silence.

"Please don't think that I'm a terrible woman. When you were born, I was not married to your father."

"Yes, I understand. Go on."

"Do you really understand what I am saying? This is one of my mortal sins, that I had a baby with a man who was not my husband. Then my baby was taken from me. If you hate me now for what I just told you, I deserve it."

"Frances, I figured that out a long time ago. It doesn't matter. It's all history now. It doesn't matter to me that you and he weren't married. I'm not ashamed and you shouldn't feel so guilty. It's in the past. I am not going to worry about something I cannot change. I wish you could do the same."

Frances continued, "I wish I could make you understand. Your father was the nicest man and we fell in love. It wasn't right but it happened. I was wrong because I was already married with three children but my husband had left me and I was raising them alone. I didn't know where he was. You don't understand because you are not a religious person. I couldn't get a divorce because of my family and I was a Catholic. Otherwise I could have married your father. Do you know what would have happened in those days if I talked about getting a divorce? My family would have tried to take my children from me. I was so frightened of my family. I wasn't bad. I was always a good mother to my three children.

"Ever since I got your first letter, I've been reliving the past that I remember very clearly. There are many other things that I've forgotten and I am trying so hard to remember people's names and events. I think about your father, something I haven't done for many years. Don't get me wrong, I never forgot him. It makes me sad to think about him and our time together. I haven't seen him since those days but I know he's still in Hartford. Everything gets so mixed up in my mind. I don't know where to begin so it makes sense to you. I feel like my head is going to explode and I'm going to drop dead."

Please, not now, I thought. As I listened I realized how Frances had been keeping secrets for years just like me.

I said, "Look, it's okay. We don't have to talk about it right now. Tell me what you can when you are ready."

"No, no, no. We have to talk. I owe this to you. But first I want to know about the people who raised you. Were they good to you? They never came back and you were gone."

Frances had just revealed information about Cecilia and Hollis Sutherland that stunned me. *They never came back and you were gone.* This only raised more questions. Still, because she was upset, I told her that Cecilia and Hollis had taken very good care of me. I told her about traveling out west with them, the turkey ranch, and how I had started first grade at Prospect Valley Grade School when I was five.

Hearing about my early childhood was difficult for Frances. She kept saying how guilty she felt for not being there for me. At one point, she made a critical remark about the Sutherlands and we got into an argument. The Sutherlands were people she didn't know. They were the only parents I had known and I was defensive. According to her, the Sutherlands stole her baby. I told her that she had no right to talk badly about them. She came right back and said I was wrong and disrespectful to her. The argument didn't last very long, despite both of us being very loud. She apologized for what she had said and I said, no, it had been my fault. Eventually, we got back on track.

When she asked about Cecilia, I regretted telling her about the alcoholism. Hearing that she had left me with an alcoholic stranger only reinforced her guilt. I also should have skipped telling her about the year that I spent in Byer's Home for Boys in Denver after Cecilia and Hollis had divorced. I let this slip out in the course of telling her about my childhood.

We talked on the phone for almost three hours and neither of us wanted to hang up. I still didn't have the entire story. All I knew was that Frances had left me with Hollis and Cecilia and then they disappeared. Given how upset she could become, I wasn't sure just how to press her for more details. Frances did mention my father several times, but she revealed very little about him.

Toward the end of the call, Frances asked, "Are you going to go away like you promised?"

"If that is what you would like. I don't want to cause problems with your family."

"I was a rotten mother to you and I'm sorry. I have no right to ask, but I really would like to talk to you again."

"Well, I still don't understand everything that happened. I have a lot more questions that only you can answer. If you want to talk again, I would like that."

"I'm glad you feel that way. I feel better knowing that you don't hate me. What I should do is sit down and write a letter and try to tell you everything. That way if I get upset, you won't know."

"What about your family? In your letter you told me you were very frightened of them finding out about me. What if they did? Then what?"

"When I got your letter, I was terrified of them finding out, especially my brother. Angelo can be one mean son of a bitch if he wants to. He is usually a nice man but I don't know what he would do if he found out I had a son on the other side of the country. He might flip out and throw me out of his house. Janice would never believe it. I don't know if she could forgive me if she found out."

Then Frances said, "But you know what? I don't care right now. You came back to me for a reason. Maybe God has stopped being angry with me and sent you because I have suffered enough. Anyway, don't worry about my family. Let me worry about them. Only don't write here anymore. My brother might see your letters. I will write but don't answer. I'll call instead. I lost you once and I don't want to lose you again."

Finally, we hung up.

I was exhausted, just like that night in Berkeley with Susan six months earlier. Rolland came back into to the living room, amazed that we had talked for so long. For the next hour I tried to recount to him what we had talked about. Later in the evening, I called Susan.

Much of my past had been a blank slate. Now a small portion of it had been filled. I still didn't know the entire story of how Frances and I became separated. She wasn't my mother but at the same time she was my mother. It was hard to reconcile the contradiction.

I remembered the anger I had before I met Susan. I was fairly certain that I had come to terms with my anger before I started my search. But after this phone call with Frances, I knew that any anger I once felt toward my mother was now really gone.

When I began this search, my plan was to make a brief contact with her and my father. Once they had answered all of my questions, I would again disappear from their lives. I had no expectation or desire to develop a relationship with either of them. But the telephone conversation with Frances abruptly changed everything. I had no idea what was next. The only certainty I knew was that this telephone call was just the beginning.

# *Chapter Five*

After our initial talk, Frances called daily for the first week. The calls were shorter and she cried much less. She said that she had to hear my voice "so I know I'm not dreaming all of this." We continued exchanging information. In addition to her frequent calls, she was also busy writing letters.

I never knew what stationery Frances would use until I opened the envelope. Most of the paper appeared to be whatever was within her reach. She never worried about the size or whether the edges were evenly cut or what the paper's original purpose had been. For her third letter she used green lined paper that looked like it had been hurriedly pulled from a discarded accounting ledger. Her stationery was all function and no form.

Her letters included notes in the margins at the beginning and the end of the letter, or wherever she could find the room. These notes were confusing because I was never sure where the letters ended. Sometimes when there wasn't enough room, she pulled out another piece of paper, added her afterthoughts and then titled the page, "The End" or "Read this last."

\*\*\*

*June 2, 1976*

[A note at the top of the letter read: *I hope you are not a sensitive boy.*]

*I'm not a slob. Don't judge me by this letter.*

*My dear James,*

*In my heart I would have loved to write my dear son, but what right have I to say that? Ever since I heard your voice Saturday evening* [our first call] *I have felt guilt roaring through my bones. There hasn't been one moment of the day that you are not on my mind. Somehow it is like you are haunting me. I can see you in front of me all the time. I already know what you look like. I cry so much that my eyes are ready to roll out of my head.*

*All I can think about is leaving you, a fat, healthy baby boy to some alcoholic. But who am I to condemn this woman when I did so much worse? All I think about is who took care of you when you were sick, when you had the measles, when you cried, or got hurt. Then they threw you in some home for boys with no parents.*

*You expect me to not have any feelings. God is picking at my bones. He has his way of punishing me. You keep saying I shouldn't feel guilty. You will never know what has happened to me. There were times I thought of you and said to myself, he is 19. I wonder if he is in the Army. Sometimes I worried that you were killed. Don't think that there weren't times that I did not just wonder.*

*Jim, don't misunderstand me. I am so happy but so confused. I don't know what to do. I'm happy but also I am so sad. My heart has been thumping from the day I opened my brother's letter. I would never in a million years open a letter that did not belong to me, but when I saw the name Sutherland, I got weak in the knees. I knew it was you. I destroyed the letter so no one would see it and I memorized the address.*

*What kills me is I have devoted my entire life to my children. I loved them very much and worked hard for them. I gave them everything. I spoiled them. My sisters called me a bad mother but my children and grandchildren love me very much. When they make mistakes, I always tell them that they take after me. There is so much to tell you that can't be put on paper. It would take years to tell you my life story.*

*I should see a doctor because my heart is thumping so hard. Now I am getting so nervous. At present I'm under so much tension. I do hope someday I can see you for God only knows how long before I drop dead.*

*I can't write a letter that makes sense. I haven't written a letter in years. I can't even spell anymore. I was always a poor speller. I just want to hold you in my arms and beg—I keep thinking of you as a little boy— forgiveness. I love you more than I love my other children, for all the love you never got from me while growing up. Jim, you missed a lot growing up away from me. I know I can never make it up to you—never, never. The best part of life is growing up. Going to school, laughing, crying, your first date, fighting, playing. And with you, I missed it all.*

*I spent most of my life devoted to my children, taking them to the park, movies, plays, and historical places and many more places. All I can think about is you as a sad little boy. I just can't make myself believe you are grown.*

*I have so much work around this house right now that I should not be writing letters. But I've got a feeling you may want to hear from me. Though I may be wrong. Remember you are in the best part of your life so make the most of it for there is nothing like your youth. Stop thinking about me and more about yourself. My life is over and the few years I have left I go to my grave with tears in my eyes over you.*

*Love to my darling boy*
*Mother*

*A hell of a mother I turned out to be. This is me, Jim. I hope you can understand the writing. Read it over and maybe you can make it out.*

\*\*\*

During one of our phone calls Frances opened up about her daughter Janice, and her husband and three children. I was glad to hear about another person to whom I was related by blood.

Frances surprised me again in a later call when she told me she also had another son. She had never mentioned him before and seemed uncomfortable talking about him. His name was David, and he was two and a half years younger than me. Because there were no other kids at Mountain View Ranch, I played alone with imaginary friends until I started the first grade. One of my pretend creations was a brother with whom I shared secrets. I knew that I really did have a brother somewhere and this feeling stayed with me for years. When Cecilia was drunk and abusive, I thought that if I had my brother with me, things would be okay. I envied the boys at school who did have brothers. I was astonished when I learned about David. The brother I had always imagined really did exist. I wanted her to tell him about me right away. She said she would eventually but she had a number of reasons why she wanted to wait. The calls and letters continued.

*June 7, 1976*

*Dear Jim,*

*Please excuse whatever I write on. I've sent you letters telling you about myself. What I wrote I have never told your brother or sister. Somehow I feel you are brighter and more understanding. I am very high-strung and a very nervous person. I get carried away and my writing becomes messy because I am shaking all over when I write to you.*

*You said you would like to meet me. Believe me, I also want to see you but are you sure this is the best thing for you? You asked me to tell Janice and David about you. You have to know that this would be very hard for me. I will in time. I love you more than I love them. For years you missed so much and so did I. I never tried looking for you because I knew I would never find you. But I never forgot how I had lost you. That pain will be with me forever.*

*I am a simple woman. I'm not wealthy. Actually, I'm broke. As I told you, I live with Angelo in his big house and take care of his two children. They are spoiled and treat me like a servant. I don't tell my children this or anything else. At least here I live independently and do not have to ask my children for anything. For as long as I live I shall never live with my children. I would jump out a window first. They would drive me crazy. Maybe I would drive them crazy first, I don't know. I could never stand anyone watching me all the time. Especially now, I don't want anyone on my back as old as I am.*

*Janice is married to Stanley, a good Polish fellow. He is the greatest. What a good husband she has in him. He works very hard in a factory where he has worked for a long time. They have their own home and have three children. Janice works nights at an insurance company.*

*Your brother David works for the State of Connecticut. He is a drug counselor. He thinks he is an artist and does a lot of what he calls art. I call it junk. He wants to buy a farm and put bums on it to work. Every bum that comes by, David helps out. I don't know what he has on his mind and I never question him. When he talks about buying a farm, I tell him not to look at me for I only have seven dollars in the bank. I don't know what I do with what money I have.*

*I guess I am always spending on grandchildren or myself. If I buy something, my sisters still say, "What do you want that for?" Ever since we were little they have watched me, and what I do. Even as an old lady, I do like I did when I was younger when they ask their questions—I don't answer them.*

*I don't have a lot of new clothes but when I buy myself something I buy good quality. I had to go to a wedding in April. One of my sister's sons got married and all she did was brag, brag, brag what a good girl he married and she comes and tells me. I went out and bought earrings for $30 to wear to the wedding and my sisters flipped out. "Why did you buy such gaudy earrings?" They hate it when I wear big loop earrings. They say I look like some gypsy. So what if I do?*

*My sisters are all comfortable and have good husbands. They waited and got married at 28 to 30. But the best years of their lives flew by. Even now as old and ugly as I am, I am fatter than all of them and they still watch me and they still ask me stupid questions. They are jealous of me because I have always been the most free. They wear pantsuits. I only wear dresses. I have enough sense to know that no fat lady should ever put on a pantsuit. My sisters are very stingy people.*

*There is only one brother who likes me and he spends everything he makes. I am like that and so maybe that is why he and I like each other. I never could save. I have enough insurance to bury me, and that is all. None of my children will fight about my money when I am gone.*

*When Doug died three years ago, everyone was shocked when I told his wife, Janet, to find another husband and blow away from here. I told her that nothing could bring Doug back. She got married again recently. She moved to Florida and is sending for the three girls when school is out on June 22. I also told Janet if her new husband was no good that she should leave him and find another and never stay alone. My sisters are raking her over the coals because she married again and left Connecticut. What the hell do they know what this woman has been through, losing her husband and the father to her children? I love my two daughter-in-laws.*

*So give me some time. Don't push me. I will tell Janice and David about you. I know you are anxious. And I know you said it would help me if I had someone here to talk to about you. Just give me time. I am anxious to let the world know you are mine.*

*Are you happy? I am.*
*Love to my baby.*

***

In the early weeks I didn't mind Frances' frequent calls. She had no one with whom she could share her story. She also called a lot because, as she had requested, I was not answering her letters. She was worried that Angelo would find out about me. Ironically, charges for her phone calls started appearing on his phone bill, which created problems later.

When she called, I tried to convince her that she needed another ear besides mine. She mentioned a woman named Mabel, who had been a friend for over 40 years. Frances eventually confided in Mabel and the phone calls became less frequent. But now they were replaced by calls from Mabel. She was a lovely woman and overjoyed with the story Frances had shared. Mabel was religious and told me how much Frances had suffered when two of her sons had died. She saw my return as a miracle that Frances deserved. What amazed Mabel was that Frances had kept my existence a secret from even her.

A relationship was developing between Frances and me. I encouraged her to talk with Janice. It was only a matter of time before word about me got out. I felt that despite the initial shock, Janice would understand because she had three children of her own. She would recognize the guilt Frances suffered over the loss of her child. A few days before I received the following letter, Frances called and told me more about my half brother David. It was a very difficult conversation for her. I now understood why she was reluctant to tell David about me right away. The entire story emerged as the letters continued.

***

*June 7, 1976*
[Second letter on this day]

*My son I love you regardless of what I am. I am the bad seed*

*My dearest,*

*After speaking to you last night, I don't want you to have the wrong impression of me having two sons out of wedlock.*

54

*I have four sisters and four brothers. My mother and father were married up in Boston. My mother taught school and my father was a businessman. As far back as I can remember, my mother was singing and dancing, and as I grew up I was the spunky one. My four sisters were very shy and would hide when we had company. I was a little different. Mother took me to dancing school where I became a ballet dancer. I loved ballet. When I danced my heart and soul were in it. My sisters would just stare and call me fresh. I was the favorite of my mother and they did not like that. When my mother died in 1928 I was 15, the ballet lessons stopped. My father never approved of it but I still went on dancing in my own way. I was young, healthy, very thin, short, and wiry. When I was 16 nothing could keep me down. We had a big house and when everyone was sleeping, I would jump out one of the windows, climb down a tree, and go to the park and dance and dance and dance until I was all in. I would sneak back home and my two older sisters would be crying and I ignored them and hopped into bed and went to sleep.*

*I hated school. I would go and dream all day. When it was time to learn to sew, I went to the gym instead and climbed ropes, swung on the bars, and exercised.*

*My father was very strict. No one could go out. So every chance I'd get I would sneak out. One day when I was 17, I met the man I thought I wanted to be my husband. There was a skating party at the trade school and the girl I went out with told me about it so I climbed out the window and off I went. Paul was a skinny kid in trade school learning to become a plumber. He was the first boy that attracted me. All I did was tell him lies. I told him I was hungry and my father was so mean. I had no mother. He felt so sorry for me. I was innocent and stupid. I thought if I got married, I could leave home and stop looking at those four old maids (my sisters). I talked Paul into marrying me. I was 18 by then. We went to a small town and got married. He had a Ford and it was February and snowed like hell. After we were married, I became frightened and cried. When he stopped the car, I jumped out and ran. I'll never forget how he ran and couldn't catch me until I fell. This was February and he graduated in June. He wanted me to tell no one that we were married until June. So he lived at his house and I went home to mine.*

*We lived apart about four months. After he got out of school he came to my house with $100 and wanted me to go with him to New York and I said no. I was frightened of what we had done. My father had a big house and yard and I ran away from Paul, but he chased me and put me in his car. My father was working in his store. My sisters didn't know what was going on and they ran around the house screaming as my new husband chased* me. They called my father but by the time he got there, Paul had put me in his car. I was fighting and beating the hell out of him. I pulled his hair and scratched his face and tried to get out of the car but he would not let me go. He said, "I never thought I married a wild Indian."

My father, who did not know this man, grabbed Paul and I thought he was going to kill him. Paul said, "I am married to your daughter." My father said, "You both get the hell out of here now." My father's hair turned white overnight. I loved my father and I was always his favorite. I love my father so much. He gave me everything. And it never left me that I had hurt him so much by what I had done.

Paul and I were dumb kids and we lived in one room, then in two rooms and then in three. When I had my first baby, I was 19 and my sisters came to visit. They did not approve. I had not changed. As a girl I loved nice clothes, expensive ones, good creams for my face. I always wore earrings. I loved to dress. Not my sisters. They were plain but pretty. I was always ugly. Always looking to buy something for myself. When I went home to pick up my clothes, I had 20 skirts and blouses, shoes, tennis racket. I had beautiful broaches. My father had given us everything.

I loved my husband very much until my sisters started to come to my house. They tried to boss him around. I was having babies and they were crying because I had no nice things. Paul did not make a lot of money and so there was not enough money to buy me nice clothes. My sisters drove him nuts when they told him to take better care of me.

This was in bad times [1931] so I told my sisters to take care of my children and I would go to work and I did. Every time they came to my house they would tell my husband to stop having children. I had three by that time. If I had stayed with him I would have had 20! He started to drink and when I came home from work he would be drunk. I didn't mind him being drunk but could not stand the smell. My sisters continued to interfere and that drove him even more nuts. I will tell you more in the next letter.

If you want to write to me once in awhile, write to me at Mabel's house. Ms. F Roccolini c/o of Mrs. Mabel Ruggio. She is my friend. I am going to tell her about you. She knew your father.

This letter is so bad. I just sat here crying and shaking. I thought if I wrote I would get you out of my mind for a while. I got you out of my mind all right, but I started to cry when I started writing about when I was first married.

*Frances*

***

Another letter arrived the following day.

***

*June 8, 1976*

*I didn't sign my name because I can't stand for you to call me*
*Frances or Ms. Roccolini and I have no right to ask you to call me mother.*

*Dear Jim,*

*Now that I told you about my past, I will tell you more about your family.*
*I will start with your brother David. He's a bit of a ding-a-ling with big*
*dreams. He wasted eight years of his life on drugs and the time he spent in*
*prison because of them. Sometimes I think he hates himself for that time he*
*can never have back. He was 32 on March 21 or 23. I can't remember. I*
*know you were born on the 21st. I don't know where the hell you got the*
*idea that you were born on the 26th. It may have been over 30 years ago,*
*but I was there and I remember.*

*Back to David. He is tall and thin and maybe weighs about 170*
*pounds. I can't tell. He has brown eyes and his hair is light brown. If he*
*puts on a few pounds he goes into a panic. His two greatest fears are get-*
*ting bald and getting fat. Sometimes I don't see him for a week or two at*
*a time. He only graduated high school. He is not too dumb but I love him*
*very much anyway. Sometimes I think I love you more. I get along well with*
*him, except when I tell him to please get married. That is the only time he*
*storms out of here.*

*When he was younger, he was very fussy about his clothes. Now he*
*doesn't seem to care and is always in jeans or cut offs. The only thing I*
*can't stand is when he shows up in my house with his damn dirty sneakers.*
*I go crazy and always get after him to get rid of them. He looks at me, and*
*laughs and tells me I don't let him live his life and he is not a baby.*

*Sometimes when he goes out with girls, he tries to dump them after-*
*wards. He has a very bad habit—he dumps them on me and Janice, your*
*sister. He says he doesn't want to hurt their feelings so he brings them to us.*
*He is always running away from them and I can't understand why. I guess*

57

he just lives the way he wants. I don't approve but I never say anything to him. I am just glad he is not lazy. When he comes to see me here and if I am cleaning the range, he will take my cleaning rags away from me and starts cleaning it. He will also shine up whatever I was cleaning. Then he will wash my dishes, wash the floors and walls, vacuum, and haul out the trash. It drives him nuts to see me here working hard for Angelo and his ungrateful kids. One thing I like about David is that he works fast, just like me. Not like Janice. She is pokey and moves like a blind snail. I end up screaming at her, "For God's sake, can't you move any faster?" All she does is STOP and say, "Ma, stop swearing." I tell her to go to hell.

Now as for your sister, Janice, sometimes she drives me up a wall. She spends more time in church where she prays and prays. I think she is saying a lot of prayers for me, and that is why she is in church so much. I tell her she is nuts. I could never live with her, even though she said I should when I am older. I have to say she has a clean house—too damn clean sometimes. But this is all my fault. I was too hard on Janice when she was growing up. I relied on her to take care of everything when I was working. I would go crazy if I came home and the house was not clean. She comes here with Stanley sometimes and tells me she is going to help. This is after I have already cleaned this house. This house is clean but not enough for her. We argue all the time about whether or not this house is clean. In the end whose fault is that? Mine. Sometimes Stanley tells her to leave me alone. He really is a saint. I admit that I can be a slob. I can sit for a couple of days and do nothing. But then when I get the bug, watch out. I will work like hell for three days straight. Usually when I do that I end up sick for five days.

When I get finished writing about Janice, me, and David, you may want to run the other way. I am sure you must have been raised differently and lived a very different life than we did.

As for you, Jim, I am sorry to tell you this but you need to know since you are looking for facts about your heritage. We are all fat in our family. We are thin when young and as we get older we put on weight. My brothers and sisters all did. I am sorry to have to be the one to let you know this, but you need to know because the same thing will probably happen to you. Don't be surprised. Your father was thin. He had a brother named Andrew and Andrew was fat. However, you couldn't be sure he was really fat because Andrew was also very tall. Andrew had black curly hair and he was a good-looking Greek. Your father's other brother was bald, with squinty eyes. He was a bad-looking Greek. Your father fell somewhere in between his

*two brothers in the looks department. I still remember your father's square
jaws and his eyes. They were too big. My eyes were always too large too. All
my children inherited my big eyes.*

*Love to my baby.*

***

There was another letter in the same envelope. With no greeting,
Frances begins.

***

*I killed my husband. He died broken-hearted. We didn't get along because
I did nothing but make fun of his family and laugh at him. He drank
more and more. At night I would come home from work, put my children to
bed, do my housework, and then turn on the radio and dance all night by
myself. One night it was dark and my husband was sober for a change. My
hair was very long and he always told me to braid it, but I would keep it
in a knot on the back of my head and hanging down my back like a horse's
tail. On this particular night, I started dancing and he got up, grabbed
me, put his hand on my mouth, and pushed me onto the bed. He held me
down with his two legs on my back and took a pair of scissors and said," If
you yell I'll stick this in your neck." Then he proceeded to cut off all my hair
off my head. He hated my hair. He hated to see me dance. I guess that was
the way he showed me that he loved me because he was so jealous of me. He
did not want other men to look at me. He was jealous for what? It was so
stupid for him to cut my hair like that because I never looked at another
man. He was the only one I loved.*

*The next day I tied my hair, or what was left of it, in a kerchief, I went
out the door with my children and went home to my father. This was a very
hard thing for me to do because I was very proud. In my haste to get married, I hurt my father so much and returning to his house was very painful.
I cried for days. I couldn't go back to work for about two months.*

*Eventually, my hair grew back and I had it trimmed and went back to
work. My husband came to the house looking for me. My sisters would not
let him in and they hid my children from him. While my sisters helped me,
they never tired of throwing it in my face for years afterwards. Living with
them was hell at times. "Don't do this. Don't do that." I saved my money as*

*I worked and one day I went way out to West Hartford and found myself two rooms and took my children and beat it. I cleaned rooms for the landlady so I could earn extra money.*

*I stayed in my rooms for a month until I had enough money to pay the landlady to watch my children and then I went back to work at a regular job. Times were hard in those days but I always managed to get a job.*

*It was during this time that I met your father. Jimmy had come home from college and rented a sleeping room in the apartment house where I lived. This was because he had a job for the summer working in his brother's restaurant, the Athena Diner. The restaurant was up the street from the apartment house. I told him right off that I was married and I was not free to go out with him or anyone. He never gave up. I remember how he was so clean. That's what I really liked about him. I laughed so much when I was with him. I taught him how to dance and sing American songs.*

*Jimmy spoke broken English and I would correct him and tell him the right words. That damn Greek was smart because he always remembered what I told him. He also would dance Greek dances with his friends and sing. I was very happy when I was with him. When he had to return to school at the end of the summer, he did not go back to New York. He didn't want to leave me. We were always together. He never cared about me having three children.*

*I taught him to sing, "I'm a Rambling Wreck from Georgia Tech (and a hell of an engineer)," a popular song back then. Jimmy wanted to be an engineer and that was what he was studying at college. Your father came into my life when I was a very lonely young woman. My life didn't have much joy in it except for my children. He brightened up my life so much then.*

*I made him buy a car even though he kept saying he didn't want one and that he didn't know how to drive. That made no difference to me because I was determined that I would teach Jimmy to drive, even though I didn't own a car and hadn't driven for years. That's how I was when I was young—not thinking things through when I should. On the first day he had the car, I made him drive down our street. I wasn't actually in the car but running along side, yelling to him what to do. People screamed and ran and he ended up on the sidewalk. I told him, "Try, try again," and he did until he got off the sidewalk and back in the street.*

*Luckily we lived on a street that had very little traffic and he kept driving until he finally learned how. I was determined that he wouldn't have to depend on his brothers to get somewhere. I still can see him with that damn car up on the sidewalk and everyone screaming. We laughed so much.*

*After he learned to drive, Jimmy said he had a surprise for me. He made plans to drive me to meet his mother in Long Island. Then my oldest sister found out that I was going out with your father and all hell broke loose. Soon she had my whole family in an uproar. When they heard I was going to go to New York with him, one of my brothers cornered him and told him that if he took me out of state they would have him arrested. Of course, this ended me going to New York. My four brothers frightened him. He told me we were not going to New York. It wasn't until a month later that he told me why. My sisters made so much trouble for him and for me.*

*To be fair to my family, part of our problems were because of his family. Jimmy had come from a good family. He was young, he was in college, and he had a bright future ahead of him. His family was very proud of him. He had come to this country ten years before when he was 20. As you can imagine his brothers didn't like it one bit when they found out he was seeing me. There were a lot of reasons that were important in those days that don't matter now. I had three children and I was not divorced from my husband.*

*His brothers hated me but they never let it show when he was around. As time went on, I loved him too much to be ashamed of our relationship. If he left me it was because he didn't want to hurt his family because they meant so much to him. He was ashamed of what happened. He was like my sisters in that he would rather die than shame his family. I wish I could make you understand.*

*I found out I was pregnant with you in September. At first your father was happy. He insisted that the baby had to be healthy and drove me to see a Greek doctor for check-ups. The doctor was SO old. To this day I can still taste the calcium pills that damn doctor made me take. Gradually, things changed. Jimmy was happy about a baby until he realized what his family would do when they found out. He began to change. He was afraid of my family too, since he had already been threatened by one of my brothers.*

*We started to have arguments. Me and my mouth and temper did not help matters. He did not come around as much and that made me even crazier and when he did come back, I was not nice to him. I worried about what I was going to do if my family knew.*

*The last time I saw your father was December 31, 1941. It was my birthday. He came by and brought me a birthday cake. I had a neighbor next door, a young girl, Joanne, who had not been married very long. It was her second marriage and she had three children. Her husband was about to leave as he had joined the Army and the War had started. I told*

*Joanne about me going to have a baby and about your father. I didn't know
that she had also told her husband. Shortly after Jimmy arrived with the
cake, Joanne and her husband came in to my apartment. Joanne's husband
grabbed Jimmy and punched him in the mouth. He was stunned. I was already upset and started screaming. Jimmy looked at me, turned and walked
out the door and I never saw him again.*

*Your father was not a violent man or he would have punched Joanne's
husband back. He didn't know what happened. Joanne's husband thought
that your father was responsible for the situation I was in. Somehow he
overlooked my part in what had happened.*

*Later I read in the newspaper that Jimmy was a commissioned officer
with the Army Engineers and had been sent to North Africa.*

*I sit very still right now as I remember the times with your father. What a
life. I was hell on wheels in those days and must have driven him crazy. But
I can tell you honestly that I never regret the time that I spent with him. My
only regret is that the time was too short, that and being so young and stupid.*

*As sad as I can become when I think back, there still is happiness for
me buried in those memories. Now you have come back into my life, it is not
easy for me to face you and my past. Are you sure you want to know me?
Do you still want to see me after the things I have told you?*

\*\*\*

I found out later that Frances and my father disagreed about what
happened on the night of December 31, 1941. Their memories con-
cur only in that it was her birthday, that there was a birthday cake,
and it was the last time they saw each other. From that point on
there is little agreement about that evening.

Was it the passing of time that caused my mother and father
to recall the night of December 31 so differently? Or did each hold
on to a memory that would later justify their own actions that led
to their separation? Eventually, I was able to reconstruct what happened between them that New Year's Eve, by combining elements of
the stories each told me later.

# Chapter Six

June 11, 1976

My dear Jim,

I received your letter and was glad to hear how happy you are. Mabel spent the day with me yesterday and all we did was laugh. She is something else. I finally told her about you and it made me feel a lot better. She wanted to know when I was going to tell David. She kept hoping that David would drop in while she was here so I would have no choice but to tell him about you. Thank God he didn't show up and I was glad he didn't. I am not ready to tell him yet.

This morning, just when I was starting to write to you, David came in with a box of strawberries. The strawberries were a good excuse for him to come by. I wanted to get back to this letter but I couldn't get rid of him. He had those dirty sneakers on and a pair of overalls and no shirt. I told him to wash his hair. The temperature is 90 right now. David works the 4 p.m. to 12 midnight shift at the hospital.

He is on my back and I am ready to jump out the nearest window. He asks me if I am okay as he looks me in my face. It makes me uncomfortable. He knows me like a book and I know he knows something is bothering me. I can't tell him about you yet. For the past two weeks he has been here every day. David was always close to me. As he got older he tried very hard to get away from me. He was turning into a man and this is what he needed to do. Now I tell him to get married. As soon as I say that, he is out the door and gone. David gets very moody at times but lately he has forgotten his moods and is intent on finding out what is bothering me. David has a St. Bernard dog and has to board her out in the country because the dog is too big for his tiny apartment and he works long hours. I think that dog is the only thing he loves. The dog is always dribbling all over David and his clothes. YACK!

Mabel would have told David if he showed up yesterday. She is so happy that you have found me. Mabel doesn't think I should worry about anything. I wonder if she would feel the same way if you were HER son and that you had suddenly come back. I asked Mabel if she remembered Jimmy and she said, "How could I forget? You were out with him every night." I told her she didn't know what the hell she was talking about because he worked nights.

Most nights I called her after I put the children to bed and went downstairs to wait for Jimmy while he was in the shower getting ready for work. He had to be to work at 8 o'clock in the evening and we ran up the street to the Athena Diner. It was lucky if we got there by 8:30. When he was late, his brother would give him hell in Greek, while giving me dirty looks. I sat in a booth with a bunch of girls, who worked across the street at a big insurance company. I just sat there, waiting until he got through his shift.

I look back now and I don't how I ever did it. The next morning I would dress and feed the children, take them to Mabel or the landlady, and then run to work. I got home at 3 p.m., picked up the children, cooked, cleaned the house, washed, and put dinner on the table. Then we ate. I'd take them out for a few hours in the yard. Sometimes I peeked in Jimmy's window, thinking, "Boy, has he got the life." Sleep, sleep, sleep, and get up at 7:30 p.m. and go to work at 8. He never seemed to be in any hurry. I did this for one year and I never got tired because I was so happy to be around him.

Today when I hear my daughter say, "I'm tired," I tell her that if I was her age I could push her house across the street. I was strong when I was young, and healthy. Never sick until I was 40. David told me that his biggest fear would be to marry a lazy girl. I asked him what he would do if he did. He said, "What do think? I would be gone the next day."

When it was time for Jimmy to go back to college, he wouldn't go. This was about the time he decided that I needed to move away so his brothers could not keep an eye on us. It was easy for them to keep tabs on him because the diner was very close to the apartment house where we lived.

I moved to Hester Court and Mabel and I lost track of each other. She had problems with one of the rotten husbands she married. One day I ran into her and she wanted to move to the same building where I was living. She tried to get an apartment there but for some reason she couldn't. I told her to go to the main office downtown and bring her children. When they called her in to the office for an interview, she took her children with her. I told her to cry about how awful it was to live with all the bugs and rats where she was now living. She must have been a good actress because when she came to see me later that day, they had rented her an apartment in my building. When she came to visit yesterday, we laughed so much over the things she and I did in those days.

After I moved away from the diner, I never saw much of my family for almost 20 years. They were disgusted and ashamed of me. I married too soon, I didn't stay with my husband, and I was going out with your father. David was the last straw for them.

David was born two years after you. His father went overseas and was killed when his troop ship sank before he reached North Africa. After David was born my sisters would come and take Billy, Doug, and Janice to their houses on Sundays. But David never existed as far as they were concerned. I stayed home on Sundays with David and tried to make it up to him. He never understood why he could not go with his brothers and sister. My father died and never knew I had David because my brothers and sisters felt I had shamed the family and they forbid me to tell him.

David was six years old when my father died. A part of me cannot forgive my family for hurting David for something that I did. While that was going on, I had a bigger secret they knew nothing of—you and your disappearance.

To give you a better idea of what kind of man your brother is, let me tell you this. There are five girls and four boys in my family. Who do you think is the only one who goes to the cemetery and puts flowers on my father's grave? It is David. There was a large urn on my father's grave that got broken. Who fixed it? David. He goes on Memorial Day, Father's Day, Easter, and Christmas with flowers for a grandfather he never knew. It breaks my heart to think about that. He also takes care of the graves of his two brothers. I still cannot go see my handsome boys buried in the dirt. I cry and sometimes want to kill myself. I am a coward as I would have been dead long ago.

But I am getting side tracked again. After I moved to Hester Court, I was never close to my family. I never asked them for anything. I worked all my life to take care of my children. My brother Angelo's wife left him and moved to California. She was very young when they got married and he was much older. She became unhappy and no one knows why. What I do not understand is how she could have left their two children. But it doesn't matter. Shortly after she went to California, she was found dead.

Angelo was left alone with two babies to raise. My family rallied around him to figure out what to do. They came to me and begged me to help. He needed a housekeeper and someone to supervise the children as he had a business to run. Angelo is my younger brother and I felt sorry for the children that would grow up never knowing their mother. I agreed and quit *my job, gave up my little apartment, and moved into Angelo's big house.*

*I wonder how I let them talk me into it. I don't know. Janice and David tried to talk me out of it. "Please don't go. Think it over." David kept saying, "You'll be sorry." Janice wanted me to live with her. I thought it would be better for me to take care of Angelo's house and children since I was tired of working a regular job like I had been doing for the last 40 years.*

*Today I am responsible for the upkeep of a nine-room house and two children. They are so different from mine. Angelo has spoiled them because he has so much. I think he is trying to make up for the loss of their mother. I never spoiled my children because I never had much to give them. I look at these two and I am glad I had nothing when mine were growing up. They are very selfish and don't even share with each other. They don't do anything to help around the house. I do everything. I don't mind since I am the one who made the choice to come here. Work does not bother me if I am well and I can still work no matter how old I am.*

*If I complain a little to David or Janice, they go crazy. I can't tell David anything about what goes on here. Angelo was very upset when Mabel and her husband came to visit me yesterday. My sisters always looked at Mabel like she was some sort of a freak. None of them were ever nice to Mabel. But I don't care. She has been my friend for 40 years and is more like a sister than any of them. I like her and David loves her. My sister called last night. All they are concerned about are the children. They want to know if Janice took them to the dentist. They never ask how I feel or how I am getting along. All they tell me is how easy I have it. They come up here and look around to see if the house is clean and the children have clean clothes, and remind me of how easy I have it.*

*They have no idea how much work it is to keep this house looking nice. When they come for their inspections, I don't say anything. I am on the move all the time working around here. My sisters walk in, look around, and walk out. Angelo can't understand why I have so much to wash every day. I don't answer him. I live the way I want. As soon as his children are home from school, I grab them and throw them in the tub and say, "Damn it, wash!"*

*Love, Frances*

*P.S. I told Mabel yesterday that I look awful and I am worried about you seeing me. She looked at me and said, "Stop already with the worrying. This kid's coming to see his mother, not some pin-up." I always laugh when she is around. We laughed and laughed so much yesterday. Maybe that is why Angelo got so uptight when she was here. She also told me, "It's little Jim that wants to see you, not Jimmy, so stop worrying about what you look like."*

*I also told her you wrote to Jimmy and he told you that he didn't know me. Mabel laughed at first and then she stopped. "How could he say that? What the hell happened to that damn Greek's memory? Remember how crazy jealous he was of you? And what about the times he told his brothers that he was sick and didn't go to work at night because he was afraid you would go out? Didn't know you? What a bunch of bull. You know why he said that? Because Jim coming back must have scared the bejesus out of him." I also told her that you are not finished with him and you intend to meet him someday whether he liked it or not. She laughed and said, "Boy, your new son sure is just like you." It helped a lot to tell Mabel about you. She remembers crazy things that I have forgotten, and when she tells me I start laughing and I feel better. Mabel is happy for both of us. She helps me see that I should be very happy about your return into my life.*

*I really like Mabel. She has been my friend for over 40 years. How can anyone not like her? She had a terrible life, mostly because of the three rotten husbands she had. Well, maybe two and a half. Tony, her present husband, is a heck of a nice man when he isn't drunk. I want you to know about me so that when we meet you won't be surprised at anything I say. I am a little worried for what you might think after you read my letters. You are probably wondering, "Is this woman really my mother?" There is more to tell you. I am afraid it would take years to put it down on paper. I had better stop writing and get some housework done before the "inspectors" drop in. Until next time, keep the devil out of your eyes.*

*Love, Frances*

\*\*\*

A few days later, I received a large envelope. Inside were two notes written on smaller scraps of paper, along with a smaller envelope whose yellowed color and worn creases hinted at its age. The writing on the front looked as if it had been written in crayon, and the original color was faded beyond recognition. On the back, several lines had been scratched out and were no longer readable. I wasn't sure what to expect as I opened the smaller envelope. Out fell three locks of hair, each separated and held together by thread.

***

*June 12, 1976*

*In September 1973, when I first moved into Angelo's house, I gave up my apartment and sold my furniture, thinned out my clothes, and threw away many little things I had saved over the years. I was going to throw out these three locks of baby hair that I had saved. When I thought of you in the last few years, I figured that you were married somewhere with three or four children. You should get married. It will make a great difference in your life. You don't think so, but it will. I tell David the same thing.*

*I couldn't bring myself to throw out this envelope. It was my only proof that you existed. I could not show anyone and always hid this envelope in the bottom of one of the dresser drawers. I was afraid someone would find it. Yet I did not want to throw it away. I crossed off the name "Jimmy" and your birth date a few years ago. I was worried that if I dropped dead, my sisters or my daughter would find the envelope and might be able to figure out my secret. I kept this envelope all these years.*

*The lock of Janice's hair was cut when she was one month old. Yours is the black one and I cut it when you were about a month old. The brown hair is David's when he was one year old. You had dark hair like your father and were light skinned. The writing on the envelope was in lipstick. I don't remember why but I guess I couldn't find a pencil thirty-five years ago.*

*I thought that if you were single and found out the truth, you would try to find your father and not me. If you found him, I would hear somehow. But if you were married and had children, you would want to find me and not him. I know this doesn't make any sense and I can't tell you why I felt this way. It is like this envelope. I can't explain why I kept a piece of your hair. About six months ago I was cleaning the dresser and came across this envelope. Do you know what? I almost threw it away. I thought if I did, maybe I would finally forget about you. I sat down on the bed and cried as I touched your hair but I couldn't throw it away. I am glad I didn't. Now I can give it to you and you can throw it away if you don't want it. You probably think I am some silly*

*old woman spending years crying every time she saw the lock of hair*
*from a baby she never raised.*

*Love, Frances, your mother*

[On the second scrap of paper]

*When you read me the names on your baptismal certificate, your father's*
*name was correct but mine was my maiden name. I still do not understand*
*how the Sutherlands knew who your father was. I didn't tell them. Before*
*you came back, I had this feeling that if you ever came looking for your*
*father or me you would only find him. I didn't think there was any way to*
*find me because I used my maiden name. I should have known better. You*
*are a fox just like your father. I guess you were one step ahead of me. I am*
*laughing to myself right now. Except for one thing. I am so glad you never*
*found me when you were a teenager. You would have probably chopped me*
*up into little pieces had you found me then because you were so angry. I*
*have a strong feeling that you were like me then when you were young. I*
*had a fiery temper and a big mouth that was always getting me into trouble.*
*I may be wrong. Am I?*

\*\*\*

I called the next letter from Frances the "poor me" letter, inspired
by an argument we had over the phone. I don't remember what we
said but it had to do with my father denying he knew her.

Before beginning the search for Frances, it seemed logical to
start with James Zaldonapolous. I thought he might be easier to locate. With the help of a telephone book, I learned that he still lived
in the Hartford area. I wrote him a letter about the information on
my birth certificate, and asked him to get in touch with me.

I received an answer a few weeks later. His response was short
and business like. He acknowledged receipt of my letter, said that
"its contents are being analyzed" and that he would reply "in the
near future."

Two weeks later I received another letter from him in which
he stated that he was not my father. His reasons were not substantial.
He said he was overseas in all of 1942 (I was conceived in 1941), and

that he was married in 1944. None of this had any bearing on the situation. He said any baptismal or birth certificates with his name had been obtained illegally. They weren't.

However, the last two paragraphs seemed to contradict the first part of his letter. When I initially wrote to him, I never mentioned anything about my birth mother, other than I was searching for her. The final paragraphs of his second letter reveal too much about a woman he claimed he did not know.

He stated that the woman I was looking for was separated from her husband (true) and that she had other children (true) and that one of them was a girl (true). He went on to say he had not seen her since 1941. The letter concluded with "I know she is not around this area." I felt he was trying to discourage me from searching any further in the Hartford area. Maybe he hoped that I would not find Frances. If I found her, she could counter what he had denied.

His information was enough for me to suspect he might be my birth father. Obviously my letter had shaken him. Otherwise, why so many contradictions? I decided to give him time to think about the situation. Since he had stayed in Connecticut for the last 34 years, there was little chance of his leaving. I was also looking for my mother and I wanted to concentrate on finding her.

I never hid the truth from Frances. I told her I had located my birth father and we had exchanged letters. She was curious and asked me about him. I made a big mistake when I told Frances that he said he never knew her. She was furious. I tried to tell her he said this because was he was afraid of me. I told her I didn't believe him but she would not listen to me. His denial of her reinforced the anger she had toward him over the last 34 years. All she could focus on was his denial that he knew her.

After that conversation, I thought that I might have to make an unscheduled trip to Connecticut. I imagined having to restrain her from finding him and pounding the hell out of him when she did. The last thing I wanted was for Frances to confront him and set him straight about what "really" happened 34 years ago. If I was patient and didn't push, he might decide to talk to me.

After Jimmy got over the shock of my reappearance, his attitude changed. We exchanged more letters and eventually met. He told me his side of the story. Most of what he told me about their time together matched what Frances had told me. Despite this change, Frances remained angry with him. This anger erupted from time to time as we became reacquainted.

She was jealous of what might happen if he were to acknowledge me as his son. I was sorry that she had to relive those painful memories. Here comes the son she loved and lost, but he looks and talks just like the father she now hates.

I learned from my mistake and when the topic of Jimmy came up, I was very careful about what I said. She had a habit of hearing only what she wanted to about him. Despite her anger, she was able to share her earlier memories of him. Even though she felt abandoned, she never forgot the good times they had together. Frances always spoke highly of him, especially about the traits she was sure I had inherited.

For several years after we were reunited, she only referred to him as "that Greek son of a bitch." Yet she also came to his defense if I said something that she didn't like. With regard to my real father, I never knew how she would react. It remained that way for the entire 22 years of our relationship.

Frances knew she was partly responsible for my father's leaving, and some of her anger came from her regrets. Her life might have been much different had she behaved differently with Jimmy when they were together. This is not to put the blame on her entirely. My father could have done better too.

In her attempt to answer my questions, Frances was forced to confront a painful part of her past. By looking back she started a long healing process that eventually freed her from the fear and guilt she had carried alone for many years.

Frances could be self-pitying. I imagined sad violin music playing in the background as the following letter began.

*June 14, 1976*

*Dear Jim,*

*After speaking to you last night I didn't sleep at all. How could I? I kept thinking about the strong love you must have for your father. I don't belong in your class, nor do I belong in his. You and he will be great friends some day, for you think the same way and are very smart. Not me. I was always the dumbbell. He once called me "crazy." I don't remember why. You are like him, because there are a few things you have said to me that I will never forget.*

*Don't feel badly because you have said something that hurt me. You probably don't even know what you said. Don't feel sorry for me. I am used to it. Once Janice called me a "big mouth" after I had a fierce argument with my sisters. I know how I am. When I talk I can get carried away and start speaking too loudly. David covers his ears and runs away. The three of you have hurt me—you, Janice, and your father. I never told Janice. I am only writing it down for you. If I had to tell you to your face, I wouldn't have the heart to hurt you as much as you have hurt me.*

*Sometimes I wonder what the hell I am living for. Believe me, you broke my heart and now I don't care if I ever get to see you. All I can imagine is you being close to your father. Stay there. You walked into my life one day and now I feel like you have just walked out the same way. I was so anxious to meet you and now I don't care anymore.*

*Maybe I am jealous you may become friends with Jimmy and forget that you ever found me. Who knows? I am so mixed up. I sit here and cry like a crazy person. I have decided not to tell Janice and David about you. I can't take this anymore. I am at the end of my rope.*

*You will fit nicely into Jimmy's family. You went to college just like he did. I am sure that you will have a lot to talk about. I can imagine what his other children are like if they are anything like him. I must have been crazy to go out with him. What a gullible fool I was. I hope I get this terrible feeling out of me. Believe me, I paid for the wrong I did and I am still paying. There is never an end to my tears. I can't write anymore.*

> *Goodbye and good luck with the no-good stinker,*
> *Mrs. F. Roccolini*

*I hope David doesn't walk in. I will have a lot of explaining to do. Nothing dries sooner than a tear. Why does everyone hurt me? I never hurt anyone. Why?*

# Chapter Seven

June 16, 1976

Dear Jim,

How can I be angry with you when you send me such beautiful pictures? When you were a boy, you were a dead ringer of your father. But at this age you look more like me. I can see that you are a Postiglione. You have a mouth like my father. None of his sons looked like him. You look handsome but I don't know for sure because I have not seen you in person. I can't tell if you look anything like your older brothers. David's eyes and nose are like yours.

I am shaking like a leaf. I finally told Janice and David about you. Somehow Janice didn't blink an eyelash. I was surprised. I told her in the car while I was riding with her. She wanted to know what was bothering me. We are very close and I just came out and told her. I didn't go into any details until we got home. It was so hard for me to tell her. Then right after she left, David showed up on my doorstep. That was all I needed. He brought in my mail and could see that I had been crying. He asked me why I was upset. I said nothing. When he handed me the mail, I saw a letter from you. I opened your letter and said to him, "This is from your brother." The pictures you sent fell on the floor and he stooped down to pick them up. He stayed on the floor looking through the pictures. When he stood up, I could see that he was in shock. "Wow!" he said, "I'm glad he is getting bald before me," and then he ran out the door.

This took a lot out of me but I deserved it. Janice kept asking why didn't I keep you. That I can't answer. I struggled alone raising four kids, what difference would one more have made?

I feel so weak and I can't stand up. I have a great love for my children, a love so strong you will never know. You can never know how much it took for me to tell the two children that I love about the terrible thing that I did. My love for you goes deeper because all the years you grew up without me. I'll carry that guilt to my grave because I can never make up for the years you must have suffered wondering where I was and why you weren't with me. I am a very sensitive person. When you write to me and tell me not to be upset because it is all in the past, I can't feel that way. What happened is in the present with a terrible heartbreak. This will kill me.

*I am not a hard person but I can be a loud one. Your father was soft spoken and I think you are like him. I had to go to the doctor last week. I am on tranquillizers. I hate to take them but I just can't cope. Maybe after I see you I may feel differently. My hand feels so weak that I can hardly write. I am supposed to go to Florida in August with Janice, Stanley, and their children and Angelo's children. I hate the idea of going, but I made a promise to the children. Right now, I don't feel like I have the strength to get up and out of this chair.*

*Whenever I feel like this, I write. I must put it all on paper or I will bust inside. Only you understand what I am going through and what I am trying to say. I've always been talkative. But this morning Angelo asked me if I was sick. He noticed that I haven't said much to his children lately. Most of the time I am yelling, "Did your brush your teeth?" "Did you change your underwear?" "Don't come to the table unless you wash your hands." Lately, I have said nothing.*

*I have not always gotten along well with Angelo. He is so different from me. He never has a good word for anyone. If he is home and David comes to see me, Angelo looks him up and down like David was some bum. He never liked David because of his drug problems when he was younger. Even though that happened years ago, he still holds it against David. But I am very proud of David because he just ignores Angelo. He holds his head up high. He walks in and never says a word.*

*David has never said a bad word about Angelo. David says, "He can't help himself. That is just the way he is. What he thinks about me doesn't bother me and it shouldn't bother you either." David never speaks badly about any of my sisters or brothers. He really never knew them because mostly they never acknowledged or accepted him.*

*He is very close to Janice but they fight a lot. Janice doesn't approve of a lot of things David does or how he lives. He laughs if she tells him something she doesn't like about how he looks. Sometimes he comes to her house in a pair of shorts with one leg shorter than the other. I think he does this to aggravate her. I have to admit that he is spoiled and acts like he hasn't grown up. He sings and laughs all the time. I wonder if this news about having a brother will make him grow up. David is happy when he has money, and if he goes broke he is like an insane person. He never has any money because he is always giving some bum his money.*

*One day he came here and I was crying over something the children had done. They treat me like a servant and not their aunt. They are very spoiled and selfish. Their father spoils them, but I cannot say much because they are not mine. When David saw that I was crying, he stormed into my bedroom and grabbed a suitcase and started opening drawers and throwing my clothes into the suitcase. He told me he was going to take me out of here. He said I had to leave with him because he didn't want those kids making me cry all the time. And he didn't think I should be a servant cleaning Angelo's house. I said, "No." He would not listen to me and started pushing me out of the house. David calmed down when I got angry and started shouting. This happened when I first came here. It was also hard for me at first, because I couldn't get used to being here without seeing anyone. When I moved from my apartment and quit my job, I left my friends behind too.*

*I always worked hard to take care of myself and my children. My whole life was like that. I was very independent. The older I get, the more I am that way. Someday, if I can't take care of myself I will really kill myself. I don't want anyone to have to take care of me. I hope when I die, I just drop dead. Ever since that day when David got so mad, I don't tell him or Janice what goes on in this house anymore. I am not happy here but I never tell them. Angelo does not like my friends. It hurts me how he looks at David and how rude he is to Mabel when she comes to visit.*

*This isn't my house. It seems like it isn't his house sometimes. This house belongs to his children. I have been here three years in September and I still don't feel like it is my home. For my whole life I had my own place, and did what I wanted when I wanted, and where I wanted to go was my business. Now if I go anywhere, I have to give my life history to Angelo. I seldom go anywhere except when Janice or David take me. I can't get to the bus to anywhere from this house. I am stuck in the suburbs, not like when I lived in my apartment on the bus line in the city. I was never home then, even though I didn't have a car. You better believe that if I wanted to go somewhere, I would say to hell with everyone and call a cab and I would go!*

*I loved being in the city and always lived very close to downtown. What really gets me so uptight when I think about it is that for years I waited to get old so I would finish work and retire and go where I wanted. Do what I want to do and not work and sleep when I want to and spend time with Mabel. Now look at me. I am starting all over again with two children, washing, ironing, cleaning, cooking, and serving Angelo's daughter breakfast in bed. If David ever knew, he would throw her out the window. I must have had shit in my eyes when I agreed to come here. But I am a pushover when someone is in trouble. I always have been. So are Janice and David. I sure the hell hope you are no pushover. What is done is done. Tell me who the hell ever had a happy life? Not me for sure.*

*My children will not know about my misery here. I don't want to live with Janice or I could go tomorrow. I want to live alone now that I am an old lady. I love being alone. You know more about me now than David or Janice. It seems easier to tell you. I feel better already by writing to you because you are an intelligent man and can understand how I feel. Just like your no-good father.*

*I will send the picture back later, the one when you were four years old that you want back. I want to look at it longer. I got up this morning at 4 a.m. and looked at the pictures you sent. Now I will look at them again. All I did yesterday was look at your pictures. I love you very much.*

*Love, Frances*

\*\*\*

Shortly afterwards I received a phone call from Janice, who was overjoyed to hear the news. It was the beginning of a close relationship that we have maintained. Janice told me how she first heard about me from Frances. For weeks she suspected something was bothering her mother. Frances had become unusually quiet and withdrawn. Her eyes were always swollen and red. When Janice asked why, Frances became upset and denied anything was wrong.

One morning Janice thought that a trip to the mall might cheer Frances. Speeding down the freeway, she almost lost control of the car when Frances blurted out, "You have a brother in California." Janice pulled off onto the shoulder of the freeway, thinking, "My God, this is it. My mother has finally lost her mind." When pressed, Frances began to cry, became very upset and said, "I can't talk about it. Take me home."

It was a strange ride, with Frances crying and unable to talk and Janice wondering what had come over her mother. When they arrived home, Frances stopped crying and finally revealed everything that had been going on the last month.

***

*June 21, 1976*

*Dear Jim,*

*I have made up my mind. I am not going to Florida with Janice and the kids. I am coming out to California to see you instead on August 4th or 5th. I can't wait until September to see you. I don't know what's come over me. I called Janice and told her. She is upset with me and doesn't want me to fly out there alone. She gave me all sorts of reasons why she doesn't think it is a good idea, like I am too old and would get lost. Maybe I might not like you and you might not like me. She said the first thing I would do is start arguing with you. David and her are used to me and you are not. Then she wanted to know what to tell Angelo and her kids why Grandma is not going to Florida like she has for the past ten years.*

*What the hell is she talking about? I never knew I was that bad. I know that I must have my way about this. She and Angelo will just have to give in as my mind is made up. I am one way and I can't change it. I swear and yell, and when I make up my mind to do something, that is what I do and I don't give a damn what anyone thinks. I guess Janice is worried something bad is going to happen if I go to San Francisco by myself.*

*She told her husband about you last night. Stanley said, "Not your mother. I can't believe it." My son-in-law thought Janice made up the story. "All of her life your mother took care of people when they were in trouble or needed help. Look how she loved you and your brothers and our children. And you are trying to tell me she had a baby no one ever knew about?"*

*It is true that my children were my life. And I did help out so many people, even when I barely had enough for my children. I think Stanley loves me better than David or Janice.*

*Janice just called and wants to go with me to California. She even suggested that I take Mabel and maybe I shouldn't fly. She wants me to go on the train or the bus. Janice said it's too far for me to go alone. None of her ideas are for me, and don't you tell me not to come out there to see you. It was you who found ME and now you have to face up to what I want to do. If I take a bus or train like she wants me to, I would be dead before I got there. Not for me. I am flying!*

*Of course, I don't expect to stay with you. When I go on vacation, I treat myself good and stay in a nice, clean motel. I don't like hotels. Janice is still trying to talk me out of coming. She said, "Ma, what if you go to San Francisco and he hurts you?" She has some notion that you may hurt me. If you do, I told her that I deserve it and she started crying. I told her that if it would make her feel better that she should call and tell you I was coming to visit in August. She could ask if you had plans to hurt me. Of course, she said "Oh no, you don't. You tell him you are coming out to visit him and let's see how he takes it. Make your own call." She said you probably have to work and won't have time to spend with me, and then what? If you are working, I will sleep all day. I need a good rest from the work I do around here.*

*She is driving me crazy. I will never get this letter finished. Janice called again and wants to know how much talking we could do for three or four days. She said you would get sick of me and my big mouth real fast. If you get sick of me, I will tell you a thing or two. I never stay where I am not wanted. I will call the airlines and make the reservations. Maybe they can help me figure out a place to stay. Even if I see you only a short while in the evenings, that is enough.*

*Lisa, my granddaughter, called and I told her I am trying to write a letter and not to bother me. She asked, "Who are you writing a letter to, Grandma?" I told her that it was none of her business. You know what that fresh Lisa said? "Grandma, do you have a boyfriend?" I hung up on her.*

*Janice told me that you might be different from what I expect. You have to be like me or like your father. Why would I be disappointed? Well, I hope you are not too much like him. However, I hope you are quiet like he was. I sure hope you don't have my big mouth. But I do hope your disposition is like mine. To get Janice off my back, I told her I would think it over for one week or ten days before I make up my mind. I promised that I would not make any reservations until then. But I know me. My mind is already made up. I didn't tell her that.*

*Love and many kisses,*
*Frances*

*Please don't tell me not to come after all this.*
*I hope you can read this letter because I stopped and started it so many times.*

# Chapter Eight

*June 24, 1976*

*Dear Jim,*

*I just received your letter and more pictures that you sent. The pictures are beautiful and I read the letter 10 times. After reading your letter, I called Janice to find out how you are. She gets very nervous when she speaks to you. She told me that you said, "I hope I did the right thing." Janice wants me to stop calling so much, and bothering you with my letters. Somehow she got the impression that you think this family is a bunch of pains in the neck. Maybe we are but you might as well know. This is your family. I decided not to mention my calls or your letters to Janice or David again. Let them ask if they want to know anything.*

*I hope you understand what I am going to say now. I thought it over about coming to San Francisco in August. I decided not to come out there after all. It is not because I don't want to see you. I do. But there is a reason I can't. It is not that I am ashamed of you. What I have to admit is that I am ashamed of what people would think of a woman who did not keep her baby. I know that you don't feel this way and you are happy you found me. But deep in my heart I don't have the courage to meet your friends. It has been hard enough for me to face my son and daughter about what I did.*

*Don't try to talk me out of the way I feel. I'll never change and when I do finally see you, I'll want to bury my face in shame. You wait and see. I can never forgive myself. Remember I love you very much and I am so very happy that you found me. I hope I will feel differently some day and then it would be easier for me to meet your friends and the family that brought you up. But I can't face any of them yet.*

*As for David, I haven't seen him since I told him about you. I have spoken to him over the phone since then but he seems to be very busy. I know you would like to hear from him, but I don't think it is the right time to ask. He has to work out this thing himself. I will not bring you up to him. He has to come to me. I never pushed your sister or brothers into doing anything. I want them to do these things of their own free will. I hope this doesn't sound sharp. You are part of me and if their love for me is as strong as they claim, let them show it. Time will tell.*

*David hates his job and wants to quit. I tell him jobs are hard to come by these days and he should stick it out. That advice goes for you too. Work at whatever job you have until you can find one that is what you want. Don't ever be without a job. David is a good worker but he has his lazy spells. When he was younger he stayed home and slept all morning. When he got older he got a lot of jobs but if he didn't like what he was doing, he would tell them to shove the job, come home, and have another vacation. Doug and Billy were the same way. As they grew up their eyes opened and they realized that to be successful they had to stop walking out of jobs because they didn't like something. I knew they had to work the rest of their lives and that time would come soon enough. So when they walked out of jobs, it didn't bother me. Janice would get after them and yell, "What do you think Mother is?" When Doug and Billy got married, they settled down and worked hard. Eventually they bought their own homes. I think that's what killed them, working too much—they both had two jobs. I don't believe in working that much. When a man works 40 hours a week, that's enough.*

*Sometimes I worked two jobs when I was alone with my children. I never became rich. However, I always had a little extra money. Even now, David comes up and says he is broke and I give him $10 or $20. He doesn't fool me. I know he is saving his money. He wants a farm so I hope he is putting his money away. I don't ask him what he does with his money. He doesn't spend it on women. He makes them spend on him. He works around a lot of women at the hospital and manages more time off because he is such a B.S. artist and those women really like him so they believe what he says.*

*David will never be broke as long as I am alive. I can't give him hundreds or thousands of dollars because I wasn't a scrooge when I worked. I never saved very much. I liked to spend too much. What is money going to do for you if you drop dead? I like to spend it now.*

*I always spoiled my boys. I can't say that I spoiled Janice. Somehow I was harder on her.*

*David lives like a hippie. He loves antiques and has a dinky antique shop where he works when he is not at the hospital. He lives in a small apartment connected to the shop. Can you believe he sleeps on a bed on the floor that sits on cinder blocks? He cooks, washes, and cleans for himself but on Fridays he asks me to come there and straighten things up. He doesn't fool me. He doesn't need my help, he just wants to make sure I get out of the house and have somewhere to go. I never go there unless I am asked. Once you get to know him, I am sure he will be very close with you.*

*David was never close to Doug and Billy because they were so much older. But there is only two years difference in your ages.*

*I enjoyed your last letter. I am very proud of you standing up for your rights at your job. No one can tell me you are not my boy. I feel better when I don't think about the past. I had made plans to go to see a psychiatrist about how mixed up I feel now. I knew it was going to run into a lot of money but I made an appointment anyway. When I called the office I was so nervous I forgot to ask how much it would cost. I called back later and the receptionist said the first visit would cost $75. Boy, did I snap right out of it as soon as she said that. I broke the appointment. Mabel was the one that told me to go in the first place. I know how guilty I feel but I have to figure it out on my own. Otherwise I will go broke talking to a doctor. I'm going to try not to bring the subject up anymore. Next time I call and start telling you how guilty I feel, hang up on me.*

*Stop worrying about the money that I spend calling you. First of all, Janice won't take money from me, so I'll go to the telephone company and give them $30 or $40 to put toward her bill. The only thing I hope is when she or I call that we are not interrupting your personal life.*

*Janice just called. I told her that I was writing you a letter and she got after me again. She said I shouldn't treat you like I do her and David. I don't know what she is talking about. She said you have a life of your own and I should leave you alone. She said I couldn't keep you hanging about me coming out there either. Well, I'm not and I won't change my mind.*

*She also said that all you thought you were going to do is meet me and then go on your merry way. I don't know what she or you are thinking about. She said I shouldn't feel the way I do about you. No, I told her, I should only feel for her and her brother. They can both go to hell. After I meet you I am leaving here. Damn it, I am not that old that I can't still move around. I am going on my own and away from everyone. I am beginning to believe Janice and David resent you. I am so angry. I am getting a headache. All I know is that I will see you. I am sure you are strong enough to take this. What a hell of a life. I feel like ripping up this letter but I won't.*

> *Love and kisses,*
> *Frances*

*The children are fighting right now and I am ready to kill both of them. I haven't lost my temper in years.*

*** 

I have always had an interest in antiques and "old things" ever since I was young. A few years before, Rolland and I opened our own antique shop in Petaluma, California for a short time. We didn't get rich but we had a lot of fun in an interest we shared. To learn that a half-brother I never knew shared my interest in antiques was an exciting discovery.

Another fact about David that gave me pause was our choices of sleeping arrangements. The bed in my flat in San Francisco was the same—a mattress and box springs on four cinder blocks.

***

*June 25, 1976*

*Dear Jim,*

*David called this morning and wanted me to help him clean his apartment. He came by and picked me up, but when I got there, the place was already clean. What he really wanted was to talk where Angelo or the children could not hear us. David wants me to leave my brother's house and let him find someone else to take care of the children. I won't leave. Angelo might be one big stinker sometimes, and I don't like a lot about him, but who else has he got except his family. And what about these young children? How can I just get up and go out the door and leave them all alone? Of course, I am sure they would jump on their beds if that happened because they would be so happy.*

*When David picked me up this morning, I got into his car and his radio was blasting away like always. I didn't say one word. Then David looked at me and said, "I know you Mother, and you are not yourself." I asked him why he said that. He said because I wasn't yelling at him about his radio being so loud. Then guess what he told me? He turns it up loud as soon as he arrives to take me somewhere. Then when I get in the car, he likes to hear me yell! He said that way he knows I am not sick. I wish I knew what he is talking about.*

*I think he wants to talk about you, but he didn't say anything, so I didn't either. I think he is still in shock. But there is nothing me or anyone else can do for him. This is something he has to work out himself.*

84

Janice got sick with a bad sore throat and didn't go to work last night, which is unusual for her. She works four nights a week and her husband wants her to quit but she won't. Stanley is having a hard time believing that I really had you. Janice said she likes talking to you because it won't be so strange when you come to visit in September. I left your phone number for David and asked him to call you. I was surprised when he said, "Of course I will." I should have told him the time difference. He is on a different shift these days—12 midnight to 8 a.m. So I don't know when he will call. Knowing him, it will probably be in the middle of the night when you are asleep.

As for the telephone bill for my calls last month, David told me to pay my brother what I owe and I don't have to explain anything to him. I wanted to pay the whole bill so Angelo wouldn't see the California calls. I know my brother. If he sees my calls, he will pester me about who I called in California. His phone bill runs over $100 every month. He is a businessman and he always calls New York, Philadelphia, and other places. Maybe he won't notice my calls because he makes so many. David told me not to pay the whole bill. He said to let my brother pay his own bills. Everything was all right until this damn bill arrived in the mail and I opened it. If I don't stay out of my brother's mail, I am afraid he will speak to me about it. But I don't want to explain myself and have him find out about you. Not right now anyway.

I am sending you a couple of snapshots David had around his apartment. I want you to see how much you two resemble each other and me. He said these are all the pictures he has. Everything else is on slides. The one with him in the beard is a couple of years old and the other is how he looks today.

Well, Jim, I better call Mabel. She is going crazy because she just found out her no-good husband is cheating on her. Don't get me wrong. Tony is a hell of a nice guy, but he drinks too much and doesn't know what he is doing sometimes. Poor Mabel has had a hard life because all of her husbands were bums. I told her over and over, "Who needs a husband if they are no good?" She never understood and ended up marrying another bum. I told her the ones I wanted I couldn't have, and the ones I could have were not worth having. When we were young, I was always telling her to go out with somebody. I reminded her of those days when she was crying about Tony. She got mad at me and said, "Look what going out with that somebody got you!" And I was quick to tell her, "Two handsome sons with character."

She stopped crying and we both laughed. Mabel tells everyone that she is a three-time loser, because of her three bad marriages. I guess you think we are a couple of morons.

Well, Jim I hope you don't think too bad of me. My spelling is so bad. I sent you a card the other day. After I mailed it, I remembered that I forgot to put my name on it. I am so damn nervous that I keep breaking things around me. I will be okay so don't worry. If you are like me, I know you will worry. I love you very much.

Love,
Frances

***

June 30, 1976

Dear Jim,

I received your letter and the pictures. Thank you. They were very nice. I liked them both but the one with the cat I liked better because I liked the way your beard was cut.

I have been in a fit of anger this morning. I must have written 25 letters and torn them up. I wrote about me, things I never told anyone not even my children. I wanted you to know what I am really like and then you could form your own opinion. Maybe I was coming on too strong and making you wonder just what kind of mother you found.

Janice keeps saying that you are a Sutherland and not a Postiglione. What does she know? She tries so hard to get it into my head that you are a stranger. She gets very angry when I tell her she is crazy. How could you be a stranger, my own flesh and blood? Then she tries again to explain it to me. So finally I said, "Okay, he's a stranger," so she would shut up. Come hell or high water you are my son, but I will never tell her that again. My ears are hurting because she kept on until I said, "Okay, okay."

She can't change my mind. I don't like her anymore and I don't like David either. Sometimes I don't even like you. I told her you are a Greek, a real Greek and half wop. She can't stand me when I tell her that. All I have to say is "He is Greek, Greek," and she runs away.

Jim, tell me the truth. Is Janice right and I am wrong? You won't hurt *my feelings. I told her that I love you as much as I love her and David. She said that is impossible because I never raised you. I know you have a father and a stepmother that you must love very much and that they love you. But my daughter can't seem to understand the way I feel inside.*

*You said that you have this friend who had a son she gave up and didn't see him for 20 years.* [The friend was Susan Hamilton, the Berkeley psychologist I saw before starting my search for Frances.] *Could you ask her to write to me one letter telling me how she felt when she found her son and how she feels now? Maybe you could talk to her and then write and tell me.*

*Don't let this letter upset you. If it does then I won't write anymore. I am very funny. I don't get in anybody's way and if I think I am, then they never hear from me again. Every year I spent away from you, that's how much I love you—STRANGER!*

*Frances*

\*\*\*

*July 3, 1976*

*Dear Jim,*

*I feel much better after speaking to you last night. When I talk to you, I am myself again and very happy. Hearing you say good night and that you love me is the happiest moment of my life. I wonder how you can love me since you have never seen me. I have never seen you but I miss you something awful. I'm beginning to realize that it is not you I feel so bad about. It is what your father said. In the name of God, I can't believe he thought so little of me. I cannot shut that out of my mind.*

*Janice is so right. You are not like her or David. You made that clear to me when you told me how independent you are. Well, that is good and I wouldn't want you any other way. I don't want to change your life. Be a Sutherland and I will forget that you are Greek. However, you are funny not to think you are Greek, with all that hair on your arms and chest.*

*About living here* [Angelo's house], *it was sweet revenge to have Angelo come begging to me for a change. He and I never got along before. I was living in an apartment with David. He wanted to go on his own but* would never leave me because he didn't want me to be alone. He was about 28 or 29, so it was time he got away from me.

I was happy when Angelo crawled to me for help. Once I asked him to help me when David was on drugs and he laughed in my face. For 20 years I never saw much of my family [her four brothers and four sisters] and it never bothered me one bit. The only reason I agreed to come here was to free David. I knew if I didn't break up my house, he would still be living with me. After I moved in here, I pretended I was happy. But it was David who was the happiest. Janice wanted me to live with her. Stanley said they would add a room on to her house and Janice would go back to work full-time. I can't see myself living with her or any of my children. I would jump out the window after one day in her house.

She called a few minutes ago and I am going downtown with her. Wait until she hears I want to run an errand for David. Hell will break loose. All I hear is that I always spoil him. She is the one that is spoiled. A friend of David's had a baby and he wants me to pick up a gift. He will send me a check and when I get it, I'll give it back to him and if he won't take it I will tear it up. If Janice happens to be there, they both will go crazy. Most of the time David laughs and Janice says I never taught him responsibility. Let him learn that after I am dead. The hard way. It won't kill him.

To be truthful, it is not that bad living in Angelo's house. But I have to admit the children are monsters a lot of the time. I lost all my friends because my brother doesn't want any of them around. One reason he acts this way is because my friends are poor. When they come to visit, I give them everything in the cupboards from soup to nuts and he knows it. I don't hide it from him. I tell him that so-and-so was hungry and needed something to eat. When one of my friends needs $10, I give it to them. Angelo starts shaking all over he gets so mad. I take from him and give to whoever I like. I have an understanding with him about what I wanted when I came here. He pays me. Janice tries to get me to put money in the bank. Sometimes she will say she needs $25 and I give it to her. But I know she puts it in the bank for me, because I don't save. She never needs $25 for herself. She is a fox about saving money.

Nobody I know seems to like Mabel. I told my brother yesterday that I am staying home this weekend and not going with him. He is driving Janice, Stanley, their children, and his children to New London and the shore for the day. I decided not to go with them and have Mabel come here and spend the day visiting with me instead. Angelo doesn't like that one bit. But he knows I can leave any time I want. Then he says, "Please don't leave my children." I can be mean when I want to. With this brother I don't care. I cannot forget the mean things he did to me.

The mailman just came by and I didn't get a letter from you today. Guess what? This is the first time I am writing a letter to you without shaking. I am not so nervous today. Don't worry too much about how I am and what I do because in my next letter I will turn around all I have said.

As far as yourself, go on and be James Sutherland and live any way you like. The furthest thing from my mind is to change any of that. When I see you, I will be happy and when you leave, a little sad but happy for you to go back. You are not a baby and for 34 years you have taken care of yourself. I am proud you turned out to be a good man. So my dear, stay that way. I love you very much. I have written this many times to you before. I want to kiss you on the top of your head where you are losing your hair. I want to touch your beard and hold your hands tight. After that I will be ready to die.

Take some of that hair off your face so I can see you just around your cheeks. I think they are fat. I love and miss you very much.

*Frances*

P.S. I had a good laugh last night when I remembered the first time you and I talked over the phone and you called me Mrs. Roccolini. No one ever calls me that anymore.

# Chapter Nine

What kind of mother allows strangers to take her six-month-old baby? The following narrative is pieced together from telephone conversations with Frances. It was painful for her to tell me. Several times she said, "I can't talk anymore. Let me call tomorrow and maybe I can finish." Eventually she did.

As I listened to her recall my birth and infancy, long held feelings of rejection began to fade. Telling me also helped Frances come to terms with her own guilt, and my story became our story.

\*\*\*

As her pregnancy progressed, Frances wore looser clothing. She went to great lengths to keep out of sight of her sisters and father. Luckily she did not show as much as she had with her previous pregnancies. Frances said no one seemed to notice she was getting heavier. "Maybe they did, but didn't say anything because they were afraid of my temper if they said I looked fat." My father was with her in September 1941 when she found out about the pregnancy, and stayed until he left in December.

By the time I was born in June 1942, Jimmy had been gone almost six months. He was drafted after the attack on Pearl Harbor. Although Frances and Mabel were close friends, she did not tell Mabel about her pregnancy. Mabel was in the middle of a messy divorce and Frances didn't want to burden her with additional problems. Frances confided in Helen, an older woman living downstairs in the apartment house. She was sympathetic and the only other person who knew she was pregnant.

When I decided it was time to be born, Frances made arrangements to take a few days off from work. Helen, who already watched Janice, Billy, and Doug while Frances worked, agreed to keep the children while Frances was at the hospital. Rather than go to a Hartford hospital where she might run into someone who knew her, Frances checked into the General Hospital in suburban Manchester. She knew no one in Manchester and this lessened her chances of being seen by friends or family. She was frightened, trusted no one, and took a taxi to the hospital. Cab rides were a luxury she could not afford, but when she knew my birth was imminent, she had no choice.

She checked herself into the hospital and told the admitting clerk that her husband was overseas. She used her maiden name, Postiglione, and made up a Manchester address. I was born at 4:30 on the morning of Friday, June 26. Worried about her children and her job, Frances only stayed a day and a half at the hospital. Despite the advice of her nurse, she checked out early. Frances boarded a bus with me in her arms for the ride back to the apartment in Hartford. She wanted to take a cab again but she did not have enough money for the return trip, and prayed throughout the bus ride that she would not run into anyone she knew.

Frances got back to the apartment unnoticed. She was very happy that her baby was fat and healthy. My chubby little body and face gave her joy despite her circumstances. But my appearance in her home quickly became the source of a new fear. What if her sisters and brothers found out? Her father was still alive and she was afraid of his reaction. She wasn't sure what to do.

Frances was not afraid to face the public shame. What frightened her was her family and what they would do if they found out about me. With me now in her tiny apartment, this was a real possibility. She was afraid that they would say she was an unfit mother and try to take away her other children; Janice, Billy, and Doug might end up in foster homes or be put up for adoption. Looking back at the social morés of the early 1940s and the religious beliefs of her family, her worries were justified.

Helen took care of me and the other children while Frances was at work. Helen was the only other person who knew about me. For the next few weeks, whenever a family member or a stranger came up the sidewalk to Frances' apartment, she grabbed me and the diaper bag and bottles and ran down the back stairs to hide me with Helen.

When Frances' mother passed away, Miriam, the eldest daughter, assumed the matriarchal role. Miriam kept close watch on her siblings while she helped her father manage their house. She had a forceful personality and intimidated her younger brothers and sisters.

Miriam was not pleased when she heard that Frances had been seen with Jimmy. Since she was Roman Catholic, his Orthodox religion and nationality were unacceptable to her.

That Frances was still legally married made matters worse in Miriam's eyes. She continually pressured Frances to return to her husband who had by this time been gone three years. Whenever Frances talked about a divorce, Miriam responded with threats. She would tell their father and have Frances' three children taken from her. Miriam's interference made things difficult for Frances and Jimmy. Miriam kept the pot stirred by watching Frances and reporting back to her brothers and sisters. Frances suspected that it was Miriam who was responsible for Jimmy's being physically threatened by her brothers. Miriam remained suspicious of Frances, long after my father had gone overseas.

One day, Frances saw Miriam marching up the sidewalk to the apartment. She grabbed me and ran down the backstairs to the baby hideout at Helen's. Miriam entered the apartment as Frances came in the back door. Although they were just children, Janice, Billy, and Doug were aware that there was a new baby in the apartment. Janice and the boys greeted Miriam with shouts of "Auntie Miri, Auntie Miri." Little Janice was bursting with excitement. "Auntie Miri, guess what? We have a baby. A little, bitty baby that lives with us," she blurted out as Miriam removed her hat and tossed her coat on the sofa.

"What baby? Where?" she asked, looking down at the little girl.

Janice was startled by her aunt's loud and angry voice. She had never heard her aunt talk like that before and it frightened her. She ran from the woman to hide behind her mother who had just entered the room.

"Fran, what is Janice talking about?" demanded Miriam.

Frances was paralyzed by the question but she knew that she had to overcome her fear or things would get much worse. She tried to be nonchalant.

"Oh for God's sake, Miriam, Janice made that up. Don't your kids imagine things and tell you about people and animals that they have met and played with? Janice does it all the time. You never know what she is going to come up with next."

"Well, yes, but this is different. Janice said there was a baby living here and I want to know why. Janice, come over here and tell Auntie Miri what you meant."

Janice started to cry and refused to move. This made Frances angry, but it enabled her to confront her sister.

"Well, are you happy she's crying? I told you, Janice just made that story up. There is no baby here. If you don't believe me, look around. Do you see a baby? Go into the bedroom. You are always snooping around anyway. Go ahead and be my guest. Look, damn it. See for yourself," Frances yelled at her sister.

Miriam walked in the bedroom and looked around. Frances was right behind her. In the living room, the three children huddled on the sofa. They had never seen their mother shout at their aunt before.

"Go ahead, look in the closet. Look under the bed. Look in the dresser. Who knows where that baby could be hiding?" Frances continued yelling at her sister and followed her around the room.

Miriam came out of the bedroom looking contrite having seen no evidence of a baby. Frances had the upper hand and she did not hesitate to take advantage of it.

"You come busting in here, assuming all sorts of crap and upset my kids. Now why don't you just get the hell out of here and leave us alone. What do you want anyway, checking on me all the time? Go on and get out of here. Here's your coat."

Frances took the coat off the sofa, pushed it in into her sister's arms, and shoved the shocked woman toward the door. The three kids cried as their aunt hurried down the steps and out to the sidewalk.

For a few minutes, Frances stood at the open door of the apartment, her heart pounding as she wiped away tears of relief. She closed the door and went back to comfort her children. The encounter with Miriam had put her secret in jeopardy. She had to figure out what to do next.

She considered asking Helen if she could leave me in her apartment. But Helen was much older and looking after a baby full time might be more than she could handle. What Frances needed was a safe place to hide me for a few weeks until she came up with a solution. She had to keep me from her family so they wouldn't find out. Then an idea came to her. The next day she went downtown and put an ad in the local newspaper. It read:

*"Working mother in desperate need seeks temporary room and board situation for newborn baby boy."*

In a few days, she received a number of calls in response to her ad. Among them was one from Cecilia Sutherland in Colchester, a small town 30 miles southeast of Hartford. The distance appealed to Frances and was the determining factor in where to hide me.

Frances didn't tell me how she got me to Colchester and the Sutherlands, perhaps another bus ride. She said that it was difficult to leave me with a man and woman whom she did not know. However, her recent close call with Miriam left her no other option. Every weekend, she traveled to Colchester to see me and paid the couple $10 for my board. She held me and cried when it was time to leave. Because she worked during the week and because of the distance, she could only visit on the weekend. Sometimes I was asleep when she got there, and Cecilia did not allow her to wake me. She didn't want to upset Cecilia, so she said nothing. Then another week had to pass before she was able to hold her baby again.

The few weeks turned into months. Frances didn't want to give me up but she knew she could not keep me. She still didn't know what she was going to do, but for now the arrangement seemed to be working. At some point, Helen introduced Frances to a couple she knew, Katarina and Nikos Mykonossos. They were childless and looking to adopt. Knowing Frances's situation, Helen saw a solution to benefit everyone. Frances liked the couple and they discussed the possibility of an adoption.

Frances didn't want to give me up but she had no choice. Nikos went to an attorney and had adoption papers drawn up. In the meantime, Katarina drove Frances to Colchester each weekend to see me and pay next week's board.

Although the paperwork was in process, nothing changed during the next month. Katarina and Nikos were anxious to proceed, but they realized how hard it was going to be for Frances and did not pressure her. Katarina continued to drive Frances back and forth to Colchester on the weekends, while Frances struggled with the idea of giving up her baby.

By the time I was five months old, the couple become impatient and told Frances that she had to make up her mind. They wanted a yes or no and they wanted it soon. Otherwise they were going to look somewhere else.

Reluctantly, Frances agreed to sign the papers and turn me over the following weekend. The plan was for Katarina to drive Frances down to Colchester. Frances would thank Cecilia for caring for me and take me home. Once they returned to Hartford, Frances would sign the adoption papers and give me to my new parents.

In her heart, Frances did not want to give me up. I was getting bigger. "You were the fattest baby I ever saw," she said. However, she knew I needed a real mother and not a rental. Frances took comfort in knowing that if she let this couple in Hartford adopt me, I would be close by. Frances thought she would be able to see me once in a while. But the plans Katarina and Nikos had for their new baby did not include Frances after the papers were signed. When they made that clear, Frances understood that her relationship with me would be only from a distance.

The next weekend arrived and the adoption papers were ready. Early Saturday morning, Katarina drove Frances to Colchester. The Sutherlands lived in an apartment attached to the rear of the gas station that Hollis operated. Katarina pulled her car into the driveway and the two gas pumps were locked. There was no one around. The two women got out of the car and walked to the apartment. They knocked on the door without getting an answer. The shades were down so they could not see inside. Going around the corner of the building, they found a window with a partially drawn shade. Frances' heart stopped when she looked inside and saw an empty room.

They ran back to the door and began pounding and yelling. Still no answer. They hurried out to the front of the gas station. Again, no one responded to their desperate knocking. On the door was a sign reading, "Closed." The truth of the situation was obvious. The Sutherlands had moved out and taken me with them.

Katarina lost control. It was still early morning and she ran out into the middle of the empty street and shouted, "They stole my baby! Call the police!"

Despite the theft, the last thing Frances wanted was the police. She didn't have time to think about the kidnapping. All she wanted was to get Katarina and herself out of Colchester before the police arrived. Somehow she managed to get Katarina into the car and they left the town before anyone showed up to see what the screaming was about.

They got back to Hartford and told Nikos what had happened. He wanted to call the police, but Frances feared that if the authorities became involved, the events of the last five months would be revealed. Her family would find out about the baby. In addition to their anger, she was afraid of losing custody of her other children as a result. Katarina and Nikos gave in and the police were not called. They scolded Frances and told her that if she hadn't delayed the adoption for so long, this terrible thing would never have happened. They left, blaming Frances for everything. She never saw or heard from them again.

After I had disappeared, Frances became depressed and consumed with guilt. She regretted she had not acted more quickly to facilitate the adoption. Because of her Catholic upbringing, she eventually concluded that God arranged the disappearance of her baby as punishment. She had a baby out of wedlock and it was a mortal sin. But He made sure she suffered even more. She would go to her grave never knowing what happened to her baby. This was the punishment she deserved and she never questioned His judgment. She told no one and suffered alone with the secret of the baby she had lost.

Frances cried when she talked about the events of the summer and fall in 1942. I have often thought about how many times she must have relived those five months in her mind, how many times she wept. What a burden for her or any woman to bear. She suffered alone because she could not share her pain. No one else knew her story. Eventually, she buried the memories. As the years passed, she would be startled when passing a dark eyed, dark haired boy on the street that would be about my age. Then the memory of her baby returned. Later, when she saw teenage boys on the buses in Hartford, she wondered if one of them might be me.

***

*July 4, 1976*

*My dear Jim,*

*Speaking to you last night took me back many years. At last I am alone.*
*Everyone has gone to New London. Angelo and his children, Janice and*
*Stanley and their children have gone to the shore for the Fourth of July.*
*They have done this for years. I used to go with them, but not this year. I*
*just can't. To get to New London you have to drive through Colchester. Ev-*
*ery year in the past as I rode in the car and we reached Colchester, a great*
*lump came to my throat. I felt like I could not breathe, like some big hand*
*was squeezing my throat. My heart raced and sometimes I thought I would*
*faint. Every year I dreaded going through Colchester. I sat very silently in*
*the car and prayed none of the kids needed to stop to go to the bathroom. I*
*just sat there wishing the town would disappear. Sometimes I closed my eyes*
*because I did not want to see the gas station where the Sutherlands lived.*
*Sometimes I asked, "Have we left Colchester yet?"*

*The gas station is not there but was for many years. The building*
*must have been torn down when the road was widened. On one trip Janice*
*noticed how much I changed all of a sudden and asked me if I was feel-*
*ing okay. Of course I said I was fine, but I wasn't. There was no one in*
*the world, not even my daughter that I could tell about how I was feeling*
*as the car left the town.* [When I met Janice, she told me how Frances always became uneasy whenever they had to drive through
Colchester on the way to the beach. This went on for years and she
never understood why until she heard her mother's story] *And now*
*you have come back into my life, but I don't think I could survive going*
*through Colchester this year.*

*My son Doug wanted to buy a house in Colchester after he was married.*
*When he told me, I went out of my mind. I cried so hard and begged him*
*not to. He and his new wife could not understand why I got so upset. All*
*I could manage to say was that I had a bad experience there and I didn't*
*think it was a good place to live. In my heart I knew if they moved there, I*
*didn't know if I could manage to visit them. I carried on so much that I*
*scared them out of buying the house. Shortly afterwards they found one in*
*Windsor Locks instead.*

This happened when I was 43 because Doug was just married. To be honest, I was a little disappointed that he got married so young. I hate to say this, but what the hell, it is true. Besides, Doug is gone so what difference does it make. I think I expected him to help me raise Janice, Billy, and David, since he was older and on his own with a job. But he was too much in love.

"I can't live without her." Her name was Janet. When he told me that he wanted to marry Janet and for me to say it was okay, what could I do? I couldn't say no. I said, "Doug, I got married young. How can I tell you not to?"

He had a good wife in Janet. I liked her because she always agreed with whatever Doug wanted to do. So when the Colchester house came up, Doug saw how upset I was and decided not to buy it and she agreed despite liking the house.

But that was not all. When David grew up, he started going to Colchester to swim. When I found out, I told him not to go there again. He wanted to know why and I said that I knew someone who had drowned where he went swimming and he never went back.

I cannot believe it is true. Maybe I don't have to cringe anymore about Colchester now that you came back into my life. But I still hate the sight of that town.

You said that the Sutherlands must have lived in Hartford for a while because your baptismal certificate is dated 1944. I guess when they left Colchester, they must have moved to Hartford. I had better end this now or I will have a bad day. I don't want to think about you as the baby I left with them.

Mabel is coming to visit with me. Her husband is in New York playing in some elite club. I hope he doesn't come home drunk. How can anyone live with a man that goes to bed drunk? I know how disgusting a drunken man can smell. When Paul came home drunk, even if he was passed out, I could not stand the smell and I washed his whole body to get rid of the smell in my house. Drunken men smell awful. I asked Mabel and she said she let him lie there on the bed while she slept on the couch. In my day, we were lucky to have a bed and a couch.

We called Doug "Bunny" all of his life. That was because when he was born, my husband Paul said he looked like a baby rabbit. And William was always Billy to everyone. My two sons never drank. David, I don't know whether or not he drinks. I know he likes wine. I hope that he can take it or leave it alone.

*Today I don't feel so bad. I enjoy being alone in the house for a change and looking forward to seeing Mabel later. Usually these holidays make me sad to think I have two dead sons. What kills me is that I worked so damn hard when they were growing up that I did not spend enough time with them as boys. Now when I have time to enjoy them in my old age, I had to lose them. They were almost like brothers to me. We went to the beach for swimming and I swam way out until they yelled at me, "Come back, Ma. Don't go out so far." I used to do it just to scare the hell out of them. I miss them both very much.*

*I never had a car when they were little, so as soon as Bunny was 16 he got a car. He took us everywhere after that. Billy couldn't wait to be 16 and they took turns driving the car. But that damn car started a lot of trouble between them. They stopped being good about sharing and soon had fist fights over it. Billy was younger but he was a better fighter. Bunny ended up crying and I was always getting in between them and breaking up their fights. This was probably not too smart. Once I got clobbered in the face. I was furious. They both got scared and took off running. They knew if I caught either of them, they would be in a lot of trouble. That was the last fight they had. They were 14 months apart. Well, I hope I am not boring you.*

*Before I got your first letter, I had it in my mind that God took Bunny and Billy from me to punish me for losing you. I am Catholic, but not a very good one. What I am trying to figure out is that if God punished me for losing you, then what is He up to bringing you back? Another reason I don't feel sad today is because my mind has been on you.*

*Janice said to me, "You can't cry to Jim like you cry to me and David. You don't know him. He doesn't know you." Yet yesterday when I went to pieces and called, I calmed down after talking with you for only a few minutes. I couldn't believe that you wouldn't let me hang up until you were sure I felt better. I still can't. My God, what I have missed all these years you have been gone. However, I promise I shall never call you again when I am that upset. I am very sorry.*

*I am having a hard time waiting to see you in September. If you weren't working, I would get dressed, throw some underwear in a small bag, and call Janice to come and get Angelo's kids, and be on a plane to California this afternoon. I would stay at the airport until I could get a flight even if I had to wait until tomorrow morning. This is the way I am.*

*I know I am not the family that you are used to. Ruth is your mother and Hollis Sutherland is your father and you have a sister. They are the people that cared for you and loved you. And where was I? Yet I believe you inherited some fine qualities from your real father, and I want you to know that the Postigliones are a fine stock of people. I have always felt compassion for others and I know you have a little bit of that. You showed me that yesterday. Jim, I am proud of you. I hope one day that I can see you face to face and tell you in my own way. As I get to know you through your letters and our telephone calls, I realize that I have one great regret— that I missed so much of your life. That is the penalty I must pay for not having you with me as you grew up. I hope this finds you as happy as I am. This is what you have done to me. I love you very much. This is the first holiday I don't feel I have to go to the cemetery and cry over my two dead sons. I know where my boys are and they will be happy not to see me crying for a change.*

*Frances*

# Chapter Ten

*Tell me if you like this letter.*

*July 6, 1976*

*Dear Jim,*

*Now that I have looked at your pictures and see that you look like me, I think you must be ugly. All this time I thought you were handsome but today I changed my mind. Did I tell you that you were born big? Over eight pounds, just like me. I was nine pounds when I was born and my mother always told me I was her biggest baby.*

*I'm lucky that I was never sick and if I did catch cold it only lasted a couple of days. I remember my father paid us girls a dollar to take cod liver oil. He believed it would make us fat. My four sisters and me were skinny. In those days, you were considered to be beautiful if you were fat. I don't know how I could have been thin when I was young because I love to eat. I didn't start to get fat until I reached 40 and ever since then I keep getting bigger and bigger. My sisters eat nothing and are always on a diet and you should see how thin they are. Not me. I am a junk food eater and so is Janice. I never seem to eat a meal. I just like to snack all day. I love cakes but I don't like cookies.*

*My mother and father had four girls, then one boy, then one girl and then three boys. One boy died at the age of nine months from measles. My sister Miriam is 65. Then comes me at 62. Anna is 61, Teresa is 60, Salvatore is 58, Silvia is 54, Angelo is 56, Albert is 52, and Leonardo is 50. He is the baby. They are all living. Salvatore is the only one that has been sick. He has trouble with high blood pressure. Not me. When I go to the doctor he takes my blood pressure three times. That is because he doesn't believe that my blood pressure is so normal when he sees how fat I am. I don't know why it isn't higher but it is always very low*

*I had one operation when I was 40 on my gall bladder. My mother, your grandmother, had the same operation but it was in the 1920s and she died on the operating table. Lucky for me the doctors and hospitals know a lot more these days and I made it through okay. I was in the hospital for eight days before they let me come home. Janice was upset because I was sick and could not work. She left school in her senior year when she was only 17. She worked at an insurance company and took a second job in a movie theater on the weekends. That is where she met Stanley. He worked at the theater too.*

*Janice wanted to become a nurse and probably would have had she not stopped school and gone to work. It is one of my regrets that she had to go to work because I got sick and had no money to support her, David, and myself. She would have been a very good nurse because she always cares so much about people, even more than herself. At that time Doug had gotten married so Billy and Janice ran the house for me. Billy was not married yet, but he was working. Somehow they managed to scrape some money together and sent me to the shore so that I could get well. I went when David got out of school.*

*I had a lot of nerve to be sitting on my rump sunning myself at the shore while Janice and Billy worked and paid rent on two places. Where was my rich family then? They never came near me. I think they were afraid Janice would stop working and go back to school. Then I would ask them for help. Let me tell you, my daughter and Billy never forgot how my family avoided us. Billy was very fresh and always said, "Your family stinks." My children always stood on their own two feet. I taught them never to ask anyone for anything as long as they were able to work themselves. Maybe I didn't teach them that; maybe it was in their nature to be independent like I am.*

*I came home in September. I was very lucky that I never was sick after that. I went back to work and never stopped. I tried to get Janice to go back to school but she didn't want to. She got used to making her own money, she met Stanley, and things changed for her. I look back and I am very sorry, as she loved school. At the time I didn't realize how important it was. Otherwise I would have kicked her ass back into school. Billy hated school and poor Doug went only because he had to. He was the quiet one and never gave me any trouble about school. In those days, I was too wrapped up in trying to make a living and take care of us. I missed the important things that happened.*

*David grew up alone. I remember how he sat by the door with his cat, waiting for me every night when I came home from work. For some reason I remember that all he would eat was fruit. He still likes fruit. I hate it. I would much rather eat bread and eggs and spaghetti. These are my favorite foods. I am not much of a meat eater. Let me tell you that if eggs do harm to people, they haven't killed me. I eat them whenever I feel like it.*

*My father was 79 when he died. He had high blood pressure and drank wine in his old age and maybe that's what killed him. My father was 38 when he got married. He had four brothers who lived to be over 80. When I was a little girl, they all seemed so handsome. And they also seemed to be happy all of the time. They were good businessmen as was my father. My father made a lot of money in his own grocery business. I can hear my mother calling him a dumbbell. She was a schoolteacher and always thought because of her education she was smarter than my father. But my father was making the money. She had a brother who was a lawyer. My father said that all he had was a big mouth. My mother's father had owned a nail factory in Italy and they were very well off. My grandfather's name was Andrew and my mother always said she was a blue blood because her family was rich.*

*Mother reminded my father of her blue blood until he said, "Then why don't you go back to Italy where the blue bloods are, if that's what you like. What are you doing in America?" My mother never stopped loving her native country. On the other hand, my father was very glad to be here and proud to be an American. He laughed about my mother's blue blood connections. She would get angry and call him vulgar. They did not get along when my mother put her nose in the air and ignored him.*

*One sister looks just like my mother. This is the sister who takes one look at me and all she can do is just roll her eyes. She is always telling me to shut my big mouth. That's probably because she talks like a bird. I only have one sister that I really like and get along with. Her name is Sylvia and she is the youngest girl in my family. She is more like me and we have fun when we are together. It drives our other sisters nuts because they try to act so prim and proper. Not Sylvia or me. If we are at a big family wedding or party, Sylvia will have a drink and then bug me to have one. I am not a drinker, but if Sylvia is there, I will have one with her.*

*If Janice is at the party she can get pretty uptight, just like my sisters, when Sylvia gives me a drink. David will tell her to leave me alone and I should drink all I want. None of my boys drank. I met a girl David was dating and said to her, "I am happy David doesn't drink." She answered, "Not much." So who knows? Who cares?*

*Anyway, when Sylvia says, "Come on, have a drink," in no time we get happy and start having fun. You should see my sisters. They get so upset I think they are going to pass out. For some reason, they think that Sylvia and I are embarrassing the whole family with our laughing. They are crazy. This only makes Sylvia and me laugh all the more. We have a good time especially after we have a few glasses of wine. While our sisters may not approve of how we are acting, neither of them will come near us nor tell us to stop because they know God would have to help them if they did.*

*David called me. "Mother dear, how was your weekend? I missed you. I was very busy. Are you busy today?"*

*I said, "Yes."*

*"What about tomorrow?"*

*I said, "No."*

*"Please come and dust and wash my clothes and clean my house, Ma. I will pick you up early tomorrow morning."*

*I said, "Okay."*

*He is just about to quit his job and go to Virginia next week. Jim, he is 32 but he acts like 19. He wants to visit his father's family and they are always bugging him to come down. He is lucky Doug and Billy are dead or they would kick the hell out of him if he said he was going to quit his job so he could take a trip. Doug and Billy were much older than David. He was a little brat to them and sometimes they were mean to him.*

*Janice does for him what he can't get me to do. Boy, he loves us so much when he wants something. I can't tell Janice I am going there tomorrow. She reminds him that I am an old lady and doesn't think I should do his cleaning. But she can't put that into his thick skull. He is not lazy but if he horses around all weekend and goes to work today, he wants to come home to a clean house and fall into bed and go to sleep. He lives like a hippie but he is a clean hippie. Sometimes I never see him for weeks at a time. I don't give a damn what he does. The only things that bother me about him are if he doesn't feel well or gets arrested. I suspect that he smoked pot sometimes. Once I asked him and told him that he had damn well better tell me the truth. He looked right at me and said, "Yes" and started to laugh. It never bothered me because the important thing was that he did not lie.*

*There were some things that I tried to teach my children. They were honesty, self-respect, and cleanliness. I am happy to say that all of them never disappointed me with regard to these things.*

*I never brought you up but by looking at your pictures and seeing how you trim your beard so neatly and by reading your letters, I have a pretty good idea who you are. You are smart like your father and I am a dumbbell like my father.*

*I just remembered the girl David dated for a while. He went with her a long time and she would come to my apartment and wait for him for hours until he got dressed. I thought he was going to marry her, as he seemed so crazy about her, until he found out her mother didn't like him because he was Italian and she was Jewish. He said to her, "When your mother loves me as much as my mother loves me, I will marry you." He told me he could never marry her. He said, "Ma, you should see her house." Apparently, it was a mess. But deep down he was very hurt that this girl's mother didn't like him because he was not Jewish. He used the dirty house as an excuse and stopped seeing her. She came looking for him and he had me tell her that he went away to New York to live.*

*Even now, Janice and I have one of his old girlfriends on our backs. I like her very much but David says she is lazy. He went to her apartment to see her and ended up cleaning it. While he did this, she sat down and drank coffee and smoked. That did it for him. He runs like hell when she comes around. As a matter of fact, David found her a roommate simply to get her off his back. She wanted him to move in with her to help with the rent. After he found out she was so lazy, he lost all interest in her. She always calls me looking for him. I taught all my children not to be lazy and that is why he is like that. He has been around me too much yet he tries not to be like me. That is one reason I want him to get married, so he can get away from me.*

*I don't care if he marries his best boyfriend. That's what I hear you can do in some places. Nothing surprises me anymore.*

*I have never felt that my children have to take care of me now that I am old. They owe me nothing. I made miserable lives for them in one way or another. They struggled for what they had and have. None of them had a normal life like their cousins, partly because they never had a father to help them. Bunny and Billy were lucky in that they got wonderful wives that worked along side of them. Janice has a wonderful husband and she doesn't know how lucky she is. She is not lazy. When she needs something and wants to buy it, I tell her, "Go to work" and she does.*

*David, well that's David. He had it harder than my other children and if he got married he would be happy like Janice, like Bunny and Billy when they were living. David is still a little mixed up. He bummed around for eight years after he got out of high school. That is when he got into drugs and his life went to hell. He went to Florida and ended up in a Mexican jail. That is my fault because one day I told him the truth about his father.*

*I met his father, Ted, two years after you disappeared. He was in the Army and had been a state trooper for the State of Virginia. He also taught as a golf-pro. Since you have come back, I think that David is wondering, "What kind of mother have I got?" Sometimes he calls me and says he is going to come by, as he must have a talk with me. I know it is to ask questions about you and your father. But he never shows up. He wants to know and at the same time he doesn't. But if he thinks I am going to tell him my personal business concerning YOUR father, he has a long wait. I don't know what he has got on his mind and I don't care. I kept my children clean and worked hard for them and they can never say they saw unpleasant things in my house.*

*After David was born, my life ended. I got word from the Army that Ted was killed when his troop ship sank off the coast of North Africa. He had listed me as next of kin in the event that something happened to him. The Army sent me a small insurance check that Ted had taken out in my name. I can't tell you how bitter I became afterwards. Again, I felt that God was punishing me. This time I could not ask for forgiveness.*

*All I did after that was to work very hard and mind my own business and take care of my children. When Mabel was around we went out together, but I did not drink and I could not stand the sight of any men. While they grew up, my children never asked questions about why they had no father. If they had, I would have told them the truth. I owed them at least that. But somehow the subject never came up. There was never a father around and they got used to it and didn't think much about it. If they did, they never told me.*

*I never allowed them to swear. I do and so does Janice, but not real terrible words. My sons never swore or spoke out of the way in front of me. I was strict to a certain extent with a lot of things that they could or could not do. I think they obeyed me because they were scared of me and my big loud mouth.*

*David never understands why I didn't remarry when I was younger. I almost did in 1956. Other than that, no men came near my door. I slammed it in their faces. There were men where I worked who wanted to go out but none of them interested me.*

*My sisters finally accepted being around me again when Janice got married. She had a big wedding and her aunts and cousins were invited. Before that, we didn't see much of them. I told her that she had to have a simple wedding because we didn't have that much money. Stanley's mother wouldn't hear of a small wedding. So I told her, "You want a big wedding, you pay for it." This embarrassed Janice, but I had to be honest. I couldn't go into debt for two or three thousand dollars. Of course, Stanley's mother thought I was some kind of nut. Now she and I get along very well, because we are both old ladies and understand each other. Actually, I don't understand her because she never learned English very well and still speaks Polish.*

*On Janice's wedding day, my sisters and brothers showed up. David didn't really know them. He was an usher at the wedding and had to bring my sisters down the aisle. He didn't know who was who. But I give him a lot of credit. He escorted them down the aisle like a gentleman. He just stuck his nose up in the air. That is what I taught him: Never let anyone think they are better than you.*

*At another wedding, my sisters were shocked and stared at him because he had grown a beard. They sat there staring and talking. He never cared. He usually appears at family functions, stays for a short time, and leaves. He doesn't feel comfortable around my family. Part of it is their fault for how they treated him when he was little boy. But mostly it is my fault too. I let David down. He always thought I was the perfect mother. He found out about his father, and now he finds out he has a brother. I don't know how he takes these surprises.*

*Now about your father—I think his mother was very old when she died. Or at least I remember reading it in the paper. Jimmy had a father but for some reason the father was not living with his mother. He was so crazy for his mother. When he worked at the Athena Diner that summer, he went to New York every chance he got to go see her. If he didn't go home, then he called her every night. Jimmy must have loved her very much because he talked to her in Greek for a long time. Half of the time he used my phone because his brothers got on his back for the long distance bill at the diner. They could afford the phone calls because they were getting rich at the diner. One thing I can say is that he always paid me. He was not stingy or cheap.*

*The first drink I ever had was the one that he bought me. He took me to a nice restaurant, something I never did because I could never afford it. Before we ordered dinner, he asked me what I wanted to drink. I didn't know because I had never ordered a drink in a restaurant before. I said, "I don't know. I never had one before." He didn't believe me because he thought all American girls drank.*

*Well, I'll tell you more when I see you. I can't get over how I can write like I have known you all your life. Somehow it seems like I've always* known you. I do miss you. Why I don't know. And I haven't even met you yet. That is crazy. Who knows? Please forgive me for the telephone calls. Sometimes I need to hear your voice to be sure that you really did come back.

I haven't done a damn thing around the house today and I must hurry and start with cleaning. It is Angelo's day off. How I hate Tuesdays.

Love,
Frances

P.S. My sister Teresa called a few minutes ago and told me about a wedding shower for her daughter. I am expected to show up—with a gift of course. She gave her orders for Sylvia and me to follow: "Don't drink. No fooling around. Be quiet. Don't sit with Sylvia. Don't laugh. Don't talk loud. Be sure and dress nice. And please don't wear those hoop earrings."

This is the kind of stuff I have put up with from my brothers and sisters especially. If I want to keep the peace with them, I have to do what they say. Of course, that depends on what kind of mood I am in when I get to the wedding shower. I will do whatever I feel like and they can all go to hell.

\*\*\*

*July 7, 1976*

*Dear Jim,*

First of all I am sending this picture of me. This is how I look. Fat, old, and ugly. I am deaf in one ear and always saying, "What? What?" There are a million and one things wrong with me. Wait until you see me. I hope it's at night. I got fat all over. I hope this picture doesn't scare you.

When I tell David that I am going to faint, he says, "Please don't, Ma. I wouldn't be able to pick you up." We both laugh. Janice and David are afraid I will die of a heart attack. I always tell them I hope I do. Who wants to lie in bed dying? But now I tell them, "I have to see Jim first."

When I came to live here, I was only 165 pounds but in three years I went up to 209. I have never lied about my weight or my age. The reason I gained so much weight is that I never sit down and have a meal. I snack all day and am ashamed to say that a lot of it is junk.

When I got your first letter, it was such a shock that I could not even eat junk food. My face looks terrible because I lost 10 pounds overnight. I am now down to 190. My sisters tell me that I am disgustingly fat. I know I am. Janice is getting fat as she gets older and she diets all the time. Another thing that does not help is that Angelo has more food in this house than any store. But that is no excuse for me. Sometimes I think his children eat nothing. I eat it all.

I did my housework this morning and looked out the windows going from one room to the next. I feel like jumping out of one of them right now. This is the first time I had to stay home all day. To make matters worse, Janice took my checkbook and I can't get a hold of her. I don't need the money but a friend of mine needs a loan. I am mad as hell at Janice.

The mailman came with your letter and I read it over and over again and I know I am not crazy. For a while I thought I was losing my mind because the feeling I had inside was the same feeling I have for David. I love him very much. You will never know. I feel the same way about you even if I have never seen you. I love Janice very much too, but you two are a different kind of love. I don't know how to say it. I am not going to talk to Janice or David or Mabel about you anymore. I will keep it to myself and when I see you, maybe the feeling will be different. Who knows? By the way what does Rolland look like?

I love when you tell me to write or call whenever I feel like it. That is because I love writing to you and talking to you. When I talk to you I want to reach out and touch you. The most I really thought about you, before that first letter, was in the sixties. I am telling you the honest truth. When there were those riots all over the country at the colleges, I wondered if you were out there with those kids. I watched closely on the TV for you among the young men who were running and fighting and bleeding. I froze with fright and hoped that you were not hot headed like me. I prayed to God you did not have my temper because if you did, I knew you might be out there fighting. I hoped that you were more like your father but I thought, "God help you if you are like me." When I got that first letter, all I thought was, "Thank God he is alive."

I have decided not to call collect anymore. I will have to be desperate to call. You have a large apartment and must have big expenses. Besides, you also call Colorado and your phone bills must be very large. And don't forget that coming to Connecticut is going to cost you so I don't want you paying for my calls too. I forgot to call the telephone company today for a credit card. Someone told me I could use my brother's phone but have the call put on my *credit card. I don't know how true that is but I will try. He has not noticed the calls to California yet and I hope he never does. But if he asks who I call in California, I will tell him, "My son." I wonder what he will say.*

*Now I should tell you about your sister, Janice. First of all, I am surprised she ever got married. She wanted to be a nurse so badly. I already told you she dropped out of school when I got sick. In a way, I am glad she never went back to school because if she had not been working, she would not have met Stanley. He is a wonderful man and he is so good to her. He and his family fled from Poland when WW II started, but they were captured and put in a labor camp in Germany. After the war, they went to a displaced persons camp. Then they came to Connecticut because they had relatives here. They were very lucky because his mother and father survived and managed to keep the four kids with them during the whole time.*

*Janice went out with Stanley for four years and when she was ready to marry him she said, "Mother, I don't want to leave you." When it was time for her to walk down the aisle in church, she was very scared and I thought she wasn't going to be able to. The organ played and she stood there like a fence post and cried. Bunny and Billy came to the back of the church and pushed her down the aisle. She was crying so much that Billy said, "If you don't walk down that aisle, I am going to kick your butt." I had to leave my seat and go to the back to see what was holding her up. Then I started to swear. When she saw me coming and heard my big mouth that frightened her so much that she moved. That night she called me and said she had become petrified with fear and could not move. They went to Virginia Beach after the wedding. Jim, I am glad I only had one girl because if I had another one, she probably would be like me. Janice is not like me. She is like my sisters.*

*Janice looks a lot like me when I was younger. She has dark eyes and hair. She is so spoiled and says she is not. But it wasn't me who spoiled her. It was Stanley because he is so good to her. She has three very nice children, Nicholas, Kenny, and Katie. I am crazy about her little girl. I love her so much.*

*In one of your letters you told me that you wondered for years who you were. Is this what you expected to find, an old, fat lady with a loud mouth? Are you surprised? Are you disappointed after you have heard my stories about me and your brother and sister? What did you expect? Am I anything like the mother you thought you would find? Well, I don't think I can write anymore today. When I see you I will talk to you about whatever you want to know. I think I told you everything, but maybe you want to know more. I don't know.*

*When you come back here to visit, I want to see you alone at first. I want to talk to you alone for at least a day without anyone bothering me. Then I will send for Janice and David to come pick us up. I don't know how I'll work this out, but I will. I don't want my children around or Angelo's children asking questions when I am with you. After we spend the day getting to know each other, then you can spend time getting to know David and Janice.*

> *I love you very much and can't wait to see you,*
> *Frances*

***

*July 9, 1976*

*Dear Jim,*

*I am laughing up a storm. I found out Jimmy beat it out of Hartford and is down at Old Lyme. I bet your letter scared the hell out of him. Don't ask me how I found this out. I called Long Island where his mother used to live and where he came from when I met him. I asked for his brother Georgios' number. When I reached Georgios, he told me Jimmy was in Connecticut. Don't worry, I never told Georgios who I was and he never asked. Then I called the operator and asked for your father's telephone number in Hartford and she told me there was no listing. The operator then said that he had a new number. She gave it to me but couldn't tell me where it was. That's a bunch of crap for the birds.*

*I called again and got a different operator. Only this time I said that I wanted to reach my daughter and that she was stranded somewhere and I only knew the first three numbers of the phone she called from. The operator told me that this prefix was from the Old Lyme area. Old Lyme is on the shore and is where a lot of rich people live, so it figures your father headed down there. I might be old but I would make a good detective. Don't get mad at me for doing this. I know you told me not to contact him. Well to hell with that. I did it anyway because I couldn't help myself. I am beginning to get curious about him. But he will always run away from the truth about you. I want you to know that I never spoke to Jimmy and I won't call him. I promise.*

*I hope you continue to go after him until he agrees to meet you. I don't want you to give up, as I want you to see him and find out what he is really like. With his money and education and whatever else he has, I never thought that he would turn out to be such a coward.*

*If I am writing too much, be honest and tell me. I want no lies. No one could ever hurt me. I never went out with any Italian men because they were too much like me. I always was afraid of them, yet I married Paul, who I thought was Polish because he had very light hair and was very quiet. God, I was so stupid. The only reason I went out with that damn Greek is because he was quiet. Before I met your father, I never liked Greek men. They were too much like Italian men. I am so mad right now at that no good damn Greek—your father.*

*Love,*
*Frances*

# Chapter Eleven

*July 9, 1976*

*I write letters to you every day and tear them up. I probably shouldn't send you this one.*

*Dear Jim,*

*I went to bed early last night and I can't sleep anymore so I got up. I gave the cat some shrimp and if Angelo knew he would throw me out. He brings shrimp home, I cook them, and then nobody eats them. And I am not crazy about them. So why shouldn't the cat have them? I have never seen so much food go to waste.*

*I called the telephone company yesterday. I have to do something before Angelo wises up about the calls to California. Anyway the phone company will send Janice a credit card with a code number that she will give to me. When the bill comes my calls will be separate from hers. The only other way I can get my own bill is to have my own phone. I am thinking about it. I don't mind paying to have it installed but I have three grandchildren in Florida and they are all girls. God help me if they found out that I had my own phone. The calls would never stop and I would be so broke I could never call you. It is not the phone bill I worry about. It is they need this and that and want me to send them money so they can come back here. They are 16, 17, and 19 and always want something and I am their favorite grandmother because I am always buying them something. They keep me broke.*

*They are out of school but they don't want to work for the summer. All they do is parade around in their bikinis. God, what they wear. I swear I have handkerchiefs that are bigger than their bikinis. I give them hell and tell them to go out and find jobs and go to work. These three are lazy. These are Doug's children. Doug was a hard worker before he died and he gave them everything. His wife, Janet, is English and a wonderful girl. I always liked her and we got along just fine. She married an Irish fellow after Doug died and they both moved to Florida, and the children came down after school was out.*

*Boy, did my sisters talk about her after she remarried. I told my sisters to mind their own business for a change. Why should she stay home and cry her eyes out the rest of her life? That would not make Doug come back. She and Doug were very happy and they got along so well and never seemed to be apart. They were 20 years old when they got married. Everyone in our family was very shocked when she remarried. Doug was a quiet boy and all of my family loved him.* ·

*Janice thinks I am crazy. I told her she would do the same. Stanley laughs and asks Janice if he dies, would she marry again? Janice says, "Never. Never. Never." I tell Stanley, "Yeah, not much."*

*Billy was different. He was fresh and yelled at his wife, Louise, even on the day that he died. She went to visit him in the hospital with their little boy who was six. Billy was very sick and sitting in his bed. All of a sudden, he could not breathe and he yelled at her to get a doctor. She left their son with him and when she got back with the doctor, the boy was crying. Billy had died in the short time she was gone. Louise never got over it. I had gone to see Billy the day before. It was Sunday and I stayed all day until he kicked me out. He told me to go home and yelled at me. When I left, all I wanted to do was walk. I walked three miles all the way home. I think he wanted everyone to hate him.*

*My sisters were crazy about Billy. He was really good looking. Actually, he was the best looking of my children. David is the ugly one. Doug was good looking too, but when he got sick he looked like he was 60. Janice was always very pretty, but she is starting to look like me as she gets older.*

*I get a kick out of David. He tells me that no one will cry when I kick the bucket. You know, this is the first time in a long time that I have thought about my two boys. I forgot about them when you showed up, that's for sure. I had forgotten about everything in my life when you showed up. Except the past and the terrible thing I did to you.*

*Do you know, I was thinking about Mrs. Sutherland all night* [Cecilia, not Ruth, my stepmother]. *She told me about going to Florida for a week and wanted to know if it was okay if she took you with her. I didn't like the idea, but what could I do? This was before I met Katarina. Mrs. Sutherland said that she thought your name should be Leslie. But I told her that I did not want her to change your name. I thought she might ask me if she could adopt you, but she never did. I told her that if she did go to Florida that she had to let me know where she was. This talk about Florida happened around the third time I went out to see her. I gave her my telephone number to call me* *if she needed anything. Of course, I gave her $10 for board money each time I went. One time she did call and ask me to bring diapers the next time I came out. But she never went to Florida.*

*Sometime afterwards, I met Katarina. She and her husband, Nikos, wanted to adopt you because she could not have any children of her own. Damn it, I am shaking now. I couldn't make up my mind, as I couldn't think about giving away my baby. Finally I realized that I had no other choice and I changed my mind and decided to let Katarina take you.*

*I have searched for Katarina because I want her to meet you. I called and called and found her daughter and she told me that Katarina had passed away. I just want you to know what I am saying is the truth. If only I could find Helen. She was the neighbor who lived downstairs and introduced me to Katarina and Nikos. She helped me so much. Helen could tell you more about how it was for me in those days.*

*I am a funny woman. One minute I tell you I am going to the beach and in the next five minutes I change my mind. I did this to my first husband, Paul. I married him and then got frightened and jumped out of his car while he was driving. It was snowing and the snow was very deep. We had run away to be married by the Justice of the Peace. Here I was lying in the snow and I got up and started running. When my husband caught me I told him, "I don't want to be married to you." He said, "Are you crazy?" When my mother died when I was fifteen, half of me died with her. I couldn't believe it. She loved me the most. Even forty years later I can't believe that she died when we were so young. I can't write anymore.*

*Frances*

*P.S. Wait until you come out here. The first thing I will do is pick at you. What a puzzle this letter has turned out to be. I was going to rip this up but now I am not.*

*Jim, consider yourself lucky. I can tell from the way you write that you are different than your sister and brothers and I mean your real ones. The Sutherlands did a good job bringing you up. You were probably better off with them than being brought up by a neurotic mother. Can't you tell by the way I write? I was not an easy mother to be around for my children though I loved them very much. I am very old but sometimes I still act like a child that can't have its way. Janice tells me things like this. But when you write to me you say different things like the way I would say things. I can't explain exactly what*

*I mean. When you say, "Call when you feel like it," and when you get angry and say, "Damn," I know you mean what you are saying.*

*Janice thinks that David is a lot like me. He still wants to have that talk with me. I guess he wants to know more about you and your father. I will tell him all I know about you. But I am not so sure if I will tell him about your father. Don't bring up your father with David. That is none of his business. He had his talk with me about his father when he was 17. Your father is your business and no one else's. Jim, I mean that. I don't want anyone running your father down. I have no use for the bum but only let me say that.*

*Love you very much,*
*Frances*

*P.S.S I want you to know all about me. Once I killed a dog. I was 21. I had Doug and Billy with me. I was angry with Paul, who had been drinking. I put him in the car passed out and drove from Hartford to Windsor Locks, 16 miles. I was speeding at 65 or 70 mph when I hit this poor dog and killed him. He was dead. I screamed and it woke my husband from his drunken sleep. He got out of the car and staggered over and picked up the dog and put it on the side of the road. Then he drove me home because I was crying and very upset. It is a wonder he didn't hit something because he was still drunk. I never wanted to drive again and I never did. My husband kept trying to get me to drive. At the time all that was on my mind was the only reason he wanted me to drive was so he could get drunk and wouldn't have to. I was wrong. I should have listened to him because I forgot how to drive and never did again. If I could drive, you can be damn sure I wouldn't be stuck in this house all day. I never listened to anyone when I was young and now that I am old, I still don't. Thank God you had Cecilia and Ruth for your mothers.*

*No one could figure me out. Janice is sometimes like me. She comes to pick me up and I say I want to go downtown. When we are on the highway in the traffic, I change my mind and tell her to turn around because I have to go to the mall. She gets nervous and starts yelling at me and tells me she can't turn around and I tell her to take me home. I try to think back if there was something I did or said to your father when I was carrying you. I try so hard to remember for he sure took me over the hurdles. I still can't believe it after all these years. Lately David tells me (and I don't like it) that he can't stand to be around me. Too bad.*

118

*You must have a lot of patience to be able to wait for September before coming here. You sure aren't like me. I want to see you now.*

\*\*\*

Sometime between the preceding and following letters, I received an inspirational booklet from Frances, *God is Not On a Mountain*. The twelve pages contained "Inspirational Messages by Billy Graham." I didn't do much more than flip through the pamphlet when I received it. As I was re-reading her letters some 30 years later, I took more time to examine it. I wondered why, with her Catholic background, what she found interesting in Billy Graham. Over the course of our early correspondence, she sent several other such booklets to me. I wish I asked her more about them, but I never did.

Based on my experiences long before I found Frances, I had doubts about organized religion. Much of my skepticism arose because of my lifestyle. Judgment and condemnation of others, in any fashion, by people in the name of religion always bothered me. Hypocrisy of this sort keeps me on guard whenever the subject of religion is brought up.

While I do not belong to a church, I have always felt the importance of being aware of and connected to the spiritual world. There must be many valid pathways to understanding and experiencing God, the Goddess, the Creator, the Universe, the Higher Power, or whatever one chooses to call it. I have difficulty believing any one person, and there are many, who profess that only they have the ear of God.

I once read in a periodical from the 1850s "Man will wrangle for religion; write for it; fight for it; die for it; anything but live for it." This anonymous quote mirrors much of my own view concerning organized religion and churches.

My skepticism about religion and religious people was reinforced as I came to know about my mother's life. She wasn't a perfect woman, but she was a good woman. She was a loving mother to her children. She was a generous person who helped others less fortunate than herself, even when she had barely enough for herself and her children. Still, she suffered needless shame and guilt because of a religion that is supposedly rooted in love.

Because she was not welcome in her faith, Frances looked elsewhere for her spiritual needs. For whatever reason, the writings of Billy Graham may have provided the comfort that she needed. In her later years she did reconcile with the Church. I think my reappearance helped make this possible. She felt that God was no longer punishing her. She believed that He finally forgave her. The proof was that He had finally sent me back to be with her.

***

*I should rip up this letter but I am not going to. It took me too long to write. When you read the end of this letter, I hope you won't laugh like I am doing now.*

*July 10, 1976*

*Dear Jim,*

*I just came home from downtown and I forgot to buy paper. This* [green lined ledger paper] *will have to do. I am glad to hear that you like to hear from me when I telephone. Talking to you keeps me happy.*

*Mabel called and told me she received a letter from you and she was crying. You wrote about the pictures that I had sent of Janice and David, and how you couldn't get over how much you looked like them. She was crying because you were happy to see someone that you looked like. She thought it was very sad that you never saw anyone who resembled you. She asked me why I gave you up and why didn't I come to her for help. I told her I don't know. I simply don't know. I don't want to think of those terrible days and nights I spent alone carrying you. Maybe when you were born I didn't want you. I don't know. I do know I was frightened to death. Mabel was divorcing one of her lousy husbands and she had enough trouble already. I didn't tell that to Mabel because if I did she would start feeling bad.*

*But the same thing happened when David was born. Only this time his father, Ted, was going to come back to me, and he would have. Ted was killed when his ship was sunk in November 1943 and David was born the next March. When the Army notified me, I wanted to die right then and there too. After David was born, I didn't give a damn anymore about what the hell people didn't like or thought of me. I had lost one baby because I was so frightened about what people would think. I was determined not to lose David. But this time David had to suffer in the long run.*

*I was happy to hear you stayed home over the 4th. When the express-ways are so jammed it is best not to go anywhere. I like it when my children stay home when the traffic is bad. I like to see them go where they want and have a good time.*

*Some more about David: He is having trouble because his antique shop brings him no money. Why he keeps it, I don't know. It is closed most of the time because he has to go to his other job. David hates to work for anyone. He wants to work for himself. He always dreams about being rich. I keep telling him that the only time he will be rich is if he works with his own two hands. No one will give either of you anything. If you don't have a rich father, forget it. Yes, I know you have one, but you may as well forget about him. I am ashamed to say this—your father can't stand on his own two feet. He must be a coward not to admit that he is your father. But I know you. You won't give up so easy.*

*Henry, the brother of Ted, is a very old man and he has written to David that he would like to see him. He lives in the hills of Virginia and David is going to go visit him, as he wants to know more about his father. I warned him, "David, please don't bring no old men back here." I know David. When he feels sorry for someone, and he feels sorry for many people, sometimes he forgets about me. When I tell him I am an old lady and need a ride, he says, "I wish I felt as good as you. Walk, it will keep you young." He makes me angry because he means it. Then I tell him how hard I work and he says, "Yes, yes, I already know—40 years."*

*You are lucky not to be around when the three of us are picking on each other. All I hear is, "I wish I had this. I wish I had that." I tell David to go marry a rich old lady. Then I tell Janice she should never have gotten married and had three kids. If she kept working, she would be a happy old maid with plenty of money.*

*Having a business of your own is a big headache. David is not a good businessman. First of all, he wants to start big. In business you have got to start at the bottom and build it up yourself. I am not as smart as he is, but as far as business is concerned, I was around my father for many years and I learned a lot from him. I saw the way he operated and he knew how to make plenty of money. He once owned three grocery stores in Hartford. I spent a lot of time behind the counter waiting on his customers and at the cash register. I was only eight when my father brought me down to one of the stores for the first time. He brought me and not my sisters or brothers because I was the wild child. He figured if I was with him at the store and he kept me busy, I would stay out of trouble. My father was a sly fox. When I tell David about how I learned about business he laughs and says that I am living in the old days. Today it is different and all business people rob one another. Maybe he is right, I don't know.*

*Not many years ago, I gave Angelo some good business advice. He had enough money to buy a small bar and grill. I told him to hire only his brothers that were honest. For once someone in my family listened to what I said and did what I told them to do. Doug and Billy started working nights for him. None of them drank and the money that the grill took in was unbelievable. Angelo has a lot of money today and he can thank his brothers and my sons for what he has. He is doing a very good job in holding on to his money and the only money he spends is on his children. Maybe David is right in that it is very hard to find friends you can trust when you own a business.*

*David is always fighting with Billy's wife, Louise, ever since he opened his antique store. She also has an antique shop and goes to David's and buys something for $12 and takes it to her place and sells it for $50. David sees this and goes crazy. But she is a good businesswoman and very foxy. I am laughing so much. He calls me and tells me that she is a crook.*

*Another of my brothers, Albert, is a bookie. He never worked a day in his life. Sometimes he has money and sometimes all he has is the holes in his shoes. He is my only brother that David likes or gets along with. The other day Louise called David and was crying that her kids were starving. She lies and cries broke all the time that I can't believe David listens to her anymore. Well, she had some beer steins from Germany, tall heavy glasses for beer. She cried and convinced David that she had no money. David felt sorry for her so he took them and sold them to Albert to get her some money. David got $300 from Albert and gave the money to Louise. Albert didn't need them, so he gave them back to David for his shop. Now David is trying to sell them back to her for $45 apiece and she is having a fit and they are fighting again.*

*Jim, you wouldn't believe what goes on in this place. Wait until you get here. I know that David will spend a lot of time with you and drag you all over. He really is nuts and half the time I don't think he knows what he is doing. Just you wait until you meet him. A few days with us, and you will run back to California.*

*That was a terrible thing to have happened to you in that fire. How did you get out?* [In December 1974, the apartment house where I lived with Rolland in San Francisco caught on fire one morning at 3 a.m. We barely escaped. The apartments on the top three floors were completely destroyed, including ours.]

*I was in a big fire many years ago. That fire happened in a circus tent during the war.* [This was the big Ringling Brothers and Barnum & Bailey Circus fire on July 6, 1944 in Hartford. 168 lives were lost.] *I will never forget that terrible experience. It was a hot afternoon right after the Fourth of July. I managed to scrape enough money together to get tickets to the Ringling Brothers and Barnum & Bailey Circus that had set up in a field on Barbour Street in the north end of Hartford, not far from Hester Court. I took Janice and two neighbor children with me. In those days, going to the circus was a big deal for kids. It was a big deal for my kids because I didn't have a lot of money. But that year I planned ahead and I saved a little bit each month so that that there was enough to buy the tickets.*

*The main part of the circus was held in a huge tent. I could not afford tickets to the main tent, so we had to sit in a smaller tent attached to the main tent. We got there early and though there were hundreds of people we managed to get good seats in the bleachers. We could see everything that was going on in the ring. Trapeze artists swung through the air overhead doing their tricks. We were looking up when all of a sudden we saw flames at the top of the tent. Someone screamed "Fire!" People stood up and pointed and began to run down the bleachers. It was terrible because people screamed and pushed and people were falling down, even little kids. The ringmaster came into the ring and shouted at people to remain calm, but no one listened to him. I remember hearing a band playing as the fire started to come down the top of the tent and on the sides very quickly. Wild animals started making noises and I thought what if the lions escaped? I didn't know what was worse, dying in the fire or being eaten alive by a lion.*

*Everything happened very fast. The whole tent was on fire and there seemed no way to get away from the flaming canvas above that started to fall on us. Somehow I managed to keep the children with me and we tried to get out of the tent. It wasn't easy because people were shoving and screaming. I have never been so scared. I didn't want to die in there but I was mostly scared for Janice and the neighbor kids that had come with us. I wasn't worried about myself.*

*As we tried to run—you really couldn't because of all the people—I tried to get us to the one of the entrances. Some of the animal wagons were pushed in front of the exit and I wasn't sure how to get around them. Maybe I thought we could crawl under the wagons, I don't know.*

*Then a soldier appeared in front of us. He was in full uniform and one of his arms was in a cast. He must have been on leave. He grabbed me and other people and yelled at us to go to the back of the tent. I thought he was crazy because the entrance I saw was toward the front. He shouted for us to move fast and I didn't argue with him so we turned from the direction we were going and followed him. Soon we were under the bleacher seats. I looked back and saw more smoke and flames. Jim, I cannot tell you how terrible it was. When we got to the back of the tent, the soldier pulled out a large knife and sliced the heavy canvas. He made an opening and everyone went through the flap, and was able to escape.*

*Once we were outside, I started to cry but I didn't want the children to know how scared I was so I stopped. They were scared too but they didn't have time to cry. I got the children holding my hands and each other's, and we ran like hell from the tent. You might wonder how I ran in the heat of the day. Well, I wasn't fat then and I ran like a deer when I was young. I will never forget looking back at the tent that was on fire and hearing the screams of the people still inside. I can never forget that awful sound if I live to be 100. Later they said that 168 people did not make it out of the fire and many were children.*

*For weeks afterwards, all you read in the newspapers and heard on the radio was details about this terrible fire. Some of my neighbors went to the vacant lot where the circus had set up to see what was left. But not me. I never went back there out of curiosity. Years later whenever I went down that street I got a chill and wanted to get past it as soon as I could.*

*That soldier was like an angel only I didn't have time to think about it until much later. I don't know what happened to him, as I didn't see him after we got out. Maybe it was God who sent him to save us. If it had not been for him, none of us would have gotten out alive. After that, I never liked being in a big crowd of people. Not even in a movie. If I ever go to a movie, I sit on the aisle and you can be damn sure I know where the fire exits are.*

*Going to the circus in the summer was something that all the children in Hartford looked forward to. Because of the fire and the people who died, the circus never came back to Hartford for years and years.*

*You said you don't know what you did with the insurance money you* received after your fire, but that you have greedy hands. My dear, if you really had greedy hands you would still have the money. I know what you are like and I don't even have to see you. You are just like me, David, and Janice, when it comes to money. You would rather spend it than save it. But listen to me, Jim. You have nobody when it comes to giving you money. You are working now but what if you got sick? What if you get older and can't work? I don't know about your family helping you. I am old now and how much help could I be? But remember Janice—you never, never met a girl like your sister and that is what she is—your sister.

She would take care of you and David. I always tell her, "Janice, if anything happens to me, stay close to David. That's all you have." They fight but there is no stronger love that's between them. Janice is so good and I say this not just because she is my daughter. If you were around, you would understand what I mean. And so is her husband, Stanley. As time goes by, I always remind her that she also has a brother on the West Coast and believe me that will sink in. "I don't just mean Jim, I mean your brother."

She never has a bad word about any one. I wish you could hear how she defends your father. Well, I shouldn't be talking bad about him around her. She talks so good about my sisters and takes them anywhere they want. She even takes the priests in her church where they want and they love her very much. She goes through my closets and wants to take my clothes and give them to poor people. I get mad as hell, and I have to kick her out and tell her I am poor.

It is going to be strange when you come to visit and see how we really are. I am afraid we are going to be so different from the people and family you are used to. As far as meeting your stepmother, Ruth, I can't right now. I may feel different after I see you—especially if I don't like you. Then I could go to Colorado and meet her. No, Jim, I am fooling.

It would be terrible if I looked at you and got reminded of you-know-who. God, I'd die. That is why I want a picture of you with your beard off. You already remind me of your father around the mouth. That bottom lip has got to go. I know you are like me but as far as your looks sometimes I can see the Greek in you. I don't want to talk about him.

I was very depressed when I got your first letter. Since you came into my life, I have something else to think about. One thing I am happy to know is that you got out of that fire. I would have gone to my grave wondering about you. I often thought that when I die I would be thinking about you. Before you found me, at night in bed I thought it won't be long and when

*I die I can see Doug and Billy and the baby I left. I never thought of you grown because I still saw that fat baby. I saw my mother and father and I am ashamed to say I forgot about my two sons after your wrote. Ever since you wrote to me, I want to live again.*

*Don't worry about me doing anything about your father, because I want to forget about him. I bet he is scared because he knows how I am. I bet he is looking behind his back, expecting me to jump out at him. When I write to you, I forget all my troubles but I don't forget about him.*

*My darling, don't work too hard. I hope to see you soon. Love and many kisses on your nose.*

*Love,*
*Frances*

*P.S. Do you get any complaints about your scratchy beard?*

# Chapter Twelve

Frances was angry in her next letter. Jimmy's denial that he knew her had continued to infuriate Frances. Perhaps it was my reaction when she told me that she was going to find my father and confront him herself. My fear was that Jimmy would stop communication with me. He would never meet me or tell me his side of the story. My fear also included visions of an angry Frances coming upon my unsuspecting father on a street corner. Who could predict the hell that would result from such a reunion?

Correspondence between my father and me continued. His writing became more relaxed and revealing. Jimmy did finally admit to his relationship with Frances, but his recant did not placate her. Frances did not let go of her anger when his name came up. Over the years she became less bitter, but she was very intense in those early months.

Before this letter, we discussed the huge phone bill she had run up over the last month. I suggested that we limit our calls to 15 minutes to help her save money. It was a suggestion she did not like.

\*\*\*

*July 15, 1976*

*Dear Jim,*

*I received your letter yesterday and I understand you pretty well. I wasn't going to write to you anymore but I changed my mind. I was so angry yesterday. As for your father, he is a closed chapter in my life. You have nothing to worry about me finding him and giving him a piece of my mind.*

*As for the phone calls, this 15-minute bit maybe okay with you but no one can limit my calls or how long I feel like talking. Not even you, unless you hang up on me.*

*The last time I called, I wasn't a bit pleased with the way you acted. I could tell that you couldn't wait to hang up on me. I know I call at weird times because of the time difference and I am sorry if I interrupted any of your personal affairs. I'll make a point to not let it happen again. You have to wait until September before you hear from me again. Then, as you say, we can talk. It doesn't bother me. As long as you can wait, so can I. Only once in my life did I get the brush off [from Jimmy] and I have no intention of having anyone do it to me again—not even you.*

*Don't worry. I pay for my phone calls. I take nothing from Janice. If David gives me anything, he gets it back double. I only bother them when I want a ride out of these woods. When I call Janice, she gets her nose up in the air. Well she need not worry about me anymore. There will be snowballs in hell before I ask her for another ride or call you again.*

*I don't know what she has been telling you, but I don't run her life or her brother's. As far as you, you have your mother, father, and sister and her children. You love them very much so don't think I am going to tell you what to do. You know, Jim, I am a very funny person. When you come to see me, I will be very happy. But when it is time for you to go and if I never see you again, I don't think it will bother me. That goes for David too. If he went to Alaska it wouldn't bother me. Maybe I would miss him for a few days, but I'd get over it. As for Janice, she can go to the moon and believe me I would never miss her either.*

*You have a good family in Colorado and who the hell am I? Not your mother. Well, not your good mother. Janice must make me out to be some kind of monster when she talks to you. All I can say is I did the best I could for them, and as far as you, I did nothing. So don't write to me that I can't treat you like I do Janice and David. You picked up that line from Janice, I know for sure. For the first time, I realize that none of my children under-stand me. I mean those two. You are just forming your opinion about me and you believe everything that Janice tells you. You know nothing about me. Only what I write. I don't think you and I will get along. I am hurt but I am not angry.*

*You know how hurt I am? I called Mabel and read her the part of your letter that I didn't like. Now I am mad at her too. She started to laugh and said, "That proves he is your son. That's how you sound and write. He has your blood." She couldn't stop laughing. I don't think it is a bit funny. How can she say that? Your way of life was so different from ours, and you are more like the people who raised you. Now she tells me it is all about blood. I don't believe any of that junk. You are the way you are because of how you were raised. Blood doesn't have any-thing to do with it. If it did, then you wouldn't have written that.*

*Mabel knew my children as youngsters and she tells me day and night that of all of them, you have my disposition. How can that be? If you do, God help you when you meet me. I hope she is wrong. That damn old witch. She gets on my nerves and so do Janice and David. Lately, all Mabel says is, "Oh, my God. Oh, my God," and then she laughs. She can't wait to see you because she thinks you are more like me than any of my children.*

*I know Janice is not like me. Doug was very quiet, which is not like me. Billy had a big mouth, but he was the only one. David tries to correct me and tell me not to swear and calm down. I tell him to go to hell. You, I don't know about yet. I told Mabel a few things I don't like that you said to me when you wrote or called. Now she has formed an opinion of you and thinks she knows all about you. Well, if she is right, I am afraid to tell you that I am not so old that I can't fight back. I can be hell on wheels when I get mad. I was going to say, "Don't let me frighten you," but I changed my mind. If you are really like me, then nothing can frighten you. We will see.*

*I am not a clock-watcher when I am on the phone and I am sorry you are. I won't ever call again. I'll call Florida and talk to my grandchildren instead. They never worry about how long I talk. I have you on my mind so much that I think of no one else but you, day and night. But now with the way you write and put me in my place, all I have to say is, "To hell with him and who does he think he is talking to anyway?" I am not your mother. I am just Frances. I hate it when you call me that and not Mother. I get so damn bitter at myself. I shouldn't go crazy loving you as my son because you are Ruth's son and I don't like her either.*

*GOOD NIGHT.*

*I am calling Florida and going to talk for two hours. I am going to try hard to forget you for a while. I love you very much even if you belong to Jimmy. I know you love him. I wish you could understand me. I really love you, but I hate him.*

*Love,*
*Mother*

*P.S. At least you are honest and I admire that.*

*You can still call me Frances. I don't want to embarrass you.*

*July 17, 1976*

*Dear Jim,*

*Since the Democratic convention is over, I will write to you again. I have been watching it on TV. This may surprise you, but I like politics. I don't understand them, but I like to know what is going on in this country and what they will do about it. When I open my mouth around the rest of my family, they think something has gone wrong with me. I once said I liked Jane Fonda and I do and I like what she stands for. Well, I never heard the end of it for weeks, especially from Angelo. Like he is such an expert about what is going on in the world. I thought he was going to throw me out in the street. He didn't, because who is going to take care of his kids and clean his house? I like Walter Cronkite and every night I turn on the news to listen to him. Angelo doesn't like Walter Cronkite either. Whenever I turn on the news, Angelo finds something for me to do for him or the children so that I cannot watch Walter Cronkite. One day, I finally let him have it. I told him in a loud and angry voice, "I want to listen to Walter Cronkite, so leave me alone for a half hour." Can you believe what that jackass said? "You're in love with the guy." God, I hate stupid people.*

*In my last letter, you may have gotten the idea that I was angry over you telling me to limit the phone calls to fifteen minutes. I want you to know that I am not mad anymore. After I thought about it, I decided that you were right. I called Florida three times and talked to my grandchildren. They asked me to bring them back to Connecticut. They hate Florida and how their mother, Janet, made them leave Connecticut. They hate Janet for getting married again. She married a nice fellow, but the girls don't like him. He is good to them but they are not nice to him.*

*The trouble is that Doug was crazy about his daughters. He never went anywhere without his girls. It was terrible for them when he died. At the funeral all they did was cry and call out for their father. They had to drag the girls away from his coffin and it took three men. Every time I saw them afterward, they were crying. This is why I am afraid to go to Florida and visit them.*

*Do you know they told Janet that they hate her? I tell the oldest granddaughter to find herself a boyfriend and get married. She told me that she* doesn't want a boyfriend or a wedding. I love these girls very much as they were my first grandchildren. If I knew this was going to happen, I never would have broken up my apartment to come to Angelo's house. Those girls could have moved in with me and not have to go to Florida. But to be truthful, I am too old to start over and take in the girls on my own. It would be too much. Last night they begged me to let them come back to Hartford and they told me that I wasn't too old or fat and that I was pretty. I wish you could have heard them. I had to laugh.

I have 12 grandchildren altogether, but these are my favorite. They have a brother, Billy, who is 21. He was my first grandchild but God knows where he is now. After his father died, he ran off. No one knows where he is. I was in my early forties when they were born and always with them and my son every weekend when they were little. We went everywhere. Janet was an only child and she spent time with her father and mother. She was glad to get rid of the children on the weekends. Boy, did they keep me broke. Doug liked to spend money too. He was the only one like me—spend it all in one day and have nothing to eat the next. Janice tells me I don't like her kids. This is not true. I do love them but it is different because they are big boys. I do love her little girl a lot. When the girls in Florida see me they go crazy and kiss me so much they knock my glasses off and sometimes hurt me.

I love a lot of people and love them a lot, but in my heart I love some a bit more than the others. I don't know why. David is one. I don't love anyone the same as I love him. This made Janice jealous of David. When she first got married and I bought something for David, she said, "Where is mine?" I told her that since she was married, her husband had to buy for her. This made her cry and she said that I bought David everything. She still is kind of that way, but not much. Now when I tell her I bought him something, she goes out of her mind because she knows I don't have much money and what I have I should spend on myself. She reminds me that he has a job.

I don't want you to get the wrong idea. Janice and I are very close and I love her dearly. Yesterday, she called and wanted to know what's the matter. I said nothing and she started with, "Ever since Jim came into your life, you have nothing to say to me." I asked her what she wanted me to say and she got mad. She was always picking on Billy and Doug. She always said I liked them better. You can ask Mabel how she felt about the boys. She was a girl and I dressed her like a doll when she was little because she was prettier than the boys. When I told the boys that they were ugly and she was *pretty, this made her very happy. I never thought about it at the time, but now I realize that it was very hard for her to have three brothers and have to compete for my attention. And now guess what? She has four brothers. I can't stop laughing.*

*David went to Virginia and I haven't heard from him and Janice said, "Don't worry, he won't die," and that if she went away, I wouldn't worry about her. She is right. I don't worry about her because she always takes care of herself and she has Stanley. The only time I worry about her is when she picks up hitchhikers.*

*She tries to tell me how to handle you. I tell her to shut up. I am not going to change and I am going to say what I want, feel about you how I want, and talk to you how I want. Maybe I will hurt you. Maybe love you how I want. Maybe I will kiss you. Maybe I will kick you. Maybe get angry, get happy, cry, laugh, and argue. That's me. I don't know what I'll do or how I will feel when I see you. But I can't pretend to be what I am not so I won't hurt your feelings. I am going to be myself. If you feel you don't like how I am, tell me. And I will tell you a few things.*

*Don't forget I live in Connecticut and you live in California. So who knows, we may never see each other again. To me, I love you and if you don't like me, too bad. I can't be like the people who raised you. After you see me, when you see your family in Colorado, you may appreciate them more. After all, they did a lot more for you than I ever did.*

*I am full of pain today. Yesterday I played baseball with the children because they were bored. I hit the ball and they ran after it. I batted that damn ball so hard my arms are killing me. I didn't realize my bones are so old. Swinging that bat the way I did, my whole body is sore. Every time I'd swing it Matthew screamed and laughed so much it was really funny. The balls were tennis balls and I lost three of them.*

*When I was young, my husband Paul played for the Windsor Lock Reds. I played softball for Check Bread. We took Billy and Doug in wire baskets on our bicycles to the park and played until dark. I love baseball. I don't like football. These are the things I loved when I was young. I loved to swim. I loved the ocean. I loved to lie in the deep grass. Today everybody cuts the grass. I loved to run and run. No matter where I went, to a park or to the country, I always ran. I like summer and love spring. I hate fall because it makes me sad. I like to listen to good music when I am alone. I loved to dance when I was young. Janice took lessons for 10 years and it turned out that she dances like a clumsy horse. David roller-skated for 10 years. He won many medals but when he went on to drugs, I got mad at him and threw them away. When Billy and Doug were young I had no money to pay for lessons for anything. But they were happy. Oh, I also hate to read fiction. I only read the newspapers, Time magazine, and Reader's Digest. That's all.*

*I am sending pictures of my favorite grandchildren, the girls in Florida. I want these pictures back. People always ask me how can you have favorite grandchildren? I say to hell with them. I don't know how I will feel when I see you but now I love you with all my heart. I am dying to see you. I can't wait until you get here and I am not telling anyone where you are until I see you alone and talk to you for a couple of days. I am going to get two rooms, one for you and one for me. I will stay one night and two days. Then I will call David and Janice. I have so much to say and I want to know all about you. I will get your room at a motel or hotel for one week. I already told Janice so she can take Angelo's children for a couple of days. I know if I don't see you first, I will never get a chance to talk to you once David and Janice get a hold of you. I guess David and Janice will see you and then Mabel. I will see you before you leave and I am wondering how I will feel or how you will feel about me. I can't bear to be hurt again. I don't know you yet, but in my heart it seems I know you as well as my other children. Sometimes I wake up and I can't believe this is real, that you are back in my life.*

*Ever since I spoke to you, I haven't done a thing around here. I just clean the surfaces. I can't work. All I do is think mostly of you. I write to you every day from nine in the morning until noon. Then I tear up the letters and throw them out. Sometimes I am angry when I think of your father and write terrible letters and you wouldn't believe the things I write. Why I do this, I don't know. I read them and they are awful and I tear them up. Sometimes I am happy and I write letters about the good times in my life. Then I read them and I think, "No, I can't send this. I would not want David to read this, so Jim can't read it either." On and on it goes. I hope when I see you and you have gone back, that I get back to my old self again.*

*Well, Jim it is noon and I must end. I love you very much. I sometimes want to die to think that I didn't comb your hair when you were little or kiss your cheek when you went to bed. Sometimes I slept with my boys when they were scared. Why didn't I do this to you? Don't tell me to forget. I never will.*

> *Love to my darling,*
> *Mother*

***

When I began searching for my birth parents, I imagined that once I found them, my questions would be answered immediately. However, once I made the contact, I realized that uncovering my past was not going to be simple. The story was too big to fit neatly into two telephone conversations.

Frances' letters and phone calls continued through the summer and in the process, a relationship developed between us. I did not anticipate this happening. Despite the candor in her letters and calls, I still did not feel that I knew her. I had not yet met her so the thought of an ongoing relationship was not in my plans. Because Frances had lost me once, she was determined not to lose me again. For me, it took more time to define what kind of a relationship, if any, we would have.

***

*July 19, 1976*

*Dear Jim,*

*I miss talking to you so much that I am sick inside. I don't write because I realize that you are working and have plenty to do without having to write to me.*

*David went to Virginia to meet those relatives of his father, Ted. His father's 64th birthday is today. David had never met any of them before. He came back a few days ago and wanted to tell me about his trip. I spent the whole day with him. Janice kept calling and wanted to know what we could find so much to talk about. She also wanted to know if I was going to tell David more about you. I told her probably because David was bound to ask questions about his new brother. At first David wanted me to hear everything about his trip. He went because he wanted to know more about his father and his people.*

*He found out plenty before he beat it back home fast. Ted had four brothers and one sister. The sister and one brother died from drinking too much. When I was going with Ted, I only knew the sister and the brother who is still living. The brother had saved Ted's Virginia State Police badge and gave it to David. David said that it looked like the family was comfortable and not very poor. Obviously they were happy to see David as they had known about him but had never met him. Everyone told David that he looked and talked like his father and that he had many of the same mannerisms. They said he had Ted's eyes. Of course, that can't be true because I always thought that David had my eyes. They don't know what the hell they are talking about.*

*Sometimes David was uncomfortable as they stared at him, and then insisted that he meet his cousins. This was more than he bargained for. He was shocked when they asked him if he wanted to bring Ted's body back from North Africa. David said, "These people—with the money they've got—why didn't they bring his body to the U.S. before now?" The government will pay so much and the rest is up to David, but he is going to think about it. Of course, this upset him a lot.*

*They said that the color of David's hair and his hairline were exactly like his father's. None of his uncles in Virginia are bald. Boy, did that make him feel better because my brothers are bald as eagles. They want him to come back to visit so David told them that he will return in the fall.*

*David wants me to go with him. They are very curious and want to see me. No way, never. David is happy to find such healthy, strong old men with lots of hair. He thinks he will be just like them when he gets old. David is nuts.*

*After he told me about his trip, David asked me to tell him more about you and Jimmy. I thought it was going to be hard to talk about all the things I have told you. But somehow I found it much easier to talk to him than I expected. Of course, I told him about Jimmy and he did not like hearing about our relationship. When I was finished, he surprised me. He was upset about you and said, "Please, Mother, don't hurt and upset Jim anymore." He kept asking, "Why did you let that happen to Jim?" All I could answer was, "I don't know."*

*Sometimes it is not as easy to talk to Janice as David. I hope that I will be able to talk to you as freely as I did with David. I also told David that I miss you more than him even if he went away for 10 years. He understood and said it's because of what I did to you and I can't make up for the time that I lost with you. Sometimes he is a lot smarter than I give him credit for.*

*When I was married and going to have my third baby, Janice, I told my sisters. Guess what? One of them, Theresa, had a boyfriend. He came over to my house looking for Paul. My sisters thought I should not have*

*any more babies and they sent him over to tell Paul. But Paul wasn't home.*
*The boyfriend was very mad and he grabbed me and ended up beating the*
*hell out of me. It is a wonder that Janice is alive. And people wonder why*
*I do not like my sisters. I told David and he got very angry and wanted to*
*know where this guy was. Thank God my sister never married the guy. I*
*told David he left Connecticut years ago. When you come out here I will tell*
*you more.*

*Most of all I miss talking to you but I am not going to call. I can't sleep.*
*Do you know it is 4 a.m.? I get up every morning at this time. The other*
*morning I got up at 3 a.m. I dialed your number and then hung up before*
*it rang. I didn't want you to shake me up the way you talk to me about the*
*phone calls. This is one thing I can't take. It is killing me.*

> *I love you very much,*
> *Mother*

*P.S. If David read this letter he would tear it up. He has told me not to*
*hurt you anymore. But I want you to know right away about me and what*
*I did. While I don't like your father, I do not want you to put all the blame*
*on him for what happened.*

[In the same envelope was another letter written later the same day.]

*Jim,*

*Years ago when David asked about his father, I didn't have to tell him*
*anything. It would have been easy not to tell the truth. But what right did I*
*have not letting him know who he really was? Just to protect myself? Telling*
*David the truth brought me a great heartache. But how could I lie to my*
*own son about something so important? You were different. Long before I*
*knew you were looking for me, I knew that someday you would find your*
*father. I wanted you to find him. Why I don't know. When I checked into*
*the hospital I used my maiden name to protect myself. Maybe it was because*
*I didn't want you to find me. Why? Was I afraid of what you would do?*
*Don't ask because even today I don't know.*

*When I first spoke to you I thought you were probably married. I asked*
*you why you weren't married and your answer was, "Not the way women*
*are today."*

[I did not tell her why I was not married over the phone. I knew eventually I had to discuss my lifestyle with her, but I wanted to wait until we were face to face. When we met, the topic of why I was unmarried did come up. Despite the seriousness of our talk, it had its humorous moments.]

*The girl you marry must be perfect even if it means you will be unhappy for the rest of your life. It's in you and you can't help it. Part of you is a lot like me but deep down, you are an old-fashioned boy like Jimmy.*

*Don't think my morals are low. I was far from being a tramp. I was young, healthy, and alive but very lonely. The men I went out with I could count on the fingers of one hand. For the person I was, I lived a horrible life in my youth. I suffered tremendously in my thirties. The suffering was worse as I became a woman and realizing what a mess I had made of my life. I couldn't stand the sight of a man as I grew older. I became bitter and in my forties, I built my life around my children and hard work. By the time I was fifty, I had grandchildren (my children never suffered because I was always happy around them), and my three granddaughters were my life.*

*I grew old fast and couldn't wait for the day I turned 60 and could stop working. When things bothered me I looked back and then I got a night job. Why wasn't I like my sisters? I never slowed down when I was young. Why weren't my children like me? Who was I like? I must have been like someone way back somewhere.*

*What I had in mind for you was to hurt your father but the hurt has come to me and so great that all I can say at this point is, "Here is the boy I lost." And it is slowly killing me. Yes, Jim you are not a child anymore and I am sure you understand what I am writing. I don't care what happens to me. Maybe I will feel different when I see you. Will I be able to look at you? Not knowing me, yet you worry about me paying the phone bill. If you were not my son, you could easily say, "Let her drop dead." That is the reason I will always say there is so much of you that is like me.*

*You want to talk no more than 15 minutes on the phone and I never want to say goodbye. When I hear your voice, I crumble to pieces. You say, "Forget the past." How can I? The past will be forgotten when I am dead. I have no peace of mind and don't think I will. You have to do a lot of talking to change my mind.*

> *Love to my baby boy,*
> *Mother*

*P.S. And don't tell me not to call you*
*a baby boy because I won't.*

*P.S.S. Jim, this letter may hurt you. You are very sensitive but if anything should happen to me before I see you, what I have written about myself may help you as your life goes on. Sometimes I want to take my life. I felt like this ever since my children were grown. There is nothing now. As a matter of fact, I had told Janice I don't have anything to live for anymore. Then when you came back, I started to live again. I'll be leaving August 2 for Washington, DC, then to Florida. Don't write to me after July 26. I will call before I leave. Let me know when and if that is okay.*

*Jim, I am not crazy. I know my letters may sound weird. Tell me the truth. Are you sorry you found me? Believe me, you can't hurt me by saying, "Yes." You may think I am nuts. I've heard that before.*

# Chapter Thirteen

*July 20, 1976*

*Dear Jim,*

*After speaking to you last night, I woke up feeling good. I am happy and going to stay that way all day. Tomorrow is another day.*

*I can't wait to see you. I am so happy because for the first time since we started talking, you didn't ask me to hang up. I know you are right about the phone bills. Please, when I am on vacation and I call you, don't scold me. I will not call on the weekends because I know you are busy.*

*I also was happy to hear that you went to work at fourteen, which tells me that you are not lazy. I hate lazy people. You sure fit into this family. I don't mean the Postigliones—I mean Janice, David, and me. We work like hell and then we spend, spend, and spend what little we have. That is bad. My children know no other way because they saw me do the same thing. Doug and Billy were the same. I made a great mistake the way I brought them up. Yet it sounds to me that you do the same. I always wished I were rich so I could give all my money to my children and grandchildren. Janice has to work if she wants a vacation. No vacation for her next year. They have to stay home and not spend their money as they need a new car. They drive around in a couple of junkers.*

*We drive to Florida next week in Angelo's car. He has a brand new station wagon and it's air-conditioned. If it wasn't, you couldn't get me to go anywhere, not even Florida. Angelo and Stan and Janice share the driving. I sit in the back with Mary Ann and Matthew, who are Angelo's kids, and with Nicholas, Kevin, and Katie, Janice's kids. For once I am glad I don't drive so I can sit back like a queen and look out the windows. And I can keep an eye on the speedometer and make sure they don't speed and see all the highway signs and tell them when they need to turn and what highway to go on. I don't drive but I help them. Until they tell me to shut up.*

*After three or four days, Angelo flies home. He never stays long, which is okay with me. I see enough of him in Connecticut. We always stay at motels in Disney World so we don't need the car much after we get there. Last year the admission tickets were $40 per day. This year tickets are $50. When the money is gone, we come home.*

*What I would like to do is spend one week in Miami in a very nice hotel and spend at least two days with my granddaughters. For the rest of the time I would lie around the hotel and be happy to do no cooking and no washing, and lay on the bed in the dark and listen to good music. You might be surprised I can be real lazy if I want to. But all this is one big dream that is not going to happen. Not as long as there are children and grandchildren running in and out.*

*Next year, if I am alive, I want a vacation alone for a change. If I tell anyone here, they laugh in my face. They think I will miss them if I was alone. Like hell. I love to be alone. Okay, maybe not all the time. Sometimes I can get scared and frighten very easily. But if anyone tries to break in where I am, I will be the first one to see what they are doing. I am not afraid when I see them face-to-face. I just don't like anyone creeping up on me. I am also happy you don't like to read fiction.*

*I never envied anyone. I try to be happy with what I have. Beautiful homes don't impress me and I never care what anyone else has. I am also satisfied with myself and who I am. Even as an old lady I never regret whatever I've done even if it was wrong. In my eyes, if it made me happy, then it was not wrong. And I don't care what anyone thinks. Of course, you are the exception. I was happy when I first saw your chubby little face when you were born. But that happiness didn't last very long.*

*When I am angry I do things in a fit of temper and I cry for days afterward, usually when it is too late. I have hurt a lot of people without realizing it. I can be real mean and all of a sudden I wake and say to myself, "What am I doing?" My temper has gotten me into a lot of trouble. Just ask your father.*

*Janice tells me that I should appreciate my brothers and sisters. I don't. The reason is that no matter what they did for me or gave me, they threw it in my face and I never heard the end of it. "We did this and that for you." What the hell? All they did was buy a few pairs of shoes for my children when they felt like it. They were worried about Doug, Billy, and Janice. I don't even want to write this next part. Yesterday, Theresa told me that my sister-in-law, Gloria, has never liked David. That's because David told her off one day and almost threw her out of the car. She said some bad things about me and he told her never to talk about his mother like that as long as he was around. He was very sharp to her and now Gloria hates him like poison.*

*I told him that some of what she said was probably true. He said to me that there is nothing I could do or did that was wrong. He is glad that I am not like my sisters. David can't see anything I do as wrong. The only thing he can't stand is when I yell. He covers his ears. He told me that God has to forgive him but he hates my sisters. That is the only time I see him get angry. He thinks I am good and will not believe any different.*

*Janice came in a moment ago and wants me to go with her to the mall. I will because I am feeling good. I have been feeling good because of talking with you last night. I have so much energy that maybe I will find someone to fight with later. I love you very much.*

*Love,*
*Mother*

*PS. I just can't sign Frances.*
*But you can always call me Frances.*

*When you come to visit and before you leave, you must call me Mother just once. Then I will be ready to die. I haven't got time to go over this letter. I hope you can understand it. I love you very much, more than anything in this world.*

\*\*\*

*July 21, 1976*

*9 a.m. to 12 p.m.—nothing done*
*Do you like my letters?*
*Answer me and tell me the truth*

*Dear Jim,*

*I thought you would like to see these clippings out of last year's phone book.* [Enclosed were ads for restaurants cut from the pages. On each ad, she penned a few words about having been to this particular restaurant with my father. The ads were for Great Wall Chinese Restaurant, Scarpelli's Seafood Restaurant, Marco Polo Café, the South Seas Lounge, the Ship-in-a-Bottle Lounge, and Athena Restaurant.] *The one that says Athena Restaurant used to be the Athena Diner in the 1940s.*

*That is where I met your father and where he worked when he came up from New York that summer. There were three Greek owners, Kostas, Petros, and Georgios. Georgios was Jimmy's older brother. Andrew, his other brother died four years ago. That was the last time I read in the paper that a Greek died. You can pick up the paper every night and not once do you see a dead Greek. Honestly, they live to a ripe old age. Kostas and Petros are still there.*

*Mabel's husband, Tony, played the organ for a while at the Ship-in-the-Bottle Lounge. Mabel was there one night when Kostas walked up and said, "Don't I know you?" Kostas had wanted to take Mabel out but Jimmy told Mabel that Kostas was about to get married that summer. So Mabel told Kostas to get lost. When Kostas found out what Jimmy had told Mabel, he got angry with your father.*

*Kostas, Petros, and Georgios always argued with your father. A lot of times it was over me, but I could never understand what they were saying because they talked in Greek. I was terrible and thumbed my nose at them whenever they started talking in Greek. When Jimmy didn't return to school at the end of the summer, he told me he didn't have enough money. I told Georgios that Jimmy didn't have enough money for school. Then Kostas, Petros and Georgios got together and got the money for him to go back to NYU. But Jimmy refused to take a dime and soon there was another Greek argument going on.*

*Your father was tall, dark, and stubborn as a jackass. He stood there mad as hell and ready to take the three of them on when they tried to give him the money. How he hated to work at the Athena Diner after that but he went in every night. He got so mad that he clenched his jaws together. He had a temper but not like me. He knew how to control his. Kostas, Petros, Georgios, and Jimmy were friends because they were all Greeks. I never understood why but Jimmy never went into business with them.*

*Long after he left, I heard different things about your father from people who knew him or me. He bought the East End Diner but doesn't own it anymore. It is called the Grace Lounge. About 20 years ago, I went to the Colonial Theater with Doug and Billy. They wanted me to see a play or show. Doug was married and Billy wasn't. After the show, Doug said, "Let's go out to eat." We landed in the East End Diner. Who do you think brought us the menus? Your father. I had to look again, but it was him only he was a little heavier. I know it was him if I lived to be 100. He was an old man but I never forgot his face. After he left our table, he sat in a booth for a long time. Billy said, "What are you looking at? Ma, do you* know that man?" I couldn't eat. I had only coffee. The waitress told me he was the owner of the place. That was the last time I saw him. Had I known he owned the East End Diner I would have never gone in there with my two boys.

After that night, I never went back. Jimmy didn't want to know me and I felt the same way about him. I still do. I can still hold my head up and if I should ever run into him again, I would look down on him. Thank God I never had to ask him or anyone for anything. God has been good to me.

Scarpelli's Seafood Restaurant was across the street from the Athena Diner and when Jimmy finished work at 1 a.m., we went there for coffee because they were open all night. I only went out on Thursday, Friday, and Saturday nights. He and I talked until four in the morning and walked down Ash Street and got home at about five. Believe it or not, Mabel was still at my apartment because she watched my kids. I would wake her up, dress my kids, and feed them. Then I showered and got ready for work at 7:30 and Mabel took the kids again.

I hadn't slept all night but your father went downstairs where he lived and his skinny self slept all day or until I got home from work. Sometimes he slept until 7 p.m. There were times I told him that I could not meet him every night. I had to wash, polish the boys' white shoes, and iron. He came upstairs to my apartment and polished the white shoes and helped me do other chores. At the time, my boys wore white shoes only on Sunday, but Janice wore white shoes every day.

I didn't like Jimmy when I first met him. But that changed. What made me fall in love with him was that he was so clean and when I say clean, I mean white socks, white underwear, and white shirts as white as snow. His nails were clean and his hair shined like glass. He never wore a shirt twice. I can look back and say that the time I knew him was the happiest of my life. We both were very happy but it seemed no one around us liked that, not his family or my family.

My husband, Paul, was a plumber and after living together, I found out how he really was and I was greatly disappointed. The marriage went to hell right from the start. When Paul came home from work and tried to kiss me, I was ready to jump out the window. He hadn't taken a bath. He was a plumber. You don't know how he smelled. Sometimes I made him take two baths before I let him touch my hands. Not that I am so clean. You should see me now. I am fat, ugly, and only bathe once every three weeks.

You should see what a mess this house is in. And I sit at my table every morning and instead of cleaning the house, I am writing to you. Jim, I have reached the age of 62 and who would believe I would get so lazy. I never could imagine such a thing.

When you are young you are brought up to think everybody tells the truth, then you find out that people lie like hell and you go into shock. Not really knowing my husband before I married him, I had kind of a shock once I did. But I loved him and realized that I had a tough job ahead of me if we stayed married. His people were so different from my family. My sisters never gave me a chance. He and I had enough problems but they were always there criticizing me and picking at him. This did not help us.

I wonder if I want you to be like Jimmy or not. I can't decide. You know, your father was ugly and I always told him that. His mouth was ugly and big. Is that why you won't take your beard off? Do you have an ugly mouth? Please take some of it off. I want to see if you've got a mean chin, a mean jaw, and I want to see your mouth.

You said when he wrote back to you, he said he never had a son and never knew me. Well, do me a favor. When you write back to that no-good Greek, tell him that if he doesn't see you, you are going to the Athena Restaurant and look up Kostas and Petros. That will shake his memory a bit. But they would say they didn't know me, or him either. Those damn Greeks stick together.

Your father liked to dine out. He loved to eat in nice restaurants, but he never ate at the Athena Diner. He hated that place. Kostas, Petros, and Georgios made fun of him because he was educated. They were jealous because he knew a lot more than they did. Those three were dumbbells and had not gone to school, but they always had more money than your father. Today, whatever Jimmy has, he earned himself. He had no father to help him. He had only his mother and he was crazy about her. He wanted me to meet her very badly but he made me promise not to tell her that I had three children. When he said that, it made me go completely nuts. I broke all of my dishes when I started throwing them at him. He couldn't stop me. I remember this very well because the next day, I went to get a cup out of the cupboard and I didn't have any. I only had four cups to begin with. Actually I didn't have very much at that time, except plenty of soap, but we were happy.

In the end, I never did meet his mother. I promised him that when she came from New York to visit Georgios' house, I would keep quiet about my children. Then I thought it over and in a split second I got into a temper fit to think that he was ashamed of my children. I refused to listen to him and *refused to meet her. In those days, it was almost a crime for a single fellow to go out with a married woman, especially a married woman with children.*

*Jim, your father didn't have it easy with me or his brother and friends. I haven't forgotten what Petros and Kostas did to him. Once when he carried Janice downstairs to put her in the car, and Petros and Kostas were on the porch. They laughed at him. I was too stupid at the time to realize that. I was bold, but your father ignored them.*

*When I told Jimmy about you, he must have thought three children, still married, and now another one. He closed the door on me and put it in his mind to forget everything. Jimmy was frightened as hell and so was I. He also thought about my brothers and interfering sisters. Maybe he thought they would come after him, or I would go back with my husband.*

*At that point, there was no turning back. I loved Jimmy too much. He was a very quiet man. When I was upset and started to lose my temper, Jimmy got up and left. He was thin at the time and taller than I was. Sometimes, when he got mad at my temper, he grabbed me by my wrist and forced me to sit down. I tried to get away but he made me listen to whatever he had to say. In two minutes I got over being angry. Why in the name of God would he not admit that you were his son?*

*When I moved to Ash Street, I only had Janice. Doug and Billy lived at my father's home. That was January 1939. I met Jimmy in May 1940. Paul lived in Windsor Locks. I moved to an end of the city where I didn't know anyone. I didn't want anyone to know where I was.*

*Poor Jimmy. I know he loved me as sure as the nose on my face. But it was impossible for us to be happy. He once bought me a beautiful dress when he went to see his mother. The dress was a size 12 and I only wore a size 10. We laughed so much because it hung on me like a gunnysack. He wanted me to give it to some fat girl but I wouldn't let him. It was the nicest dress I had seen. My dear, don't make trouble for him. I know wherever he is, he is dying slowly about you. He knows me and is afraid you have my temper so no wonder he pretends he has no idea what you are talking about. He is afraid you will show up at his door with my loud mouth.*

*Love,*
*Mother*

*P.S. One thing I can say is that you talk like your father, especially when you tell me to "Listen" and you mean it. He used to tell me that all the time in his broken English.*

# Chapter Fourteen

*July 21, 1976*

*Jim,*

*Janice called me and was crying so hard. My sisters have been on her back for two weeks or more. Every time they call me, I say I am busy and hang up on them. I am usually writing to you and don't want to talk to them. I usually tell them that I will call them back and sometimes I forget. Well, Janice told me to call my sisters and tell them that I don't give her any money. Can you believe they still want to know what I am doing with my money after all these years? They want to know how is Janice going to Florida and if I gave her the money. They have her so upset and she is crying. Well, let her get a good taste of how they really are. She never believes me when I tell her how badly they have treated me. She thinks they are so wonderful. I don't talk to them that much if I can help it. Except I like Sylvia. She is the only one. Why the hell do they have to keep bothering Janice and me? It's my time and I can write to you if I feel like it. I can do what I want without those nosy old bags calling me with their stupid questions. I am busy writing to you. When I finish after three or four hours, I have to clean this damn place.*

*Janice begged me to tell my sisters that I didn't give her the money to go to Florida. And if I did, who cares? My sisters tell me to put my money in the bank, every penny. They are afraid that if I get sick they will have to foot my medical bills. They are so stingy. Janice is working and that is how she goes on vacation. They want to know how much money I am taking to Florida and who I give my money to. I am laughing. If I weren't writing to you, I would be on the phone yelling at them. It is better that I am writing this letter. I'd like to tell them about you. That would give them something to talk about for years. Maybe then they would forget about how much money I have.*

*I am so happy over you, to hell with them. I have something more important to think about now besides their nosy questions. Do you know what is killing my brothers and sisters? I love to tell them that when I have no more money, I will go downtown and sign up for welfare. They go* completely haywire and start screaming. And then they rush over here and ask me if I have gone crazy. They don't want me to embarrass them. They are so afraid their fancy friends might find out they had an old, fat sister on welfare. I can't stop laughing. I have a lot of poor friends and if I want to help them out with a few bucks now and then, that's my business. They don't like Mabel and think I give her money. So what. They don't need to know my business.

Yesterday I went downtown and I paid $9 for a small bottle of body cream. I put it on my elbows. Why? Don't ask me. Sometimes I put it on my ugly legs, heels, and toes. I bought soap, three tiny bars for $7.50, and face cream for $12.50. I like the soap because it washes my face clean and gets into the pores. Now that I am getting older, I need to wash my big nose clean. I pay $4.50 for lipstick. That's all the makeup I use. This is what I am like. I bought three bras and paid $27 and the doctor told me to throw them away. I have been wearing Playtex for ten years. I had this pain and he told me it was from the bras. I told him he was nuts. Yesterday I also bought two pairs of shoes.

This is what I do with my money and if I told my sisters, they would take me to a shrink. I am sorry but I had these things all my life. If I didn't have the money, I charged them. I always had bills and worked hard to pay them. Friday I will have my hair cut before I go to Florida. For a permanent and body wave, that's $35. Now, my sisters look a hell of a lot better than I ever will. They are not fat and not half as old looking as me. They never had to work and if they want to go out and get their hair done for ten bucks that's their business. If they want to wash their faces with cheap Ivory soap, who cares? I like nice things and this is what I buy.

My biggest heartbreak is my teeth. I can't stand going to a dentist. I had a partial for my back teeth. I do have a few front teeth but two are filled. I went to three dentists and they all told me they had to come out. So I found a dentist that could save them because I can't wear false teeth. He said that I have the strongest bones and the roots are good. He is going to make a partial. I went to him four times and when he turned around to begin the work, I jumped out of the chair and ran out of the office. God knows I tried to let him do the work but got too scared. Do you know I still had to pay him—for nothing.

The minute I get into a dentist's chair, I start trembling. The last time I went he gave me a pill and then he laid the chair flat and when he sat down at my side I got so silly and started laughing so much that he and his nurse started laughing and the nurse couldn't stop. He got close to me and I told him not to breathe in my face. He said that I was impossible. He is a wonderful dentist. He asked me why I didn't come before and I told him I would rather have a baby or an operation than see a dentist. My niece works for him and her mother told me how good he was and asked me to go to him. So when you wrote, I had to do something. When you come back here I don't want you to find a toothless old hag. I shocked my family when I made the appointment because they know how I feel about dentists. I told my niece it was because I was getting married but not to tell anyone. She is 25 and told everyone secretly. Now when I go to the dentist, he looks at me funny. I know what he is thinking because my niece told him what I said. Now when I sit in his chair I feel sillier because he thinks I am going to get married. I already gave him $100 and he did nothing but fill one tooth. So how in the hell can I put money in the bank like my sisters think I should? I don't have that much.

I sat on my ass all day. It is one o'clock and Janice is still crying and I am laughing. I can get very silly sometimes. I am laughing because I did nothing except write you two letters. Angelo was mad with me this morning. When I get up, I don't leave my bedroom until I take a bath. He goes crazy. Why do I do these things? I don't know. When I get up at six, I am out of my bedroom by seven. Then he wants me to fix his breakfast. He goes crazy if he has to fry his own eggs. I wait on his two children and when they grow up, they are going to stink. They are lazy and don't think of me as their aunt, but as their servant.

Well, Jim, I have to cook supper. The children were in the rumpus room all day playing with their friends. I am afraid to go down there and see what they did. Now you know what your mother is like. When I see you I will laugh to think about the things I wrote you. Mabel told me to give you a big welcome. I told her you had better give me a big welcome. I love you first, then David, and then Janice.

*Mother*

***

*July 22, 1976*

*My dearest Jim,*

*I received your letter. I am sorry you are working so hard. Please don't answer my letters if you are too busy.*

*Your letter did not upset me. You wrote what you felt and if it makes you feel better, I am happy.*

*I see a very lonely man that wants to see his mother. He has wondered for many years where she was and who she was and who his father was. Though you had two parents who raised you, you were still alone. You must have done a lot of thinking about why you were not with your real parents.*

*For the last two months, I have done nothing but hurt and be upset and I probably make you miserable because of how I am feeling. But I am amazed that you that still want to see me. Jim, they don't make them like you anymore. Is it possible that you are my son? Maybe you found the wrong mother. All of this has made me so anxious, nervous, and tense. Please forgive me if I hurt you when I am writing or talking to you. I am an old, frustrated, broken down, wrinkled, fat lady and sometimes I hurt people. Even when I was thin and not so wrinkled I hurt people, like your father.*

*Jimmy comes to mind every time I write to you. I was just thinking about his fingernails. They were so clean. I didn't like his face, but I fell in love with his fingernails. I am laughing again. I bet you think I am some kind of a loony, but who cares. When I see you, I will explain about Jimmy and how you are his boy. I know because you are so much like him in a lot of ways. All these years I was right when I thought about you being smart like he was. I love you. God, what I did to you. But I am still in a good mood.*

*Mother*

***

*July 25, 1976*

*Dear Jim,*

*Everyone is sleeping but I cannot stay in bed. For too many years, I have always gotten up at 5:30 or 6:00 a.m. I always get up at the same time no matter where I am. Janice goes crazy when we go on vacation because I get up so early. This time it won't be too bad in Florida because I have my own room.*

*David visited me on Friday and got a little fresh with his mouth. I didn't like the way he was talking so I threw him out. Yesterday I was surprised to see him at the door laughing but I was still mad at him and I wouldn't unlock it. The only way he got me to let him in was to tell me that he had talked to you.*

*I already told you that your brother David is crazy. He is always moving around here, there, and everywhere. Lately he has been acting free and happy. I am glad that he never listened to me about getting married. I see now that he would make some girl miserable. I can see the girl trying to tell him to stay home. He sat me down and said, "Mother, tell me your love stories." This drives me crazy. He thinks nothing about asking me about your father and his father, and how we met and where we went and on and on and on. Sometimes, I can't take anymore and I tell him to get out. He said that when he talked to you, I told you I was fat. He asked me why and then tried to tell me that I am not fat. Well, if 190 pounds for a short lady isn't fat then that guy is blind and doesn't know it. He starts to tell me how beautiful I am and because I am so beautiful, that is where he got his good looks. Oh, brother. Does he ever love himself.*

*He tells me that he talked you into staying with him when you come here. Oh Lord, Jim. For once listen to me. When you are in bed, you can expect people to walk in and out of his shop that is on the second floor and right into the bedroom that you can see from the shop. Strangers can see you in bed. He has a kitchen, a bathroom, and a workshop in the bedroom so there is dust flying all over the place. When Janice and I go there, Janice wants to cry because his place is such a mess. It isn't dirty, just stuff all over the place. I keep my mouth shut when I go there. He is happy in that small apartment.*

*He has a closet for his clothes, mostly t-shirts and cut off jeans. I swear he can dirty 15 towels a day. He does laundry himself and when everything is washed and dried, it is as stiff as boards. All he thinks about is jumping into his car and singing his way to heaven. He got a night shift job because he says the days are too beautiful to be working.*

*I am telling you this so you can make up your own mind about staying with him. I won't tell you what to do, except you better think about it. He is nuts. I know once you get here, he will be with you every day. He told me he is going to tell everyone who sees you that you are his brother. He can't wait to rub you into my sister's faces.*

*I am not telling them anything. Maybe they will pass out when they get a look at you. He doesn't give a damn about anyone. I tell him, "David, what are you talking about? You can't just go parading Jim around every-where and showing him off to my sisters. How is he going to feel with those old bats staring at him? And what about me? What do I say to them?" He looked me in the eye and said, "Mother, you haven't done a damn thing wrong. Why do you have to hide Jim from your sisters?"*

*Here I am getting ready to go on vacation, and then it won't be long before you are here. I want to see you in the worst way and David can't wait for you to get here. But I don't know about his plan to show you off to my family. I am very upset with his crazy ideas.*

*I'd rather you stay with Janice or at a hotel, and have a little privacy. You won't get much at David's. I should see about getting you a hotel. I want to talk to you without some nut coming in to say, "Jim, let's go." You don't know David. You can't tell him anything.*

*He is going back to Virginia and wants me to go with him. His father's family asked him to bring me and not to come without me. I told David that if he does, he is going to be a sorry boy. They only want to see the woman that their brother knew. David likes them and says they are very warm people. David is like his father who was a little crazy too and always talking and a very happy guy. Everything was a joke to him. Maybe David isn't like me after all. I will be happy if he goes to Virginia and stays there. He will give me a rest.*

*As for your father, he was much different than David's. He was seri-ous, quiet, and easygoing. He sat down and studied you. When he came to my apartment, he sat back and looked and stared at the simple things I did. He noticed everything, even when I made a bed. When I changed the bed on Tuesday he asked me why I did it again after I changed the bed on*

Friday. How did he know? Just to shut him up, I told him that the boys had been jumping on the bed.

Jimmy thought he knew everything about everyone who lived in that apartment house simply by looking at them. When he met a person he didn't like, he let me know. He lived on one side of the building and I lived on the other. On the side where I lived there were 15 rooms that were occupied by single girls who worked at Aetna Insurance. These girls were from 25 to 40 years old. Sometimes he talked to them and if he found out one had a date with a fellow one night and another fellow the next night, he called them bums. He told me stuff like "Mary McGinnis is going steady with Richard." I didn't care who people dated. These two people eventually did get married and your father almost died. He didn't understand because Mary had boyfriends before she married Richard. Your father really did just get off the boat when it came to things like that. Yet as upset as he got about who the girls were dating, it never bothered him that I was married although I was separated.

Many times at night I walked Mary to work at Aetna Insurance because it was late and she was afraid to go by herself. I had someone watch the children while I was gone. We would go by the diner around 11 p.m. and sometimes stopped in so I could see your father. When he saw me with Mary, he couldn't work anymore because he was so angry. His mouth and jaws tightened so much that he couldn't talk. This was before she married Richard, and your father thought she was a bum and that I should not hang around her. Whenever I stopped in the diner, his brothers kept an eye on Jimmy like a hawk. When he got off work at 1 a.m., we walked back to the apartment house. He would be wild and ask me where I had been with Mary. For some reason he hated the Irish and the fact that she had some boyfriends made him hate her more. He would come back to my apartment and see who was with my children and then asked them what time I left.

Jimmy was very jealous, narrow minded, and so old-fashioned. Yet he walked around with his square shoulders like he was perfect. He was very straight when he walked. He was also dark. I had never gone out with dark men. I never intended to go out with him because I didn't like dark men. I always called him ugly and he called me "Funny." He couldn't say "Fanny." He sat and read for hours and if he didn't understand something he would ask me, no matter how simple it was.

Everything he did was okay with me. He always asked me, "Is this right? Is this wrong?" He called me the smart American. I wonder how *old he was when he came to this country. Jimmy wanted to learn to dance and I taught him on his night off. We had a great room in the apartment house. It was like a clubhouse. In the evening everyone who lived there came down and sat and talked. That is where I taught him to dance. He didn't care who was around as long as he was learning something. One day Petros and Kostas came up and watched me teach him. They laughed and mumbled in Greek to each other. But he never stopped dancing and when I started to he wouldn't let me. He held me tighter and said, "Keep dancing." Then Petros and Kostas talked to him in Greek. Pretty soon they were arguing and getting louder. I think they were giving him hell. Jimmy said to me, "Keep dancing. Keep dancing." Finally they left.*

*Petros and Kostas were always nice to me but I know they didn't like Jimmy seeing me. Your father probably isn't friendly with them any longer. If he is, it would surprise me. Your father got so uptight around them. Georgios never liked me either, but he always spoke to me like a gentleman. I think your father was the oldest of the family. I am not sure. Georgios always spelled his last name differently than your father spelled his. I have always wondered why.*

*When I went out with your father, it caused a lot of trouble with his Greek friends. His family wanted him to marry a Greek girl and my family wanted me to move back in with my husband. I didn't care what anyone thought, but Jimmy worried about hurting his people. He had a strong will, and did as he wanted. But this time he was not strong enough to stand up for himself. As much as he tried to pretend otherwise, he went through a lot of hurt about me. Anyway, what is it they say about time is supposed to heal all wounds? I wonder if it did for him.*

*I will write again before I leave for Florida or I will call.*

*Love,*
*Mother*

*P.S. As I wrote this letter, all I did was cry about what happened over 30 years ago. Jimmy was a good man. He put himself into a situation that was hard to get out of. No two families were so unalike as his and mine. They never knew each other. This is how good families were in those days. Parents told their children what to do even after they were grown up and the children listened. Your father listened to his family. Of course I didn't listen to mine. I still don't.*

[The following page was included with the letter.]

*END*

*I am going to the beach with Janice. I never go with anyone else. I never went with my sisters and their families. I don't go with any friends either. When I was younger, I went with Billy and Doug and their families. Sometimes David comes by and wants me to go with him down to the Sound. But I never go. He is too young to be dragging an old lady with him and I tell him to go with his friends. He always manages to find Janice and me when we go together. While most people like to bring food and eat at the beach, we don't. For some reason, we don't like picnics. We don't like camping either. When we do go on a picnic, Stanley laughs because our picnic lasts about five minutes and we run into the water. Mainly I hate picnics because I can't stand ants and bugs. Janice and David are like me when it comes to crawly things. We would rather spend our money in a nice restaurant rather than sitting and eating with a bunch of bugs. My whole family is like that. Now I see my grandchildren acting the same way. Nobody wants to go home and eat. I hate to cook and always have. Poor Janice didn't have a mother that taught her to cook so now she doesn't like to cook. But she likes to eat. Stanley settles for anything—eat out or eat in, he doesn't care which. She is lucky to have a husband like that.*

*It is funny. She married a man that could hardly speak English. A lot of times he says the wrong things and gets his words mixed up, but she loves him very much anyway. They get along so well. I like it especially when Stanley tells her to leave me alone and not argue with me. When they first got married, he tried to do everything Billy and Doug did. Sometimes Billy did something wrong and Stanley did not realize it and he followed Billy and did the same thing. Janice would be embarrassed but poor Stan would say, "Well, that's the way your brother did it so I thought that was the way to do it."*

*Love,*
*Mother*

# *Chapter Fifteen*

*July 26, 1976*

*Dear Jim,*

*Talking to you on the phone made me happy again. You are excited about coming here, and when you told me you were getting nervous, I knew you were my boy. I get a kick when you say, "You are not listening." For some reason I do listen to you and that is not like me. I never listened to anyone in my life except maybe your father. I guess I love you too much for all the years I missed with you. I am listening.*

*I envy Ruth, a woman whose place I could never take. She had the pleasure of kissing you and hugging you as a child and putting you to bed. Why couldn't I have done that? I raised four kids alone. What difference would one more have made?*

[Ruth did not have the pleasure of hugging and kissing me as a child. For two years after Cecilia left me at the café, my life was turned upside down. Hollis returned from Oregon and had to be surprised to find me waiting for him. While Hollis meant well, he was unprepared to care for me. He made arrangements to board me with various people, because he was working two jobs. I don't remember how many places I lived during that time, or who I lived with.

Eventually Hollis rented an apartment in the poor section of Denver known as Five Points. We lived there for six months while he worked nights. My best friends were an African American brother and sister living in the next block. Hollis made arrangements for me to go to their apartment after school and have dinner with the family. Before dark, their father would walk me back to our apartment. Hollis arrived home around midnight. The next morning while he slept, I woke up, fixed my breakfast, and got ready for school.

We were fine until a few well meaning, but nosy old ladies in the apartment house reported us to the State Child Welfare Division. They were upset that I lived without a mother and with a father who was seldom at home. Later Hollis told me that the women didn't think it was right that I had "Negro" friends.

After a hearing with officials from the child welfare depart-ment, my father was ordered to provide me with a better home envi-ronment. I was placed in Denver's Byer's Home for Boys. I was eight years old. It was a home but I am not sure it was better.

Byer's Home had been a Denver institution since 1900, lo-cated near Alameda and Broadway on the southern edge of down-town. Not much had changed in the fifty years before I arrived. The building was a large converted Victorian house with a sign out front that said: "Denver's Byer's Home for Boys." I was ashamed of my new address and always entered and exited the house quickly in hopes that no one would know that I lived there. Byer's housed 10 to 15 un-happy boys, ranging in age from 6 to 18. Like me, their parents were no longer in their lives for reasons we children did not understand.

Daily routines were strict and enforced by the intimidating Uncle Avery. He kept a black whip hanging on the back of his office door and frequently used it on boys who misbehaved. A young wom-an named Miss James was the cook. A fat, friendly housedog was the recipient of a lot of love and attention from boys who received little love and attention themselves.

It was at Byer's that I first learned about sex from stories that I heard from the other boys. Some of the younger boys may have been victims of molestation by the older ones. I was an embittered and very angry eight-year-old kid who felt alone. As a result, I was not afraid to defend myself. This combination served as my protec-tion, and I don't remember being bothered by the older boys. The home was a fearful place for a young boy to grow up. I was lucky that I only spent a year there.

Alameda Grade School was a few blocks from Byer's. It be-came a happy refuge for me during my confinement at the home. Going to school was a great escape from my unhappy childhood. Whenever I entered the schoolhouse, I forgot that I had no parents and that I lived at Byer's. For seven hours each weekday I was in a happier and more interesting world. My teachers were wonderful individuals whom I loved and who, unlike my parents and Uncle Avery, were interested in me, and what I had to say. I still owe a debt of gratitude for the help and encouragement I received from those teachers. Each one had a positive and lasting impact on my life. I learned self-worth and they inspired me to always do my best.

I loved being in school because it took me away from the chaos of childhood and the strife at home.

Sundays were visiting days. Parents were allowed to visit and the boys could leave for a day's outing. Boys whose parents did not come were sent to the local movie theater for the afternoon. With the house empty, the staff had time to mop and clean. The Mayan Theater was an Art Deco palace a few blocks away. Sometimes my father came, but usually I ended up at the Sunday matinees. When my father did not show up, I was more sad and alone as I watched other boys leave with their parents. Yet going to the movies provided a wondrous, though temporary, escape.

There were between seven and ten boys for our excursions to the Mayan, and an older boy had the responsibility of accompanying the younger ones. He was given money for our admission, a dime each, and he made sure we got back to Byer's after the movie. One Sunday afternoon stands out clearly in my memory.

The management of the Mayan was familiar with us, and arrangements were made that when our group arrived we did not have to wait in line. We were immediately admitted. This made the cashier's job easier by taking our admission dimes all at once rather than ringing up the tickets one by one.

On this Sunday we were led to the front of the line, and one boy with his mother protested loudly. "Mommy, why are they getting in front of us? We were here first." We could not help but overhear his mother's response. "Sweetheart, those poor little boys have no mommies or daddies to take them to the movies." I was crying as we entered the dark theater. The movie was *The Wizard of Oz* and there couldn't have been a better choice to help me forget the woman's off-hand remark. To this day, *The Wizard of Oz* is one of my favorite films.

I did learn a valuable lesson while at Byer's: I could no longer depend on the adults around me. Cecilia and my father had abandoned me, and I was frightened of Uncle Avery. At that age I did not understand that the State of Colorado had made the decision for my father to put me in the home. I decided that I was the only one who could take care of me. If this was how parents treat kids, who needed them? Much too soon I learned to be independent and count only on myself.

Years later on a visit to Denver I drove by to see the home

and Alameda Grade School. A Taco Bell had replaced Byer's Home for Boys. The granite fortress-like school still stood, but it had been converted to luxury condominiums. The memories of sad young boys from nearby Byer's were now part of the building's forgotten history. The Mayan Theater has survived. Renovated and restored to its former Art Deco glory, it is now a Denver landmark.

When Hollis married Ruth I was allowed to go live with my new stepmother and father. I don't remember saying goodbye to Uncle Avery but I was glad to get away from his threats of the whip. My happy moment did not last very long. Like many children with a new stepmother, I was less than subtle in letting Ruth know that I didn't like her or my stepsister, Bev. It was a bad way to start the relationship and it didn't improve as I grew. Frances' fantasy about my childhood with Ruth was just that, a fantasy.]

*Janice just called. She is crying, "Where is my brother?" Her husband's car broke down and so he took her car and now she is stuck at home looking for David for a ride. Both of Janice's cars are junkers.*

*David and Janice are arguing a lot and David is the cause. Janice can't stand it when he starts calling himself a pastor. He wrote to the Universal Life Church and they sent him a paper that made him a minister. What the hell kind of church is that? Janice said that he is not a minister of any church that believes in God. But then David brings out his piece of paper to show her that she is wrong and that he really is a minister. I don't understand this Universal Life Church ministry that he keeps talking about. For once I have to agree with Janice. I may not be the smartest person but I understand why she thinks he is making fun of God. She takes her religion seriously. I think he is nuts like this so-called church that is calling him a minister. If David is a minister, then I am the pope.*

*Janice cries when she needs help and if Stanley is not there, she looks for David. When David is in trouble, he runs for Janice. Neither one of them would go to my sisters or brothers if they needed help. Now she doesn't have a car and has to take her two boys for music lessons so she looks for David. This is my fault. When they were children, Janice took dance lessons for a year; Billy and Doug took horseback riding lessons. I wish I had the money that went for those lessons in the bank. But I am not sorry, even though not one of them stuck it out to the end. I spent a lot on these kids as they were growing up because it made them happy and brought me a lot of pleasure. Mabel always told me I was wasting my money. She seemed to forget that she wasted her money on her husbands. How can anyone say you waste money when you spend it on your children that you love? We had some damn hard times when it was the Depression and I remember Mabel stealing sometimes— but not me. I never did.*

*I still think that I haven't done enough for Janice and David, let alone you. Jim, you will never understand me but remember this when I am dead and you are married with a lot of children. No matter how you were brought up, you are me inside, I mean the Italian descent and that you would die for your children. There won't ever be enough that you can do for them. Remember what I tell you. You will spoil them and love them and swear that you will make good children out of them. But only God knows whether that will happen or not.*

*You are a very warm person because you are Italian like me. That is why I love you so much. I like warm people who have feelings. So when you die, I will see you in heaven. The only thing that will keep me from entering heaven is that I gave you up. That was the biggest sin that I committed.*

*I must talk to you about your father again. Please try and see him when you come here. I want you to. This is beginning to be important to me. No matter how it may hurt you, you must come down off your high horse. Don't be like me. Sometimes it doesn't pay to be too independent. If he refuses to meet you, I will get a good attorney after you go back to California, and he will be sorry he didn't see you because then he has to see me.*

*I am not as dumb as you, Janice, or David think that I am. There are a lot of things I want to say but I can't express them. Your father and I drifted apart, and I want to know what he says about why he left. Who knows if he can remember but how could he forget? He isn't that old or sick. That guy is as strong as an ox. These damn Greeks never die.*

*11:30 a.m.*

*Janice just got her car back and so she came by and picked me up to go to the bank and get my traveler's checks. The teller asked me if I was over 65 and I said 69. I am getting to be a good liar. I saved ten bucks. To hell with them. To go on vacation you must have a lot of money. I may as well spend what I have got on myself. I may sound selfish and when I die, to Janice and you and David, I leave my love. When I get back from vacation, I am going to get rid of my so-called friends who always want to borrow a buck or two, which I never get back. As far as the grandchildren, they can*

go to you-know-where. Let them work and buy their crap. I am becoming a
mean old lady and I am going to keep my money for myself.

When you get this letter you won't be able to answer because I won't
be home. I will call you when I am in Florida because I want to hear you
say, "You are not listening." I get a big kick out of that. What am I going
to do when you get here? Then I will have to listen to you. Maybe there will
be days I won't get to see you. I will leave that up to David. I am seriously
thinking about having you stay in Hartford rather than Rocky Hill. I love
you so much.

Love,
Mother

P.S. When I carried you, I ate nothing.
I drank milk and ate oranges. This is the truth.

Here are some more things you need to know about your mother. My favorite food is bread. I hate soup. I love eggs and I like milk. I hate beef. I like
chicken or turkey. I hate seafood or fish. I love cake. I hate cookies. I love
spaghetti, shells, and ravioli. I like cheese.

I only like to hear Johnny Mathis sing. I hate country music—some of
it is okay. I don't like Ronald Regan. I like Jimmy Carter. I don't like fruit,
except cherries. I only drink coffee once a day. I don't smoke.

If I had my way, I would drink. Someday, I am going to go away by
myself get a hotel room and order in some drinks. I would like to just sit
around having some drinks, but not get drunk. When I have a couple of
drinks like at a wedding, I get very happy. David doesn't care but Janice
goes out of her mind. I don't like the taste but it does change me and then I
feel good and laugh a lot.

Oh, I like cold cereal. I hate grapefruit—Yack! I tried hard to like it but
I don't and I won't eat it. No more room on the paper. Most of all I love you.

*July 27, 1976*

*Dear Jim,*

Look at the picture I found. This is Miriam, the sister that Janice told we had a new baby in our house. I was so scared of Miriam I couldn't sleep nights. She never worked a day in her life and still has the first dollar her husband ever earned. She is mean, mean, mean.

Miriam is the godmother of Doug's daughter. Doug loved her. She told him that when we were young, she was good and I was the wild one. She is three years older than me. I look like her mother. She has all her teeth and no cavities. Mabel and I were talking about her the other day about her teeth and her hair. She has no gray hair and I don't think she dyes it. What really kills me is you look like her, her eyes and her teeth anyway.

David swears when you come, he will take you to her house and say, "This is my brother. Remember the Greek guy you chased away from my mother? Well here is his son." He wants to do this so bad. She will remember all right and then probably drop dead and David would go to jail for murder.

I told David you are not coming here to get mixed up with that kind of baloney. For years, Miriam tore my heart apart. It is too bad I wasn't as narrow minded as she is. I wonder what I would have been like. Hell, I am glad I wasn't like her. So take a good look at the picture. This is your aunty.

*Love,*
*Mother*

*July 27, 1976*

*Please enjoy this letter.*

*Dear Jim,*

I have written you everything about myself and so much about Janice and David. We are not going to be like strangers when you get here. You tell *me that you might be scared when you are here and a little worried at how strange it will be to meet us. If it is strange, then it will only be for a minute. I want to give you time to think things over after you meet us.*

*Yes, I agree that you should stay at a hotel while you are here. Stay in Hartford when you arrive and I will get a room in the same hotel. I already told Janice so she can take care of Angelo's children at her house, and tell him that Mabel and I are going to the Cape. To hell with him. I hope when you get here it is not too late because I won't meet you at the station. It's in a terrible part of town that is dirty and lots of bums hang around. This is what I hear. I haven't been there for years. Catch a cab to the hotel and I can meet you there.*

*I will get a room under your name and you can go there first. But when you come to see me, you better be ready to talk. You will be so tired after you see me that you may want to sleep for two days. If this doesn't suit you just say so.*

*Then David and Janice can come get us and take you to a motel in Rocky Hill near Janice's. I want you to be comfortable and if you are any-thing like me you enjoy being alone. I know it would be too hard for you to walk into Janice's house and be at home. But she means it when she says you can stay at her house.*

*When I call, let me know if this sounds okay with you. I am not trying to tell you what to do. I am just trying to make you feel like you will not want to leave. I decided not to go to Virginia with David. I have to be here when you arrive. Believe me, I never want to lose track of you again.*

*If I come out to California, I don't want to stay with you or any of your friends. I don't care how big your house is, I could never stay with you. I live here, Jim, and have one reason for hating it—I have to live with An-gelo and his kids. The children bother me a lot. They run in and out and get on my nerves and I yell at them. Then I want to cry because I feel so bad they have no mother. I told you she committed suicide a few years ago.*

*I never lived with anyone except my children. After Doug, Billy, and Janice were married, David wanted to go but he wouldn't leave me alone. I couldn't live with him as he got older. He came home with a bird and said it was a present for me. But the truth was that he wanted it so bad for himself. He knew I hated birds. All I did was clean up birdseed all over the floor and clean the cage. David came home from work and talked and talked to that damn bird all night. God, I couldn't wait to get away from him. I couldn't use the phone because he lay down on the bed and talked all night. Many nights I went into his room and he was fast asleep with the*

*phone in his hand and I had to hang it up for him. If he wasn't talking to
that damn bird he was on the phone talking to his friends.*

*When I came here to live with Angelo and his children, I knew it would
free David. I was ready to get a smaller place anyway. Angelo has a bad
habit. I have my own room and sometimes I sit in here and talk on the
phone. He never raps on my door. He just opens the door and walks in. I
hate that. I have trained the children to never come into my room if the door
is closed. They have to knock. I can be in my bathroom in my nightgown
combing my hair and Angelo walks in and I yell at him to get out because I
am not dressed. He wants to know why I am combing my hair if I am going
to bed. Then I started wondering myself. It is just a habit after I wash it. I
like to look in the mirror and see myself, and how old I am getting. I discovered I am growing hair in my chin! I have always liked lots of privacy.*

## 7:00 a.m.

*I had coffee and was thinking about Jimmy. For some reason, I always con-
nect you with your father. You both disappeared from my life at about the
same time. As long as I can remember I never connected my children with
their fathers. I wanted so much for you to be like him. That was my reason
for giving you his first name on your birth certificate. I knew that someday
I wanted to tell you everything. Only I didn't know you weren't going to be
around for 34 years.*

*I am going to a psychiatrist and see if he can figure out what made me
connect you to your father. I've got to find out. About Jimmy—everyone
in those days left their doors unlocked when they went to work. When your
father went to work, I went to his room and took his after-shave lotion and
splashed it over my arms. I never had the money to buy cologne. Then I
went upstairs and if any of the girls were there they asked me what I had
on. I did not answer and put my nose in the air and went back to my
apartment. Every chance I got I'd sneak down there to steal some of his
after-shave. You don't know how happy this made me. Was I ever dumb.*

*After doing this a few times, one day the bottle was empty and stayed
that way for a long time. Your father was a fox. I think he enjoyed me being
so dumb. Then on Sunday he brought me a small bottle of perfume and
laughed like hell. He knew that it was me who was taking the after-shave. I
told him that I like cologne and not perfume and I had the last laugh on
him. He didn't even know what cologne was. He got so mad because I had*

165

put one over on him. He tried to take the perfume away. I screamed and it scared him so that he ran out. He couldn't stand my yelling.

He was funny. Jimmy was afraid of what people in the apartment house thought about him. He wanted people to know that he was not hurting me. Everyone who lived there knew him and how I liked to yell. Every time he came to my apartment the first thing he said was, "Shhhh. Don't yell. Keep quiet." When I opened my big mouth that drove him up the wall.

Why did I do this? He was the opposite of me, and I liked to tease him. Many of the girls in that house would have given their eyeteeth to go out with him. I laughed so much when they called, "Oh, Jimmy." He wouldn't look at them. Then he told me they were bums and I had to explain that they just liked to have a good time. All he said was, "Bums, bums, bums." He wasn't in this country too long, yet he was in college. He knew nothing about American girls. In fact, he knew nothing about a lot of things. He didn't speak English very well. I am very talkative and he stayed up at night and listened to me talk, talk, talk, and never said one word. He walked up the street to the diner alone to go to work. Then he came back alone. Kostas and Petros had a car and they drove and he never got in their car.

Kostas married someone's Greek sister and he cheated on her like hell. Petros also married a Greek girl. He ended up miserable and finally divorced her. Kostas' sister married Jimmy's brother, Georgios. All these people came from Greece. They should have stuck their heads in it.

The last time I saw Jimmy, the girl next door, Joanne, and her husband were at my apartment on my birthday. He wanted to say something. I remember that I had told Joanne I was going to have a baby. Her husband was in the Army and was home that night. He was drinking. When Jimmy came in, her husband stood up and clipped him. Jimmy lifted his arm and with his other arm pushed him against the wall. He walked out and I never saw Jimmy again. I said, "Let him go." That was December 31, 1941. Jimmy couldn't take what had happened. This is true. Someday, I am going to go see him before I die. I want to know what happened that night, what he wanted and why he never called me. He never came back or told me how he felt. He couldn't take it. You talk just like him.

Love,
Mother

# Chapter Sixteen

*July 27, 1976*

*Dear Jim,*

*I found this picture of Doug and Billy with my sister Sylvia and a friend. The man holding my boys is my brother, Salvatore. It was taken in the late 1930s on my birthday. I have a very poor memory sometimes, but this picture has brought back plenty to me. I called Sylvia to ask her when it was taken. She said, "Can't you remember your own birthday?" What I wanted to know was the year. She is 13 months younger than me and sharp as a whip. I have been through so much hell lately I couldn't even remember the exact day you were born. Right now I am feeling terrible.*

*Mabel is no help when I try to remember dates. Whatever I tell her about something, she swears by it because she thinks she remembers. She is an old lady of 68 and has a worse memory than I do. I never call my sisters for anything but I had to find out when I moved to Hestor Court. I asked my sister when I moved to Ash Street because she was taking care of my two boys when I was working. You know what happened? She wouldn't give them back to me. She didn't want me moving out by myself. I moved to my father's house after I left Paul and she still lived at home. She told me that I had to go back to Windsor Locks and live with Paul's people because leaving my husband was my fault. After I had moved away from Paul, he could not afford to keep a house and had moved back with his parents.*

*I would have died before I went back to Paul and his family. So I found a place of my own and went back to my father's house and told my sister that I had come for my boys and she better let me have them if she knew what was good for her. Then I left with them to my new place. I never told my family where I went. But they snooped around and found out I was living on Ash Street. That was in 1939. Janice was born in November 1938. I left her at the hospital nursery until January. Sylvia told me yesterday that the reason I wouldn't go back to Paul's family was because I didn't like their table manners. She laughed.*

*I stayed on Ash Street 1939 and 1940. That is when I met Jimmy and he used to carry Janice around because she wasn't walking. I am so mixed up now. If I met him in 1940, that made Janice three years old. She couldn't walk at the age of two and some quack of a doctor told me she would never walk. Mabel got her walking.*

*I lived with Jimmy in the same apartment building from May 1940 through February 1941, when I moved into Hestor Court. He came to visit me in a green car. During the summer of 1941, my brothers would come to see me once in a while. They were only kids then, 16, 18, 20, and 22. The first time Jimmy saw them he asked me who they were. After I moved from Ash Street, Jimmy changed and became very jealous. He did not trust me, and was sorry that I moved because he couldn't see me as often. It was his fault. He made me move away from the diner so that his brothers could not be snooping on us all the time.*

*Those rotten Greeks, Georgios and Kostas, must have found someone's Greek sister for him to go out with after I moved away. In September, I found out I was going to have you. Jimmy told me I was mistaken. I told him I was not. I certainly knew I was going to have a baby. He was happy at first. Then he became miserable and was not the same man. I remember that fall. He wore a grey raincoat that made him look taller. Jimmy became quieter. I am the first to admit I was a son of a bitch. I was so independent. It made me angry because I felt that he was letting me down slowly and trying to disappear. For the life of me, Jim, I do not know why I felt like that and acted like I did. Whenever he came to visit, he left me money. Most of the time I threw it at him as he was leaving. When I cleaned my apartment I always found money that he left on the shelves when I wasn't looking.*

*The last time I saw him was December 31, 1941. I worked the whole nine months I carried you. I weighed 128 pounds at nine months. When I kept the money he gave me, I put it in a jar and I thought someday I would crack the jar over his head. In the end I was lucky. The money paid for the hospital bill when you were born. Months later, I found $600 stuffed inside an old blue sugar bowl on the top shelf in my kitchen. At first, I didn't know where it came from. Then I knew Jimmy left it for me to find after you were born.*

*I don't understand why he tells you that he never knew me when I spent two years with him. I swore that I would get even with him. But that was when I was young and very angry. When I got older I forgot about getting even with him. What for? But now, when that no good bum says he never knew me, I want to find him and smack him in the mouth.*

*The only thing I was happy about was that your name, James*

*Zaldonapolous, Jr, was on your birth certificate. I thought that one day you would not rest until you found him. What I didn't count on was that you would find me, too.*

*I cry so hard when I think of him not wanting to meet you. Never mind the hurt he gave me but he never should hurt you. I never had anyone that was so good to me, and my children. He was so kind. I can't begin to tell you how good he was to me.*

*Jimmy had to go into the Army because he knew damn well what he did was wrong. He wasn't drafted like he said. Even though he talked about us getting married, I never expected him to marry me. Maybe if I had a divorce but that wasn't possible. Still, I didn't expect him to run away.*

*Who knows how Jimmy felt about me. If he hated me or couldn't stand the sight of me, he never showed it. I feel better that I called my old witch of a sister. She wanted to know what was so important about the date I moved to Hestor Court. I told her Mabel wanted to know and my sister said, "Is that one still around?" I can't stand her.*

*I want you to know the truth about your father and if he gives you any dates, give them right back to him. I don't want you believing any lies he might tell you. I love you very much.*

*Love,*
*Mother*

[On a separate page and in the same envelope was the following.]

*Jim,*

*I just remembered something. I hope you haven't written to your father yet. Your father knows my married name was Roccolini. He also called Katarina's daughter and talked to her.*

    [Why did my father contact Katarina's daughter and how would he have known about Katarina? He was overseas when Frances became acquainted with Katarina. Frances never mentioned that he knew this woman.]

*Katarina's daughter mentioned David to me. How would she know him? I never said a word about David to her. Jimmy must have told her about David when he spoke to her. Somehow he thinks that you are David.*

*Over ten years ago, David was on drugs and he was arrested a number* of times and his name appeared in the paper. Because your father knew my name was Roccolini and knew I had his baby, he must have thought that David was his son. No wonder he doesn't want to have anything to do with you.

Write to him about how I left you in the care of the Sutherland's and how you disappeared. Tell him that, Jim, and how you found me. Tell him that David is my youngest son and not you. He knew about Doug and Billy dying. Tell him that you lived in the West all your life, where you were raised and went to school, or he is going to think you are some kind of bum because of what he read in the papers about David.

Tell him that I agreed to see you one time and then you will go away. If I can meet you face to face, he will be a coward if he doesn't do the same thing. All of this about him mixing you up with David just came to mind.

Love,
Frances

\*\*\*

July 29, 1976

Dear Jim,

Everything is one big puzzle. About your father—understand that he is a very intelligent man and will try to confuse you. Many times he did this to me in a joking way. Now he wants to convince himself that you are not his son.

First of all, when I went to find Katarina, I called her home and a girl said Katarina was no longer living. I was surprised that Katarina had a daughter, Andrea who is now 30. I told her daughter the whole story when she asked why I was looking for her mother. Then she asked me, "Was his name David?" Why would she mention David's name?

Katarina's husband, Nikos Mykonossos, is over 75. I then asked her to speak to Nikos and ask if he remembered Jimmy. She said that Nikos was too old and he could not remember things that long ago. He could have known your father and not told her. Those Greeks stick together. They were businessmen who came from Greece and New York to settle in Connecticut, and sat for hours talking in the Athena Diner. Jimmy told me he was not interested in their talks. He was too interested in school.

*When David was nine, he took up skating and by age 12 he had won the Connecticut State Championship. He traveled over New England and his name and pictures were in the paper all the time. Of course, my name appeared as him being the son of Mrs. F. Roccolini from Hestor Court. Jimmy must have seen this. How in the hell could he forget my name when it took him a week to learn how to pronounce it? For that whole summer, David's picture and write-ups were in the paper. About 20 years ago, I ran into Petros from the Athena Diner. He asked me about my boy and said that he had seen the articles about David's skating. How would he know about David? He didn't know my name. That is the reason your father wrote he was married in 1944, because that was the year David was born. Yet what in the hell did he think I did with you? Maybe he thought I went back to my husband, or lied about David's age.*

*When David was small, he asked me about his father. I told him that Ted was killed in the war on a ship. He always asked me if it was a big ship. When David was seven years old, the police came to my door and told me that Paul [Mr. Roccolini] was dead. That was in 1951. I had not seen him since Janice was born in November 1938. He came to the hospital drunk and he told me to name her Janice. He ran out for fear that my family would see him.*

*After the police left, Janice started to scream at me. She had heard the policeman tell me that Mr. Roccolini had passed away. She was 12 and said, "I thought my father died in the war." Janice had listened to me every time David had asked about his father and naturally assumed that he was her father also. You can see what kind of hell I put Janice and David through.*

*As David grew he never talked about his father. When he was 17 and in his last year of high school, he said, "Why did you always tell me that my father died in the war?" I sat him down and told him the truth about Ted and about Janice's father, Paul. He was very confused but I could not lie to him. A few months later he graduated from high school even though his grades were terrible. After that he never was the same. He never talked to me and started going out with a bad crowd. Soon he was into drugs. I lived with the fear that he would die. He kept getting arrested and his name appeared in the paper. Don't think your father didn't see that.*

*You have a birth certificate with his name on it. Why in the hell did I call you Jimmy Zaldonapolous, Jr.? I could have made it easy on myself to say that you were Mr. Roccolini's child and tell David the same thing. But you should know the truth about who you are.*

*When there was the draft, I thought that you might show up on ac-*
*count of your name. The Sutherlands had to tell you something during*
*the Viet Nam War. Didn't you register when you were 18 and show a birth*
*certificate—that you didn't have? I never understood why I never heard*
*from the Sutherlands. You had to know by then that you were not a Suther-*
*land, and they had to find me to get a birth certificate. I kept expecting that*
*I would hear from them. But I didn't. Then I started thinking that if you*
*found your father, he would know where I was.*

*I don't care what anyone thinks of me at this age. You and David must*
*know that I will not pin anything that is not true on an innocent man. I*
*love you, you are my son, and I did a great injustice to you and David. I*
*can never tell either of you how sorry I am for hurting you. But I am not*
*sorry for having both of you.*

*Frances*

[On a separate page in the same envelope was the following.]

*You should see Jimmy at least once. I may be dumb, stupid, and never*
*cared for school but I can look back and be proud of my father whom I loved*
*so much and for what he taught me. One of the things I learned from him*
*was to tell the truth. I always tried to do this. For most of my life, it was the*
*truth coming out of my big mouth that put me in a lot of trouble. But as*
*long as I spoke the truth, I could hold my head high. It wasn't always easy*
*but that is how I was. Obviously, Jimmy Zaldonapolous doesn't think the*
*same way. He isn't worth the dust off your shoes.*

*When you go home to Colorado to see Mr. Sutherland, put your arms*
*around him and no matter how old he is, kiss him on his forehead and say,*
*"Thank you father. I love you." This man is your real father and the only*
*one you will ever have.*

***

*July 30, 1976*

*Dear Jim,*

*I keep thinking that each letter I write to you is my last come hell or high water but nothing can stop me from writing.*

*Okay, I agree that if you are more comfortable staying by yourself and not with Janice or David, then you will stay at a motel. The only reason I suggested the Hilton was because it is close to the train station. You will probably be very tired and in no mood to travel further. Whatever you want or wherever you want to stay, have your way.*

*Jim, I always worked hard for what I had. This was not a bad thing. What was bad was that I always wanted and wanted. And then I wanted more than I could afford. I don't know why but that is why I've always been broke. For the first time (I don't mean when I was single) I have a few dollars in my pocket. And like I was when I was broke, I spend everything Angelo gives me. Janice is not like me. She works hard and manages to put her money into the bank. However now as she gets older I see she is changing and getting to be more like me.*

*If a person says very little to me, but it is something nice, it makes me happy. My granddaughter told me that she wants me to live with her in Florida. She said that as soon as she gets an apartment she wants me to move because I worked too hard all my life and it's time I stopped. She said she loved me very much. Jim, I am so happy to hear these things. I never knew before that she thought this much of me. I'll always carry what she said in my heart, even if it never happens. To me this is love. I don't always expect them to run in and kiss me. But this is the kind of love I like.*

*It is raining for a change. We haven't had rain for weeks and we sure need it. I can't wait for Sunday. Not so much to go to Florida, but to get away from this house. I am going to do something this winter other than look out at the snow. I may go back to work for two days a week. Angelo will not like the idea, but I am thinking about it. David wants me to run his junk store. I told him I would, but on one condition. I want a gun. There are more bums hanging around there and I trust none of them. I tried to get a gun from Angelo and he said I am too nervous to have a gun. He said if I saw someone that scared me I would shoot them, and think about it after. What the hell is he talking about?*

*I am too lazy and have to get up now. I am tired of writing. I was so happy when I first got up. Now I am sad. I will finish later. I am going back to sleep.*


*Everyone is still sleeping because it's raining. When it rains, people out here like to sleep. Last night the children stayed up to watch the Olympics. I wanted so badly to go to Canada this year and see the women gymnasts. I was going to go with a friend of mine, Janice's mother-in-law, Lillian. But Angelo told me it was too late to get tickets. Then Doug's wife, Janet, was remarried and her children cried all the time and told her how much they hate her and that they were not going to Florida. Then David asked me to go to Virginia with him to see Ted's brother. Then the biggest and best thing that happened—you walked into my life. So it wasn't only you, it was also David wanting me to go to Virginia. And that's why I never made it to the Olympics.*

*I have written twice a year to Ted's family in Virginia. I knew only one brother, Henry, because he came up to visit his brother before he went overseas. I also met his sister who is no longer living. David never seemed to care about them until recently. I like Virginia and have been there many times. If David decides to live there I think he would like it. I don't know if that is what he has in mind and it's none of my business. As it stands, I am not going with him. I don't want to think about more new people in my life. Right now, I want to think about you even though you live far away.*

*Janice has me around even if we do argue all the time. But I love her, and she loves me in her own way. But sometimes it seems that I do noth-ing that is right to her. She thinks I am making a pest of myself with you. I said, "He has to take me as I am and I will not change. If he doesn't like it, let him go fly a kite." Then she says, "Oh, poor Jim." And I say, "Don't say that!" And she says, "Oh my poor brother. He does not know what he is in for." Then I tell her, "Go to hell!" Jim, I am mean. Just you wait and see.*

*I never bother David and Janice with my problems. Lately, I am quieter than I ever was. It scares the hell out of everyone: David, Janice, Angelo, and even Stanley, I think. When I go out with Janice she says, "What's the matter with you?" Then she stares at me and says, "Mother, don't feel so bad over Jim." She can read my mind. Then she talks to me like you do and tells me not to dwell in the past. A few weeks ago when we were down at the beach, Janice asked me what was on my mind. We sat alone enjoying* the sun and the waves, and I didn't say a word. She asked me again and I said, "I wish I married old man Sutherland." She said, "Mother, that is the first time I heard you say you wish you were married." Now she really thinks I am nuts.

Every so often, she says, "I know who David takes after." You will see he looks like me. Yet when he went south to see his father's relatives, they all said he looked like Ted. They asked him to change his name and bring his father's body back to Connecticut from North Africa. I wish I could have seen his face when they said that.

When I think of you, I think about what you have told me about yourself. Last night you were trying to say something and I didn't give you a chance. Now I wonder what it was you wanted to say. When I asked who dressed you and you came up with a quick answer, "Maybe I dressed myself," and started laughing. Jim, I could have died. If you ever see your father, show him those pictures of when you were little. He will die. I had better end it here. I just want to hurt him! But I can't because it would hurt you.

I've paid over a hundred dollars for the bills, but I don't remember a greater pleasure than talking with you. So don't worry. It is my pleasure and I will give less to my poor friends. When you go back to California, I promise that I will only write once a week and then once a month, then once a year. I might even forget about you. What do you think?

I will cut down on my calls. All joking aside, it does cost a lot but as long as I have a dollar, I will call to hear you laugh. If you are happy, then I am happy. I know I am taking too much of your time and do not want to take you away from your family in Colorado. If I know you, you only think about coming out here and then going back and getting back into your old habits.

You will appreciate your father, mother, and sister more once you see how we are. This hurts me that I could never take their place. You can never know how I feel because you are not a parent. You would be a good one. Why don't you get married? If you don't get married soon, I will find you a wife. I once asked David why he didn't get married and he said he loves his money too much. He asked me how could he take his pay and hand it over to some girl. He is greedy. I said that if you see anything you want in his junk store (it is one room), he should give it to you for nothing. He started laughing and could not stop. He said why not. I am always bringing strangers up there and I take anything I want for them. I know I could have anything I want, but who the hell wants that junk? I don't.

If Billy's wife, Louise, sees something in David's store that she wants, he won't sell it to her. So I have to go take it and then give it to her. She is a bigger crook than I am because she takes it. You will love her. She is crazy too. David will take you up to her place and say, "Louise, this is my brother." She will laugh and say, "Oh no, David." And he will say, "Oh yes, Louise."

He keeps trying to get me to work in his store. I would give it all away and then give him my money. Somehow he knows and he doesn't trust me, but he still wants me up there.

Well, Jim, I must end. I will write again but I don't know when or where from. Keep well and don't get sick so you can come to see me.

I love going into stores. I always find something to buy. Last night when you said you were going to the store, I thought to myself, "I hope he is not like me, just going to the store to buy something to eat." I love you so much.

Your loving mother

# Chapter Seventeen

*July 31, 1976*

*Dear Jim,*

*I hope you are not like the rest of my children. All of them were self-conscious. I was the same way and even more now. They never had any confidence in themselves. Maybe it is because when they were young I had to spend most of my time working. I always expected them to keep a clean house, etc. I never praised whatever they did. I never left them alone after school and always had someone to watch them. David waited for me and never went where he was not supposed to go. Janice was very frightened and nervous. While I was working I depended on her to get most everything done around the house.*

*When David wasn't clean, I gave him a beating. I remember once Janice brought him down Main Street wearing white short pants and they had chocolate all over them. I went insane and smacked her. I still remember how mad I was, but it was the last time I hit her. Even now, if Janice does something I don't like, I'll jump at her and she will run. So does David.*

*When I was young I was very conceited. However, I was very self-conscious about my eyes and nose. My nose never bothered me, but my eyes were so big. If anyone looked at me, it seemed as if they were staring into my eyes. I was happy when I got older and I had to wear glasses. I still hide behind them. My eyes seem smaller and there are wrinkles around them. I am still self-conscious and if anyone looks at me too long, I turn away.*

*As far as being conceited, all my boys were. Doug was when he was young. Billy put me in debt all the time for what he wanted. One time he made me buy him a camel hair coat for $125 to meet Louise. Billy was good looking. He didn't have a big nose like the rest of us. I was making $45 a week. He also worked part time for the coat and gave me $2 a week until it was paid. Then he wanted a new suit.*

*This bad habit of wanting things was my fault. I don't know where I got it, from my father or my mother. My father was almost 40 when they were married. My mother called him "a man about town." She was 14 or 15 years younger than he was.*

*Then there is David. Mabel has a beautiful granddaughter and I have tried to get him to hire her for his junk store. I made the mistake of saying that she is beautiful, he said, "No. I don't want her falling in love with me." I said, "Who in the hell do you think you are?" I told Mabel and she couldn't stop laughing. Mabel is real dark and tall and she has long hair and big eyes just like mine. Yuk!*

*David likes dark haired girls; Doug and Billy liked blondes. Louise dyed her hair so much for Billy that now it is like straw. She was a dirty blonde when he married her. She was beautiful but now as she got older, she turned into a tough old bird. Just like me.*

*As for you, all I remember is that you had a round face and you were very big for a baby. You looked like you were already six months old when you were born. Katarina loved to hold you when she took me to Colchester. But that Mrs. Sutherland went crazy when she saw me coming. You kicked like hell and once when I picked you up, she said it was time for you to go to sleep and she would not let me hold you. That was on the last visit to Colchester. That is one memory that will always be in my mind no matter how bad my memory gets. I can't write anymore.*

*I love you,*
*Frances*

*P.S. Oh, I forgot about Janice. She was not conceited but she never had any confidence in anything she did.*

*If your eyes are like mine, God help you if your father sees you. He will look straight into them and scare you to death. That was the only thing he liked about me. I used to put my hands over them. He had a bad habit of staring right into my eyes. Your father had large brown eyes too, but they narrowed when he laughed and looked very small.*

***

*August 4, 1976*
*Orlando, Florida*

*My dear Jim,*

*We arrived at 4 a.m. Angelo and Stanley drove for 22 hours and we only stopped to eat. We did not stop in Washington, DC, but we will go there when we leave Miami. We will be here until Friday or Saturday. Angelo has to get back to Connecticut in seven days so he left us and went to visit his friends. He says we can do what we want when he leaves. We traveled 1,400 miles and what a sore behind I have.*

*This place has eight swimming pools. People in Florida are so wealthy but they don't impress me in the least. Janice and Stanley are having a good time and so are their children and Angelo's children too. I would rather be here with my three granddaughters in their torn jeans, down at the beach in my bare feet. I sure hope these three weeks go by fast. This is the kind of vacation I wanted to have when I was young. Who the hell wants it now in my worn-out old age?*

*Love,*
*Frances*

***

*August 4, 1976*
*Orlando, Florida*

*Dear Jim,*

*When Billy died, I stuttered so much that I stopped talking. The same thing happened when Doug died. Words just wouldn't come out of my mouth and when they did, I stuttered. This happened again the other night when we talked. I am sorry I cut you off because I started to stutter and cry. I started to think of what Jimmy and me did to you and we robbed you of so much.*

*I used to envy women like Jimmy Carter's mother and the women in the seminary where I worked. They watched their sons graduate, and some became priests. Women like Rose Kennedy. These are the women that I envy when I read about them. Then look at what appears at my doorstep! I can't believe it. Yet you are not my son. I often thought about you and how I wanted you to be. Yet I can't say Mr. Sutherland and Ruth made you like you are. I know they helped but you are Jimmy Zaldonapolous' son and you are very determined in what you do, just like he was. And determined like I am.*

> *Love,*
> *Frances*

*How can I ever sign "Mother"?*

\*\*\*

*August 10, 1976*
*Miami, Florida*

*Don't write to me until I get home.*

*Dear Jim,*

*If I have anything left when I die, Janice and David get it and you also have your share. As it stands now, I don't have anything. David asked me to help him buy a piece of land. I asked him what Janice and Jim would get out of it and he said he was going in with two other people. As long as you and Janice get nothing, David gets nothing from me.*

*After I see you in September, I shall always know in my heart that I have another son and I will always know where he is. Don't think that I have ever forgotten you. This is the reason I have been so miserable for many, many years. As for Jimmy, let him drop dead.*

*This is the first time that I have listened to anyone and that is you. But let me tell you, this is eating my heart out. As much as I want to call Jimmy, I won't for your sake.*

[We had arguments about her wanting to call Jimmy and give him the hell that she still harbored. I did not want to scare him away before we had the chance to talk. He was very guarded in his letters and I tried to let him deal with the situation at his own pace.]

*I hope you are never like him. When I see you, I hope and pray that
you will remind me of my side of the Postigliones and not be anything like
him. No matter what you do wrong, always admit to it no matter how
much it hurts. I don't pray very much but every night when I go to bed I
say, "Please God, don't let Jim look like his father. That is all I ask." You
sound like him when you talk and the way you talk. When you get angry
at me, you say, "What do you mean by that?" And you sound like me.*

*I love you very much and when you say that over the phone, I hope you
mean it. Time will tell.*

> *Love and many kisses,*
> *Frances*

*P.S. I am not a kissy person. I never kiss my children.*

*Remember you are a Postiglione. They are good people. Not matter what
I say about my brothers and my sisters, Postigliones are clean and honest
people. They are strong-minded and loud—well, some of us are loud. They
are not lazy and always help someone in need. They are a little narrow-
minded, except me. I know in their eyes I was the bad one in the family, but
I never thought so. I am a good person and I know it, so to hell with them.*

***

*August 20, 1976*
*Fredericksburg, Virginia*

*As soon as I get home, I'll send the pictures I want you to send him* [Jimmy].

*Dear Jim,*

*Last night when we spoke, you told me about writing your father. I never
had anything as far back as I can remember that made me so excited,
happy, and I don't know what else. I was happy for you because I know
how much you want to see him.*

*After we talked, I came back to my room, showered and washed my
hair and then rolled it up. Then my head started pounding and it would
not stop. My heart was beating a mile a minute. I thought I wouldn't live*

*through the night. I unrolled my hair but I still couldn't stop the pounding. If it had been any other time I wouldn't give a damn but all of a sudden I want to live. Finally, I did go to bed and went to sleep. I had some pills but I did not want to take them. I cried and cried thinking about this for a while and then the pounding stopped.*

*I can't take any more from Angelo or my sisters. They criticize every-thing I do with the children. Everything I do is wrong. Janice is never pleased with how I dress the children and she says I am being too hard on them. David is the only one that tries to get me to leave Angelo's house and stop taking care of his children.*

*As for Jimmy, I hope he comes alone to see you but if he comes with some-one I hope it is not a lawyer. If it is, you can handle it because you have his brains and my guts. He has a lot to gain if he meets you alone. One way or another he will be happy because if he had any doubts about you, he would have had you arrested by now. As for myself, I don't give a damn what he has to say about me. He is nothing. I never knew I could fall in love with such a weakling. I have forgiven him, but God as my judge, I shall never forget.*

*No matter what I say, he is your father and you must love him in your own way. Never forget him no matter how much he may hurt you. Don't be like me and be so independent and tell him to go to hell. That is not right. There is enough love in you to share. He may be hard to take but after he sees you, he might change. I always had it in my mind that you belonged to him and not me. This hurts me now but that's how I felt sometimes.*

*Love,*
*Frances*

\*\*\*

*August 21, 1976*

*Dear Jim,*

*The ride back to Connecticut wasn't too bad. We stopped in Washington, DC, and went to some historic places for the kids. We ran into a lot of traffic from New Jersey to New York. I've never seen so many cars on the highway. No wonder men drop dead so young from the rat race in those big cities. Now I know what David means when he talks about not wanting to work all the time.*

*My head is giving me a lot of trouble. I am very happy that you found me but when I think back to the past, all I can do is cry. Jim, don't feel bad because I am happy about you but so damn ashamed of myself. I don't even want to look you in the face because the time has come and soon I will really be seeing you. I wonder if I did the right thing when I wrote so much about Jimmy and me.*

*My letters to you are the only letters I've written without someone standing over me, telling me what to write or not to write. I love to write actually. Something happens when I get everything about how I have lived on paper. When I put it in letters, I feel better.*

*Here are the pictures you sent me of when you were little. Send them to Jimmy but tell him he can only look and not keep them. I want the pictures back.*

*I think he will send them right back. Jimmy won't want his wife to see them and who knows if he will tell her about you. I want him to see you as a small boy. You are his boy but all he deserves is a dead rat. He can never be half the man you are because of what he did to me and in return what I did to you. My crying days haven't even started. I love you very much.*

*Frances*

\*\*\*

*August 23, 1976*

*Dear Jim,*

*I don't think it is a good idea that you call here. Call Janice and if you can't reach her, call David. Angelo shouldn't have answered my phone but I wasn't home. He said someone called but when he asked who it was they hung up. He asked me who it was. I told him, "How in the hell should I know?" But I thought maybe it was you. That was a close call.*

[I had called Frances and Angelo answered. I was totally unprepared. He demanded to know who I was. I did the only thing I could—I hung up. I called her back later to tell her what happened.]

*Calling David is okay but half the time he is busy as hell and might forget a message. I can't remember, but when are you going to call?*

*You only have to meet Janice, Mabel, David, and me when you are here. Don't worry about anything else. I know how you are feeling about meeting a bunch of people you don't know, but don't get nervous. Do whatever you like and go wherever you want after we talk.*

*Last night I wanted to call but I have made up my mind not to. So I went to bed and was sick. I hate that I have no willpower. That is my downfall. I break down very easily. Anyone can come to me and lie like hell and after a while I believe them and they can talk me into anything. David goes crazy when I give money to someone with a hard luck story. He has a friend that can't keep a job. He is young and when he is broke, I help him out when I can. When David finds out he wants to break my neck. But David is just like me and he is always helping out bums. I know that I have no willpower or I would not be so fat.*

*I will get you a place to stay. Hartford is better for a couple of days, or at least until you see your father, then go on to Rocky Hill. In Hartford, you can get around easier by walking or taking the bus. In Rocky Hill, the only motels are on the highway and you will be stuck in your room until someone comes for you. David works at night but he can take time off while you are here. Janice has a car and she can take you anywhere you want to go.*

*Jim, I thought about asking David or Janice to let you take their car. But I didn't. It is up to them to offer. I never interfere with their business, their homes or their cars, or what they earn or spend. We are very close but I cannot tell you what either of them earns, what they save, or what they owe. Living today is hard and as sure as I am sitting here, you have to scratch hard to make a living. I can tell by the way you talk that no one has ever handed you anything for free either.*

*I expect my children to do the right things while you are here. This is what I want, but they are grown and it is up to them. They hurt me plenty but I say nothing. I am sure you won't be disappointed in them. As for myself, you will find it hard to understand me. First I want this and then I change my mind. I am like hot and cold water but I am sure the short time you will be here, it won't kill you.*

*Well, Jim, all I can say is that I love you very much, as much as David and Janice. Except at this point because I never had you near me, I love you more.*

*Stop worrying about meeting Jimmy. I don't like what he made you go through to see him. Making you answer all those questions on a piece of paper and send it back to him. He acts like you are some kind of criminal. You are a good man and did wonders on your own. I always thought of you growing up and running wild somewhere. I always had the feeling you were wild. Maybe because I remember how I was when I was young. I am glad that I was wrong. Going to school as you did, I am glad you never had time to get into trouble. I love you very much.*

*Mother*

*P. S. Those pictures are very important to me. I am talking about the ones of you when you were a boy that you sent to Jimmy. Don't think I am selfish. I want the two small ones. I don't care about the big one. You gave them to me and they mean a lot.*

*If I don't get them back I will be very hurt. I know you think I got my nerve giving you an order. Well, that is what I am doing. I expect you to obey it. Get mad? I don't care. I love you so much. I don't know why I am so angry right now. Please forgive me for writing this way. All I can say is I am sorry. But I want those pictures back.*

\*\*\*

[This is the last letter from Frances before I left for Hartford.]

*August 25, 1976*

*Dear Jim,*

*I am sorry I was so sharp when I wrote about the pictures. I can't bear the thought of Jimmy touching them. I can't even think about him being near you. I have no right to feel like this because I've been just as bad as him. I don't even know how the hell you can stand to come here and see either one of us. Thank your lucky stars neither of us brought you up. You have turned out to be a fine man without our help. If I had brought you up, you would probably be a gangster.*

*Mabel and Tony were here yesterday. I laughed so much. We talked about you and she told me what to say and what not to say. She said I had better not lose my temper and Tony laughed so much. He said, "Mabel, do you think she listens to you?" Tony can't wait for you to meet me. Everyone, David, Mabel, Janice, and Tony have opinions about how I should be with you. You can take me as I am. What the hell do they think? That I am going to change?*

*I want you to know one thing—your father did not leave because of the way I am. That was the reason he loved me. Jimmy liked everything I did, everything I said. The more I talked, the more he loved me.*

*So, if you are anything like your father you will like me. But God help me if you are a Postiglione. Remember you are half Postiglione. Sometimes I think you are like my sister, Mary. She whispers when she talks. When I get loud she makes like she is going to pass out. She married an Irishman. He is the only man to hit me. She has one son and two daughters.*

*Janice thinks I am going to be hurt after you leave. She doesn't know what hurt is. If I never see or hear from you again, I had it coming for what I did. But I love you no matter where you are.*

> *Love to my baby,*
> *Mother*

*P.S. See you soon.*

# Chapter Eighteen

Unlike most people traveling from the West Coast to the East, I took the train. My relationship with the friendly skies got off to a bad start in 1963, when the four-engine plane I was riding in got caught in a thunderstorm over the Colorado Rockies for over an hour. My seatmate was an elderly woman who held my arm in a death grip as the plane was tossed and the tops of mountain peaks appeared much too close to the window. She confided, "My husband died in a plane crash and I always knew that is how I would die." We did land safely despite the landing gear that had been damaged in the storm. The experience of seeing foam trucks, ambulances, and fire trucks waiting for us on the field left its mark on me.

As the years passed, I tried to overcome my fear by downing tranquillizers and finally spent $300 for a "Fear of Flying" seminar at the San Francisco Airport. Nothing worked. Eventually I gave up and learned to live with it. By the time of my trip to Hartford, I had quit being embarrassed about not flying. I enjoyed traveling across the country at a civilized pace and am still fine with the choice I made years ago.

Whenever I traveled by train, I kept a journal. I knew that this journey was going to be more memorable than any I had taken in the past. I was about to meet my mother for the first time, so I wanted to remember the details and share the experience with Rolland when I returned. As soon as I got on the train, I started a journal using a ballpoint pen and a spiral notebook.

\*\*\*

Saturday, September 11, 1976

I left at 10:30 a.m. on the bus to Oakland, and transferred to the train (no station or direct service to San Francisco). Since the trip will take three days and nights, I spent the extra money for a room-ette in the sleeping car. That is a better alternative than trying to sleep upright in a coach seat every night. I need to be alert and fresh when I get there. Naturally, I have mixed feelings now that I am headed east and into the unknown.

Abandoned piers, abandoned railroad cars, and an abandoned ferryboat pass my window and remind me why I am on the train. It's a cruel word when I see it written down but it is correct. Jimmy abandoned her and Frances abandoned me.

I expect Frances is freaked out, knowing that I am on my way to meet her. I wonder what I will find at the end of this ride. I have a mental picture of Frances from the telephone calls and her letters. But what about David, Janice, and Mabel, and God knew who else?

I try to imagine what my father is like. I am uncomfortable about Jimmy because of his resistance to meeting me. But I didn't give him a choice. I am tired of his attitude and determined to meet him. He can decide how easy or difficult it will be. I expected him to show the same courage Frances has shown. I am not sure if he read my letter as a threat or if he feels ashamed, but he has reluctantly agreed to meet me. With his reply, he included a three-page questionnaire about me—obviously on the advice of an attorney. It annoyed me but I filled it out and returned it as he asked.

Rolland, it was strange not to have you there to see me off when I boarded the train. It was okay but lonely. The cool, gray summer skies and your absence put me into a quiet mood that remains with me.

On a deserted road partially hidden in the tall weeds, a pile of abandoned cars from the late 1940s glides by the window. The forces of rust and decay are at work. One day they will disappear and no one will know they were there.

\*\*\*

Sunday, September 12, 1976

Wyoming looks like my fifth grade geography book said it would. The landscape is familiar because I have seen it on previous train rides to Denver. The sun is rising in the east; it is overcast and the view out this window is one of peace and quiet.

I haven't been away from San Francisco in a long time. It has been months since I last crossed the Bay Bridge or the Golden Gate.

I need the break from work and my routine. Still, leaving my familiar world is jarring. The rest of the country does not act or look like San Francisco, and the transition reminds me that I live on a small and unique island.

I am not as apprehensive as I was yesterday. I have thought about Connecticut, Frances, David, Janice, and whoever else might come out of the dark past.

So far the trip is boring. I have come this route at least ten times since I left Colorado in 1963. Once I reach Denver and head for Chicago, it will seem like this trip to Hartford is really happening. Right now it's just another trip to Denver.

I am not frightened about meeting Frances and Janice and David. It will be interesting whatever happens. I try to imagine how they are and I can't. This visit will end in disaster if we don't like each other.

I wish I knew how I'll feel a month from now. Whatever I find on this trip will not make any difference in who I am. My life isn't going to change. Still I can't help but wonder if I missed out by being raised by Hollis, and not Frances.

I worry that they may not accept me. That is a possibility after they know about my lifestyle. I will not hide it. Maybe I won't like any of them. That would be awkward but I have to remember they are strangers. I am not sure what to do if it all goes wrong once I get there. Stop. I am giving myself a headache.

I visited the bar/lounge car and didn't stay long: Too many old people, too many teenagers, and too much cigarette smoke. I haven't spoken to anyone since I boarded. If this continues, I might cross the whole country without speaking to anyone.

***

Later in the afternoon: The front range of the Rockies came into view, and this means we are in Colorado. Sad memories of Mountain View Ranch and Cecilia come back to me. In the distance over the mountains is a gray curtain of rain.

***

At Denver, I jumped off the train and ran into the station to call Bev, my stepsister. I updated her on my progress. I can't reach Ruth. I will stop in Denver for a longer visit on the way back from Hartford. Denver looks small after San Francisco and San Francisco will look small after New York. The yard crew added a club car and vista dome to the train. Why? It will soon be dark and there is nothing to see on the dry, flat prairies of eastern Colorado.

***

Somewhere in western Nebraska: It is pitch black outside. On the horizon there is a storm north of us. Every minute or so giant flashes explode in the sky. Bolts of lightning give a split second impression of daylight over the passing landscape. I am lying in the berth enjoying Mother Nature's show. I am very tired. I wonder if lightning ever strikes moving trains.

***

Monday, September 13, 1976

Near Galesburg, Illinois: It is hot and humid and we are an hour late to Chicago. About 20 miles back I asked the car attendant why the train had slowed to a crawl. He pointed to a small fortune in marijuana growing along the railroad tracks. The pot was left over from World War II when it was grown for hemp. A slow train going through the marijuana allows some of the crew to lean out and grab a few handfuls. He added that it depends on which engineer is in charge whether or not the train slows down or speeds up. No doubt my age and beard made him feel safe about revealing this information.

***

Leaving Chicago in the afternoon: I can't get a sleeping accommodation to New York so I am back in coach. What I want is a hot shower and a bed. I must be two-thirds of the way to New York. My brain is spinning the closer I get to Hartford. I'm not sure what to do when I reach New York. I told Frances that I'd see her on Wednesday and now it looks like I will arrive on Tuesday.

*** 

Tuesday, September 14, 1976

Central Pennsylvania: I didn't sleep much last night sitting upright. The train follows a small river and it's so foggy that the other side is obscured. I am glad to be off the train today. Still not sure what I should do other than shower and get out of these clothes. Unfortunately, that isn't going to happen for a while. When I am clean again, I will think a little clearer.

The fog lifts and reveals rolling hills dotted with small farms. The old towns are quiet and the forests very lush. This view could be the set for a Civil War movie.

*** 

North Philadelphia, 11:00 a.m.: The train moves slowly through slums that seem to go on for miles. Many buildings are abandoned and those that aren't should be. There is a mixture of drab factories and depressing tenements, one after another. The air is smoggy in every direction. I am used to trash and junkyards along the roadbed, but seeing this blight on such a massive scale is disturbing. Trenton is the next stop.

*** 

I have been in New York since 12:30 p.m. It is unbearably hot and humid. I found a room for the night and called Frances and Rolland to let them know I am here. I walked to the Greyhound station and bought a ticket for an early morning departure to Wethersfield. I could take the train, but that means another transfer. Taking a direct bus will be faster and easier.

It is strange to be in the middle of this huge city and its madness. The size is overwhelming. All of San Francisco can fit neatly into one corner of Manhattan. Too many homeless people on the crowded streets, and many seem mentally disturbed. Graffiti everywhere. New York is not like I remember when I was here in 1968. I am too tired to navigate my way through throngs of people. If I weren't so focused on meeting Frances, I might feel differently. I don't want to play tourist. All I want is a bite to eat, a shower, and to sleep in a real bed.

***

Wednesday, September 15, 1976

10:00 a.m.: I left New York early this morning on the Greyhound, going up 8th Avenue through Harlem and out through New Rochelle, White Plains, and New Haven. I am excited and scared, anxious about meeting people I don't know. The thought that I am soon to meet a stranger who is my mother is unnerving. Mothers are always there. You never meet them for the first time. The idea is unreal and at the same time very real. And there is no doubt that it is about to happen. This is the event that I have imagined and anticipated for the last five months. Still, I can't help thinking, "What am I doing here?"

***

Noon: Janice was at the station to meet me. I saw her on the platform as the bus pulled in and knew immediately who she was. I can't explain what came over me. For the first time in my life, I saw someone who looked like me. I was already overwhelmed and hadn't even left the bus.

As I came down the steps, Janice recognized me and made her way through the crowd. She was friendly and chatty and that made me more relaxed than I expected to be. She was as nervous as I was. Janice was there with her husband, Stanley, who told me that Frances had decided that she was too anxious to come to the station. Frances wanted them to meet me first, take me to the hotel, and then go back and pick her up. It is a lot of unnecessary running around but that is what Frances wants. They dropped me off at the

Ramada Inn a little while ago and I checked into a large and comfortable room.

I was in the hotel dining room having breakfast. I was hungry since I didn't have time to eat before leaving New York. I called Frances to tell her I was at the hotel and waiting to see her. She sounded nervous and not at all like the woman I have talked to so many times. I cannot believe this is really happening.

I have no idea what to do if Frances passes out. She warned me that she might. What if I pass out? I have to calm down. I have spent years wondering who this woman is and months preparing to meet her. I traveled over 3,000 miles to get here. I am scared, but I have to see this through. Anyway, it's too late to do otherwise.

It could be paranoia, but Janice gave my bags a thorough going-over with her eyes as we loaded them in the car and again when we when we arrived at the Ramada. I wanted to tell her, "If you're looking for weapons, I didn't bring any."

\*\*\*

4:30 p.m.: It has really happened! Thirty-four years after we were separated, Frances and I meet face to face. She walked into the dining room while I was eating. I didn't see her enter because I was engrossed in the newspaper. She came to my table and stood there quietly. I wasn't aware that she was there for a few seconds. When I looked up and saw her in front of me, my heart leaped into my throat. I jumped up and managed to utter, "Frances?"

"Yes. Please, finish your breakfast," she said.

"Sit down. I'm almost done."

Frances sat down in the empty chair and waited. I was too keyed up to finish, so I asked for the check. As we waited, she sat staring at me. I chattered on about my trip from California to break the awkwardness of the moment. Even though I was expecting her, it was still a shock to see her in front of me.

She listened to every word and watched my every move. The only thought that kept going through my mind was, "This is my mother. This is my real mother." As with Janice, I was overwhelmed to see another face that looked like mine. Seeing us together, you might guess that Janice and I are related. But if you looked at me and then at Frances, there is no doubt that I am her son. As I watched her sitting there, it was like looking into a mirror and having my own eyes stare back at me.

Frances isn't the aged hag that she told me she was in her letters and during our phone conversations. She wore a tailored blue suit with an orange neck scarf, blue shoes, and silver earrings. Her hair is gray and appeared recently cut and styled. She wears glasses and is short and heavy, but not nearly as gross as she made herself out to be. She is very stylish for her age.

I kept looking at this stranger, knowing that she is really my mother. I have not had a mother since Cecilia left me in the café when I was seven years old. Ruth came into my life when I was too old and hurt to let her be the mother replacement that she tried to be. Cecilia was my last mother. Now I have another, but this is the real one. Not everyone gets to have three mothers in one lifetime.

The waitress brought the check. Frances and I headed down the hall to my room. So far our meeting wasn't as tearful as I imagined it might be. This was a happy occasion and I didn't want to cry.

Once we got to my room, Frances' quiet demeanor disappeared. She relaxed in the privacy of the room and I did too. She began with, "Tell me everything about yourself." I started to talk but she immediately interrupted me with her questions. Before I could finish an answer, I would think of a question for her. The conversation changed yet again. Our exchange was so similar to our first telephone conversation—both of us talking about everything at the same time.

When she became excited, she jumped from her chair, moved around the room, waved her arms, and talked much faster. Her eyes grew bigger to make her point. Watching her animated state held me transfixed. I can be the same at times, waving my arms and making my eyes wider to emphasize an important point. As a child, Hollis and Ruth frequently told me, "Stop talking with your hands." I heard the same thing in grade school, and once for punishment I was told to sit on my hands and "now tell us what you want to say."

She was telling me about the jobs that she had had when the phone rang. I heard the voice on the other end and it was Mr. Zaldonapolous. The timing couldn't have been worse. I stumbled through the conversation because of the awkward situation.

Frances was here and Jimmy was there. He was calling to see if he could meet with me tomorrow. I said yes to get him off the line as quickly as I could. I had visions of Frances grabbing the phone and cussing him out. I explained that I had just arrived and didn't know what my plans were. He promised to call later in the evening to set a time. I didn't say a word about Frances being in the room. My impression was that he sounded very business-like considering the circumstances. He had a heavy accent even after being in this country for 40 years.

It didn't take long for Frances to realize who was on the phone. She rushed to the door and left the room. She is very bitter about Jimmy, as demonstrated in her letters and our phone calls. She must be curious about how his life turned out; he might feel the same way about her.

I got off the phone and asked Frances to come back into the room we could pick up where we left off. She was not as relaxed as she had been. I told her that Jimmy wanted to meet me tomorrow and changed the subject.

After a few minutes she calmed down and the phone call was forgotten. We had come to my room at noon and at three o'clock Janice returned to pick her up. The time we spent talking had flown by.

This afternoon I finally met my mother. I am not used to the words "my mother." Linking them to me is strange. Frances is very much like her calls and letters. She resembles me or I resemble her in so many ways. Kind of scary. We only spent a few hours together and already I see many similarities. I believed I was unique until today when I met the woman who gave me some of my originality. I did not grow up with her and that makes this much stranger. I wonder how much of my makeup is heredity and how much is environment. This is something I never thought about before.

Frances is a strong woman, even at her age. It is clear that she was devoted to her children and now I see why she feels so ashamed about losing me. She must be strong to have kept me a secret for all these years. Frances had to be tough to deal with David when he was on drugs. She never gave up on him even when he was at his darkest point. Frances has also buried two of her sons. That loss is unimaginable. Her life has not been easy.

As I listened to her, I wondered what it would have been like to grow up with her as my mother and the rest of the kids. She must have been powerful in asserting her way with her children.

My independent nature was a result of how I grew up. As her child, I would not have become as independent as I did. Hollis provided for me but he was not always there emotionally. I developed my independence out of necessity—more or less on my own. I had a lot of freedom from parental control very early and figured out what to do by myself. Most of the time I made the right choices.

As result, I knew who I was and what I could do long before most children. Had Frances raised me, I never would have had that freedom at such a young age.

She has so much guilt about me and I wish I could make her understand that it isn't necessary. Several times as we talked she broke down and wept. Sometimes this made me cry and then I would try to talk us out of the situation. I told her the most important lesson I learned from Susan: "You cannot change the past. It's done and over, and you can't go back and rewrite it." This will not make Frances forget her guilt or make it disappear. She will eventually have to forgive herself.

Her guilt affects her thinking about me. When the subject of swimming came up, I told her that I never learned. She said, "That's my fault." She was bothered that I didn't know how. I explained that the polio scare had closed all public pools when I was old enough to take lessons. I added that living far from any ocean in Colorado also affected my interest in swimming. France said that she is a good swimmer and made her children learn.

According to Frances, my being unmarried is her fault too. I skipped and hopped around that topic, as it is too soon to go into the real reason. We were already covering enough ground for the first meeting. I am ready to answer her questions when we get there. But for now, I will wait until she knows me better.

Although I did not spend much time with Janice, she seemed friendly though a bit reserved. I can't expect her to trust me yet. After all, I am a stranger from the strange land of California. I am not sure if she is jealous that I have shown up and thinks that I want to take the attentions of her mother away from her and David. I do, but only for a little while. I see how Frances can embarrass her. Frances doesn't hold anything back when she talks. Frances knows she does this and I bet sometimes she does it on purpose. I will reserve judgment about Janice until I spend more time with her.

I have yet to meet David and Mabel. That should go well if they are as easy to engage as Frances. It was a bit awkward at first but once we started talking, it went very well. Then there is Mr. Zaldonapolous. Now that promises to be interesting.

***

Thursday 2:00 a.m.: David called at eight o'clock this evening (Wednesday) and said he would pick me up after he got off work at 11:30. He arrived at the hotel in a battered van whose appearance matched its uncomfortable and noisy ride. Despite this, he is very proud of his wheels. It is hard to describe my emotions as I climbed into the van and saw my features on a total stranger. The face and grin were mine and at the same time, not mine. The very first thing that happened was we both started laughing for no reason. I liked him immediately. He has an easy going and down to earth demeanor. He told me of 100 different ideas and schemes for making himself rich. So far none have worked out but he isn't giving up. We drove across town to the building where he lives. His apartment and small antique shop are on the second floor directly above a neighborhood pizza parlor. The place was not the dump that Frances had described. I walked up the stairs surprised to find his apartment reminded me of my flat on 14th Street in San Francisco. There was an amazing similarity in how both places are furnished, with vintage furniture in the rooms and curios hanging on the walls and scattered on tables and shelves. Like me, he has an eye for antiques and collectibles.

He also has an artistic side, something Frances had not said much about. He showed me several metal sculptures he created. I should get photos of some of them before I leave. David is into smoking grass and he was surprised when I told him that I don't anymore. He is friendly but I'm not sure what went through his mind as we talked. It is possible he was as nervous as I was. He didn't say anything that revealed he was. He acted very normal in what was a highly unusual situation. As far as I can tell, he didn't hold back when we talked. We spent a great deal of time at his apartment as he showed me photographs of his friends and his dog, Bea, a St. Bernard. He boards her at a nearby farm because of her huge size versus the size of the apartment and because his work keeps him away from home most of the time.

I can't say that I know him or have figured him out, but how could I after a few hours together? I was often surprised when similarities in tastes and how we do things came up in the conversation. When I walked into his apartment I thought, "This looks like where I live." Like the similarities in our bedrooms: we both have no bed frames for our beds, just a mattress and box spring balanced on four cinder blocks. We are similar in that we talk fast and move quickly. That we both have beards could be coincidence and nothing more. He is 32 and I am 34.

He didn't appear too surprised about my sudden appearance in his mother's life. I assume he is okay with me. David wants to pick me up in the morning and introduce me to a woman who works with him at the hospital. I want to get to know him better. This is the brother that I imagined I had, long before I knew about Frances or Jimmy. As a small boy on the turkey ranch, I often imagined I had a brother somewhere. I cannot explain why, but I knew that David existed long before I met him.

Frances told me in one of her letters that David seems lost. After meeting him I understand why. At times he does seem lost. There is a childlike quality about him. Sometimes it comes out in what he talks about and how he talks. He has a lot of big dreams. Some are not very realistic but he believes in them, like a child who believes in Santa Claus. David is searching very hard for a goal. Maybe he wants to make up for the years he lost while he was on drugs. I don't know the whole story, but he spent several years in a penitentiary because of drugs. He didn't tell me; Frances did.

To watch David you get the impression that he is a busy person. He has an energy that reminds me of Frances. Of course, he is more laid back, but he has her drive and passion. As I watch them, I see the same energy that has always been a part of who I am.

# Chapter Nineteen

Thursday, September 16, 1976

11:00 a.m.: I am in a bizarre dream. Nothing is real, including time, which is accelerating. Yet everything and everyone I encounter here has the feel and look of familiarity. At times I am sure I am going to wake up in my bed on 14th Street in San Francisco. Frances called after I woke up with a series of rapid-fire questions about how I felt about her and what impressions I had of David. She wanted to know what we did last night and everything we talked about.

David came by at 8:30 this morning and despite our late night visit, he was in fine form. I needed more sleep but David had other plans. Soon we were off in his van. He had errands to run but didn't elaborate and I figured it was his business. I was just glad to be spending the time with him. I don't know the city so I have no idea where we went. He made a number of short stops at various businesses. At each stop, he told me to wait in the van. I had no idea what he was doing and he didn't offer any explanations. I was curious, but I thought it rude to ask.

One stop was at a liquor store in a rundown part of town, and he invited me to come in with him. The man behind the counter was about our age. David introduced me with, "Cousin Richie, meet my brother Jim from California."

I don't know who was more surprised, Cousin Richie or me. Richie's mouth dropped open and he stared. When he recovered, he tried to act cool.

"So you're from California, huh?"

"I got in yesterday."

I may as well have told him that I arrived in a flying saucer. The surprised look never left his face. Richie was speechless as he looked at me and then to David for an explanation, but David did not offer one and I didn't know what else to say. Then as quickly as we had come in, David rushed me out before Richie could recover and ask any questions.

We got back in the van and David said nothing more about Richie. He smiled and seemed pleased with the commotion that he had caused. Did I mention that he drives like a mad man? We talked about everything and anything. I still have that feeling of his being lost. He isn't headed toward any particular destination, and instead goes in ten different directions at once. If I didn't know better (and I don't), he acts like he is on speed.

He continued with his errands, stopping at the back entrances of about five or six more businesses, while I waited in the van. Sensing my curiosity, he told me what was up with his running around.

David is running numbers for his Uncle Albert, who is a bookie. This news startled me. How long before we were pulled over by the police because of David's crazy driving? I envisioned being arrested, booked, and sentenced as an accomplice in Uncle Albert's numbers racket. None of this happened despite David's driving.

I brought up the subject of being gay. I wanted to get it out in the open and determine if this was going to be an issue for David. He didn't seem surprised or upset. It was me who was surprised by his non-reaction. Once it was out there, I let the subject drop. He has been around and could know other gay men. It is possible he doesn't consider it a big deal. I have to wait and see if my being gay makes any difference in our relationship. Anyway, it is better I am not hiding that part of my life from him. I asked him not to say anything to Frances as I plan to tell her later.

I wished David wasn't so stoned. His power of concentration is pretty bad due to the pot. At times I was frustrated talking with him, as he couldn't stay focused. No wonder he was unconcerned about what I had revealed about myself.

When he finished his errands for Uncle Albert, he drove to the state hospital where he works as a drug counselor. I found that ironic. David was once into heavier drugs than pot, so no doubt he knows what he is doing with the people he counsels there. Who better to see through the bullshit coming from junkies in recovery than a recovered junkie? We cruised through a multitude of offices in the facility where I met many of his co-workers. He kept introducing me to staff and patients as his "brother from California." It sounded strange but I got used to it. One of the people he especially wanted me to meet was Sondra, a bit of a crazy, over-aged hippie. She was very nice and knew all about my return. Sondra and David are very close but not in a relationship. She is older than he is. She is also a drug counselor and his supervisor. David said she was instrumental in getting him on the staff after he had kicked his habit.

As we ran through the offices people lit up with smiles when they saw David coming. He is well liked by everyone we ran into.

I wished that we lived closer so I had more time to know him better. I want to find out what is behind his continual movement and unbelievable energy. I used to think that I moved fast until I met him. I just want to figure him out. But I know all my questions about him won't be answered in the short time I am here.

After the hospital, David brought me back to the Ramada Inn and we had a late breakfast. He told me more about his life and he wanted to know what California was like. David had smoked another joint before we sat down to breakfast. He got pretty high and I had to wait until he mellowed out a bit. Again, I would like to talk with him when he isn't stoned. I was annoyed and frustrated with him and his lack of concentration. He smokes too much pot but I didn't say anything. I have reconciled myself to being in the van with him while he is stoned. I don't like it but if I don't go, then I miss out on time with him.

Mr. Zaldonapolous called and had the desk clerk page me. Bad timing again on his part. He was on his way over for our meeting, so I cut breakfast short and hustled David out of the hotel. Mr. Zaldonapolous was abrupt over the phone and he sounded stressed. This made me more nervous than I wanted to be.

***

3:30 p.m.: Events are happening so fast, it's difficult to get them all down here. Mr. Zaldonapolous has a heavy Greek accent and it is hard to understand him over the phone. He sounds like a gangster from a 1930s crime movie. When he called, David was with me and I made the mistake of mentioning this and it upset him. He insisted that we be alone when we met. I explained that David was leaving as we spoke. But this was not enough and he decided that he did not want to come to the hotel as we had previously agreed. He came up with a new plan to meet in the parking lot of the restaurant across the street from the hotel. I was pissed that he didn't trust me, but I didn't want to scare him off so I agreed.

Around 11:00 a.m. I walked over to the restaurant. I felt conspicuous as I waited in the parking lot. His gruff demeanor and gangster sounding voice kept running through my mind and my imagination kicked in. At any moment I expected a large black limo to slowly drive up beside me. A Mafioso type would roll down the window and thrust out a blazing machine gun, mowing me down. The car speeds away as I bleed to death on the pavement.

A few minutes later a large vehicle did appear and pull up alongside of me. Not exactly a black limo, it was a new blue Lincoln Imperial. The window rolled down but no machine gun came into view. Instead the driver, an older man, asked, "Jim?"

"Are you Mr. Zaldonapolous?"

"Yes. Get in."

I got in and we shook hands. I was nervous, but not as much as he was. He drove the big car out of the parking lot and to the highway heading south. Better to take me away from the hotel so Frances will have a harder time finding my body and pinning the crime on him.

We exchanged chatter about the traffic and the weather. After a few minutes, he admitted to being nervous and asked me if I would mind if he pulled off the road. He was finding it hard to drive under the circumstances. I told him I understood. He pulled into the parking area of a strip mall and stopped the car. At least there were potential witnesses going in and out of the stores should he panic and decide to shoot me there.

Jimmy looked straight ahead and tried to catch his breath. What if this old man has a heart attack? He noticed a payphone near where we had parked and said, "I must call my wife. She is afraid that you have come to harm me and made me promise to call her when I picked you up and let her know I was safe."

I felt embarrassed and a little foolish about what I had been imagining. I assured him that I had no such intention. I told him to call and let her know that there was no need to worry.

So Jimmy had told his wife about me after all. Interesting. I sat in the car and studied him as he talked in the phone booth. I looked for similarities in his walk, mannerisms, or physical appearance that

I could connect to myself and saw none. He finished his call, came back to the car, slid into the driver's seat and started the engine. Then I noticed his hands on the steering wheel. It was like seeing my own.

The call to his wife put him at ease and he began speaking in a more relaxed manner. We were back on the highway headed south. The tension in his manner and voice were gone. Of course, I was relaxed knowing there was no machine gun in the car and I would return to the hotel still breathing. But I was still apprehensive about the circumstances and purpose of our meeting.

As he talked, I continued to look for indications that I was related to this stranger beside me. In addition to his hands, his forehead, thin black hair, and square chin bore resemblance to mine.

Jimmy had no hesitation about recalling his past. I kept quiet though I wanted to interrupt him with questions. He was an immigrant from Greece. Both parents had emigrated and settled in New York on Long Island prior to his arrival. They made great sacrifices to send for him in 1930 when he was 18. He did not want to disappoint them or make them feel that their efforts had been wasted. Jimmy quickly learned English, got a job, and went on to college where he studied civil engineering.

In the summer of 1940, he had a good future ahead of him. He moved to Hartford on advice from his family to work at the Athena Diner. The diner was partially owned by his older brother, Georgios, and the job helped him earn enough for his last year of college. Two other men, Kostas and Petros, were also part owners and friends of his brother. While he worked at the diner he met Frances, who lived in a nearby apartment house.

This very attractive woman fascinated Jimmy. As he got to know her, he marveled at how hard she worked, not only at her job but also raising two boys and a girl on her own. She was devoted to her children.

Jimmy's account pretty much paralleled what Frances had told me. He remembered her temper and that her family scared him. When I asked him about her family, he said, "The whole family was crazy." Her sisters watched Frances like hawks, even though she worked and took good care of her children. Her brothers had physically threatened him a number of times when they found out that he and Frances had been seen together.

Even after all these years, he remembered a lot about her; too much not to have been intimately involved with her. "There is no doubt you are her son," he said. "Looking at your eyes is like seeing her again."

Frances worried that he thought that I was David, but when I asked him, he said no. He knew the difference in our ages. He had read about David's troubles with drugs from stories that appeared in the newspapers. The stories reinforced his negative opinions about her and her family. All of this happened years ago and it is unfair and unfortunate that he still feels this way. I knew that I would never tell Frances that he had these feelings.

When Frances became pregnant they both were scared of what her family might do. He was also concerned about his family's reaction. Georgios was aware that he had been seeing Frances but didn't know the whole story. Despite his fear of both families, he felt a responsibility to help her. He insisted that she see a doctor friend of his for prenatal care because he wanted to be sure that the baby would be born healthy.

As he talked about this part of the relationship, it was as if he were someone else. Jimmy described events as if he were not personally involved, but only a bystander. He seemed emotionally detached. This was how he dealt with his shame when confronted by a past that he had tried to conceal. Like Frances, he had kept their secret.

His version of the last time he saw her was not the same as hers. Both stories start on her birthday, December 31, 1941. Her friends in the apartment house had planned a party and Jimmy had brought a birthday cake. Frances had told me about the birthday cake, and also that shortly after Jimmy arrived, the husband of one of her neighbors had punched Jimmy in the face.

According to Jimmy, the party was in progress when he arrived. Frances seemed upset but he didn't remember why. She was three months pregnant by then and it could have been about the baby. Frances had told me that she thought he wanted to tell her something, but she never found out what it was.

Shortly after he arrived, Jimmy and Frances started to argue. He decided to leave because he didn't want to have a scene with her in front of the others. He did not mention being punched.

He put on his coat and went to the door. As he walked out, the birthday cake came flying through the air, and hit him on the back of his head. Cake spattered everywhere, but mostly it rolled off his head and down the back of his coat. He did not stop to wipe the cake off his head or his coat, but just walked out the door. It was Frances who sent the cake hurling at him from across the room.

Jimmy knew that he was in an impossible situation and that it would never work out with her no matter what he did. Most threatening to him were the families—his and hers. Due to their Roman Catholic religion, her family was opposed to her getting a divorce. Jimmy thought that they hoped she would reconcile with her long absent husband. His Greek Orthodox religion was also a barrier. While Jimmy and Frances had talked about marriage, they knew the obstacles they would face from her outraged family.

He also feared his parent's reaction if they learned of his circumstances. They would never accept his marrying a divorced Catholic with three children. Had they married, it would have alienated him from his family for the rest of his life. This was a step he could not take.

Another factor in his decision, despite what Fanny believed, was that he had just been drafted. World War II disrupted the lives of many people. It was an event he never expected. No matter how he felt, Jimmy knew that he was soon going off to war.

Then there was Frances. She was far from meek and mild. Frances had a quick and fiery temper that had caused him any number of problems during the course of their relationship. When he thought of marriage, he envisioned a much quieter girl. His family expected him to marry a Greek girl, which he did a few years later. Though he was not emotional as he spoke of their past, I did detect some sadness as he recollected the night of Frances' birthday party that led to their separation.

When the cake hit him that was the end. He walked out despite her pregnancy. If he had any guilt about leaving her, he did not talk about it. I tried to understand how he must have felt at the time. He made his decision, didn't look back, and figured that he would never have to. Until now.

While it was cold for him to have walked out on her, I have a better sense of why he did. Frances doesn't think things through before she speaks or acts. She is in her 60s but I can imagine what a fireball she must have been as a young woman. As I listened, I felt some sympathy for Jimmy.

He told me an interesting side story related to the end of their relationship. Again, Frances had already told me this, but I was glad to hear his version. It shed light on his character, despite his leaving her.

Being drafted he knew he was not going to be around when I was born. Frances would need money when the time came. He could not give her any money before he left and expect it to be there when she needed it. She would have spent it in one day.

A few days before the party, he hid $600 in an unused sugar bowl on the top shelf of a kitchen cabinet in her apartment. It was unlikely that she would find the money right away. By the time she did, I would have been born and Frances would be in need of the money.

Months after Jimmy had left, Frances was cleaning the top shelf and found the sugar bowl. At first she could not figure out where the money had come from, but eventually she concluded that it could only have come from Jimmy.

After telling me all that he remembered about Frances, he spoke about his wife and family. While he was home on leave in early 1945, he married a Greek woman, as his family had expected him to do. So Frances was right in her assumption.

When I had written him that I was coming to Hartford, he reluctantly told his wife the story and that I had contacted him. As he expected, she was not pleased to learn of his secret. She made him swear never to tell their children about me and he agreed to her demand. It was a small price to pay to keep peace in the family.

Jimmy has four children and is very proud of them. I am sure that they respect him a great deal. What would they think of him if an unknown son had appeared? I understood his uncomfortable situation. From the beginning of my search, I had been concerned about causing problems for Frances or Jimmy with their respective families. Frances was able to tell everything to her children. Due to the promise he made to his wife, Jimmy cannot be as honest. It bothers me that he cannot face his past openly. Now I will not have the opportunity to know my half siblings. I should pity him, but I can't. Despite my disappointment, I will respect his decision. Jimmy then spoke about his mother—my fraternal grandmother—who is still living and 93 years old.

As a newly arrived immigrant he put himself through school and had a very successful career as a civil engineer. He was involved in designing a number of the freeways in Connecticut. During the War he designed airfields for use by the Allied troops when Italy was invaded in 1943.

The conversation then turned to me. He had many questions about where I grew up, where I went to school, and what I did for a living. Jimmy did not like San Francisco. There was something about me being from California that made him uncomfortable and I am not sure why.

Had I been a doctor, lawyer, or other professional, he might have been impressed and more interested. Three of his four children are college graduates, except the youngest who is still in high school. The elder children are professionals and this is a source of pride for him. My job in the micro-processing department of Bank of America for the last eight years doesn't compare to their careers.

Once he learned that I was not as successful as his other children, his interest in me seemed to wane and that was just as well. As a result, the subject of my marital status never came up. I doubt Jimmy would have been able to accept my sexuality. This is not a kind thing to say, but he struck me as a judgmental person with rigid and traditional beliefs about the world and how people should act. I find this ironic, considering his secret past.

The conversation started to drag. He answered most of my questions, and didn't seem to be that interested in me. Jimmy asked if there was any place I wanted to see in the area. All that came to my mind was Manchester General Hospital where I was born. If he thought it an odd request, he didn't say and he drove there and parked across the street. It is an ordinary hospital on the top of a hill surrounded by a lovely park. As we sat in the car he became very quiet. I wondered if he was thinking about Frances, coming here alone, checking in, and leaving a few days later with me. I felt sorry for Frances and a bit of contempt for Jimmy. The feelings faded as he drove back down the hill into Manchester.

We stopped for lunch at a local café and the conversation picked up. I wasn't sure what he thought of me, but he seemed more comfortable as the afternoon wore on. As we ate, he asked if I planned to see other parts of Connecticut. I said that I was told not to miss Mystic Seaport. Then he enthusiastically offered to take me there and show me around next week. His offer surprised me. He had recently retired and purchased a home near Old Lyme so he knows the area very well.

As we finished lunch, Jimmy had another surprise: he wanted his wife to meet me. I was taken aback at the suggestion, but I agreed. I was having a hard time reconciling my thoughts about him. First, he seemed to dismiss me because I was not a professional. And now he wants me to meet his wife. Given what he said earlier about his promise to her not to tell their children, I wonder how she will react to his idea.

In his first letter, he denied being my father or knowing Frances. But now he confirmed much of what she had told me. Yet for all the talk he never said, "I am your natural father." He admitted the fact but never said the words. If he still has doubts about my being his son, why does he want me to meet his wife?

Almost three hours passed. Jimmy needed to get me to the hotel, as he had to drive back to the coast. At the hotel we made plans to meet again. I will call him on Sunday about the trip to Mystic. He made me promise that I would be alone when he came to pick me up. He is concerned about running into Frances and her family because he thinks they are still crazy. This is how he remembers her sisters and brothers, hot tempered and unpredictable. I wanted to remind him that everything happened over 30 years ago. These people are older and could be nothing like he remembered them. Frances did tell me that her family did not like him because he was Greek. But I didn't say anything. What was the point? We'll see what happens on Sunday.

Despite spending the afternoon with him, I am bothered by his inability to say, "I am your natural father." It is strange considering what he told me about Frances and their time together. Jimmy confirmed most of what she has told me, so I know he was there. The physical similarities between us confirm the fact. If he is ashamed that he deserted her, then seeing me can only make him more ashamed. But I don't understand why he wants to take me to Mystic and to meet his wife. Thinking about all of this has exhausted me.

Frances and Jimmy are indeed opposites. He is quiet just as she said he was, and very measured in how he talks, thinking before he speaks. He is cerebral and she is emotional. If they had gotten married, my life would have been so different. Their marriage would not have been an easy union and most likely would have ended in a separation.

Frances called when I returned. She wanted to know what happened and what he said about her. I was trying to digest the past three hours and knew I couldn't tell her some of the things he said. Prior to our meeting, Frances promised that we would not discuss Mr. Zaldonapolous, but that was then. When I reminded her, she got mad, hysterical, and shouted and cursed Jimmy and me. I did not give in. I could not tell her some of what he said about her and her family. It would have hurt her and who knows what she would do when the hurt turned to anger. After 20 minutes of arguing, she finally calmed down.

I called Janice to apologize for being gone so long. She had wanted to take me to a shopping center where I could buy postcards. We talked for half an hour, and then Frances called again. She wanted to know who I was talking to and what we talked about.

I wish I had a car so I could drive around. This town was incorporated in 1643 but the area where I am staying looks like 1963. So far Connecticut reminds me of Marin County. I have to take a nap to recover from the meeting with Mr. Zaldonapolous.

\*\*\*

5:30 p.m.: After a needed rest I woke up depressed. It must be a culmination of the emotion of these last few days, meeting my natural mother, half-sister, and half-brother, and today my natural father. I have lots to think about and not enough time to absorb it.

I am confused about David. I don't know whether I am seeing who he really is or if he is hiding part of himself from me. He never stops moving and has a hard time concentrating due to the pot smoking. I resent that coming between us. There is something missing in my picture of him and I am at loss to figure out what it is. I also see desperation about him and that bothers me. I wonder if his years on heavy drugs took a toll on his personality and damaged him in ways that no one can ever know.

I miss Rolland. I wish he were here to talk to me. If he met them, we could compare notes and it would make more sense. I am very alone.

Meeting Mr. Zaldonapolous left me sad. My mistake was expecting him to be as welcoming as Frances. It is not in his nature because he is not the warm person that she is.

Up until this afternoon, I felt positive, in control, and happy with what has happened so far. Now I start to wonder why I came here to dig up this stuff. I didn't expect it to hurt. Ultimately, I will be glad that I did make the journey but for now I am overwhelmed and hurting.

Frances is like a child sometimes. She can be emotional and loud to get what she wants. If there was ever any question about my emotional makeup, the answer is partly in her personality. Although not to her extreme, I certainly have inherited some of her emotional side. Mr. Zaldonapolous is the opposite and controls his emotions. I have some of that too.

I have a better picture of their relationship after meeting him, and can see what parts of my disposition I have inherited from them. I never gave this much thought before.

I don't know if Jimmy was entirely truthful with me. I want to believe he was being as honest as he could when he recalled past events. I believe Jimmy chose to forget the painful episodes and the version I received was what he now believes happened. One of them isn't telling the entire truth. It can't be Frances. She is too much of an open book. If I had to choose, it would be Jimmy who is not being totally honest. He might have too much to lose if his children find out about me. It bothers me that he cannot be more honest.

The inconsistencies in what Mr. Zaldonapolous said compared to Frances' version confuses me. I don't know what to believe. The truth is somewhere in their stories that I don't see right now.

I should have taken David up on his offer to stay at his apartment. The hotel is nice but I am isolated. On the other hand, time away from everyone gives me a chance to collect my thoughts. Today was the first time I felt I am ready to leave.

A good cry has released some of the built-up emotion from the last few days. I don't feel good about my meeting with Mr. Zaldonapolous. It has colored the rest of my feelings about being here. I am not sure why.

7:00 p.m.: Frances and Louise are coming by for a visit this evening. Louise was married to Billy, one of my half-brothers who passed away. This is a surprise. The only people I was prepared to meet were Frances, David, Janice, and Mabel. But Frances insists that I meet Louise too. Or maybe Louise wants to meet me. Frances really likes her. I am counting on Louise to be less emotional than Frances, easier to figure out than David, and warmer than Mr. Zaldonapolous.

***

11:00 p.m.: Frances and Louise just left. Despite my reservations, it turned into a good visit. Louise is about 38. She tries to act younger and when she came in the hotel room, I was not taken with her. She was so full of herself that she couldn't stop talking about the places she's been and the people she knows. God forbid if the spotlight does not shine on her for one minute. She appeared confident but she acted like she had to impress me. She brought a bottle of California Grey Riesling wine and that helped to take the edge off.

As the evening wore on, she ran down. Eventually Louise stopped her stories and we began to talk about things besides her life. Louise was quick to let me know that she had figured out I was gay. She was cool and acted like it was no big deal. She has been around and I got the impression that she knows other gay people. The conversation went right over Frances' head as Louise and I danced around the topic. Had Frances picked up on the undercurrents of our conversation, she would not have been quiet for very long.

Frances and Louise got a bit bombed on the wine. I drank very little as I wanted to keep a clear head. They emptied the bottle before they left and became pretty silly and a bit loud. After a few hours, Frances called Janice to pick them up. We walked out to the front of the hotel and waited for her. Louise and Frances were laughing and having a good time thanks to the wine. Soon the car pulled up, and they got in. Janice was not pleased when she saw that they had been drinking. As Janice pulled the car away from the hotel, I heard them screaming at each other. Janice and Louise are completely different and I got the impression that they are not especially fond of each other. I am sure Frances likes Louise because she is such a free spirit, like Frances was when she was younger.

Later, Frances called and told me that tonight was the best time she had had in a while. No doubt the wine helped. I am not sure what Louise thought about me but we did have a rapport. By the end of the evening I liked her more than when she first arrived. I am sure I will see her again before I leave. After they left, I expected David to call or come by but it is too late now. I still want to sit down and have a conversation with him when he is not stoned, if that is possible.

# Chapter Twenty

Friday, September 17, 1976

9:00 a.m.: I am waiting for Janice to pick me up. She will take me to her house and we'll go shopping later. I haven't spent much time with her, so this will be a good chance for us to get more acquainted.

Thanks to a good sleep, I have recovered from last night's party and the emotions of meeting Mr. Zaldonapolous. I have been sleeping well because I am emotionally drained by the end of each day. Outside is gray and rainy. I don't like this hotel. If there was ever a Ken & Barbie hotel, this place is it. The staff is like mechanical dolls, moving stiffly as they carry out their tasks and exhibiting no evidence of any personality. I am surprised because they are so young. An unpleasant gay man at the front desk became unnecessarily rude with me about paying for tonight's stay. His smart-assed attitude caught me off guard. I came down to his level and I gave it right back. Can't say I am proud of myself. I got caught up in another, albeit different, emotion of the moment.

***

Saturday 1:30 a.m.: David just dropped me off. So much has happened over the last 24 hours. Janice picked me up at the hotel around 9:30 a.m. on Friday and I spent the morning at her house talking with her and Stanley. This was the first time I had time alone with them. Most of the trip has been centered on Frances and David. Janice and Stanley live in a middle class neighborhood in the next suburb over from Wethersfield. They have three children: a four-year-old girl named Katie, and two boys ages 12 and 14, Kevin and Nicholas. We spent a few hours getting acquainted before Janice drove to pick up Frances and we went to the shopping mall in West Hartford.

Since I arrived I have been continually turned around. I have a good sense of direction and can usually find my way around different cities without much problem, but not here. It is very confusing. The streets meander and not in any east to west or north to south straight line. Traveling with David in his van, I never know where I am going or in which direction. We talk and I don't pay attention to which way we are headed. I am not getting a clear understanding of the geography of the area. I usually pay attention to downtowns, important buildings, and historic markers but not here. I am too focused on the people I am meeting. Hartford and the suburbs are a blur in the background.

After spending an hour at the mall, we returned to Janice's. I never shop in malls in San Francisco. Living in the inner city I have easy access to small shops and stores right in the neighborhood. Who would want to drive all the way to Daly City just to go to a mall? Besides I hate shopping. This is one characteristic I definitely do not share with Janice and Frances. Shopping in the mall is as essential for them as breathing.

I became aware of another contrast today. During my visit here, everything has been centered on the suburban lifestyle. Suburbs rarely touch my life in San Francisco. My home is the inner city. I left suburbia behind when I left Colorado. Spending time in the suburbs and at the malls is another reminder of how different my life is from theirs.

Janice dropped off Frances, and then she and I spent the rest of the afternoon talking about our lives, our pasts, Frances, David, and everything else. She is easy to talk with and more centered than David or Frances. There is a physical resemblance between us, but not as marked as between David and me. Her facial features and hairstyle reminded me of Joan Baez. When I told her, she laughed and said she didn't think she was as pretty.

Around 6 p.m. David showed up to take me out. We went to his apartment where I am comfortable because it looks so much like mine. I took photographs and he sat down to work on a metal sculpture. I admired one the other day, so he is making a copy for me. It took a while to get his worktable ready, assemble the metal, and line up his tools and soldering iron. He spent an hour working on the piece. I watched him craft it and we continued to talk. I was surprised at how intense and quiet he was as he worked. We have the same nose, brown eyes, mouth, and square chin. His hair is much thicker than mine and his beard is not trimmed as close. Our complexions are the same. He is thinner and a bit taller. We definitely look like brothers.

I have learned a little more about Janice from spending time with her in the past few days. I already knew a lot about Frances from her letters. But my picture of David keeps changing. He is more complex and less revealing than they are. He is in a continual state of motion, always moving rapidly from one place to the next. If he has a destination, it is not evident. The most focused I have seen him was tonight when he worked on the metal sculpture.

He is warm-hearted like Frances, but also has an immature and slightly selfish side. He fascinates me because I sensed he existed long before I ever knew about Frances. While I have compassion for him, I don't like some of the things he says and does. I am not sure what I expected, or wanted. He is the most puzzling of them all. Much about him is familiar despite our separation for over 30 years. Other times, I look at David and think we were born on different planets.

Tonight David took me to a jai alai game. I have never heard of this sport, but it is big on the East Coast. Even after seeing a few games, I do not understand how it is played. The crowd was large and loud. Betting is part of the fun and David won $107. I have no idea how. David got a bit of a fat head and bragged that he knew he was going to win. I wanted to tell him that his winning was just a matter of luck. But I kept quiet because he enjoys the thought that he is such an expert about gambling.

Watching him at the game, I became aware of something else. He is streetwise in a way that I am not. That must come from how he grew up. His years on drugs and time in prison contributed to his street education. He has a tough exterior but occasionally his kinder side sneaks up on you. Every day I am fascinated to find how much we share in common because of Frances. Still we are so different since we did not share the same upbringing.

After the jai alai, David came up with the crazy idea that we should go to the Athena Restaurant for dinner—his treat since he had won. This is where Jimmy was working when he met Frances. The idea of having dinner there had never occurred to me. It freaked me out but I didn't say anything. I felt awkward even though there was no chance I would run into Jimmy. Even if his brother Georgios still owned the place he wouldn't know who I was. As I considered David's idea, I became more intrigued given the diner's significance to Frances and Jimmy. I shrugged off my doubts and said, "Great idea. Let's go."

It was midnight by the time we arrived. The 1930s diner was sheathed in metal siding and had a sign, "The Athena," emblazed in blue neon on the rooftop. The dining area was decorated in Art Deco style and did not appear to have been modernized. I wondered if it looked the same as it did when Frances met Jimmy. Having grown up out west, I don't recall being in a real diner before. Our waitress wore a nametag that said "Katherine Jones" and she was as unique as the diner.

David did not have particularly good table manners. He got a bit loud and asked, "Who owns this place? My brother knows the original owners." I wanted to kick him under the table but instead gave him a dirty look. He got the message and laughed. Katherine must have thought he was drunk, as she didn't take notice of what he had said. David was feeling the beers from the jai alai game.

As we ate, he told me about a long-time friend, Tommy, who lives in New York. Their friendship began in high school and became rooted in years of doing drugs together. Tommy is still involved in drugs so their relationship changed and David doesn't see him as much as he used to. He told me that when he looks back to when he was addicted, Tommy's addiction scares him. He seemed sad about Tommy and that part of his past, and abruptly changed the subject. I asked David about his current drug use. He told me that all he does now is pot and the occasional shot of Jack Daniels.

David kidded around easily with Katherine. He is personable and comfortable with everyone with whom he engages. If I lived here, we would either become friends or get on each other's nerves. There are times when he drives me crazy with his know-it-all attitude. He doesn't always listen. He also strikes me as someone who is unwilling to compromise. Sharing dinner with him, I was sad that we did not grow up together and that in a few days I would be going back to California. I am not sure he feels the same way because he grew up with a sister and two brothers, but I realize I missed a lot.

As we waited for the check, David laughed as he told me that he had taken the silver salt-and-pepper shakers from the table and they were in his pocket. This made me angry and I gave him more than a dirty look. I told him that he had better not steal anything.

He looked startled and sheepishly took them out of his coat pocket and put them back.

I am not sure what he thinks about me. I can imagine Frances threatening that he had better be nice to me or else. I cannot get over how strange it is to be with the brother who was in my childhood imagination.

As I write, I am sad about not growing up in this family. In one way, I was cheated out of a normal family. But how can I say that? They are not any more normal than the family I grew up in. It is possible I didn't miss a thing. The truth remains that I didn't have my real mother, a real brother, or real sister. I wonder who would I be now had I grown up in such an excitable and emotional family. Not to say that I am not excitable and emotional, but I have more control. I am homesick and need familiar faces around me for a change.

This experience has been an emotional high as well as a continual drain on my energy. Most of the mystery is over. What it means later will take some time to figure out. This past week has been like a long and bizarre dream. Right now I am ready to wake up in my own bed.

I have spent too much time trying to analyze everything and everyone I have experienced. This might explain why I am sad sometimes. I need to be away from here so I can look back at what I found. Then distance and time will explain Frances, David, and even Mr. Zaldonapolous. I am tired of thinking about all of this and I need to get to bed.

*\*\*\**

Saturday, September 18, 1976

2:30 p.m.: David came by at 9:30 this morning. It is like having a limo service at my disposal. He smiled as he bounced into the lobby, although he admitted to having a hangover from last night. "Jesus, why'd you let me drink so much?" As if I could have stopped him.

He wanted to take me out of Hartford, across the Connecticut River to South Glastonbury and see his St. Bernard named Bea. When he started working nights at the hospital, problems developed with the dog being cooped up in the apartment with no attention or exercise. His solution was to board her at a farm across the river. David is bothered about having to abandon his dog even if the arrangement is only temporary. He drives over to see Bea every chance he gets.

On the drive over, the beauty of the landscape knocked me out. The town is surrounded by forests on rolling hills and lots of green farm fields in the valleys between. There are no sweeping views in this area, no high points from which you can see for long distances like in the West. The views here are smaller in scale and more about the history of this area and its people.

For the first time since I arrived, I saw the Connecticut that I had expected. The only Connecticut I knew was the one I had seen in movies. An abundance of well-preserved and restored colonial houses were everywhere. Many were built in the 1690s through the 1700s and are still occupied. We have nothing in California that would compare to the houses I saw today.

After driving on narrow roads over many hills we finally arrived at the farm. A teenage girl named Suzann greeted us. David rushed off to find Bea, who was out running. Suzann is Bea's caretaker between David's visits. David spent time playing with Bea, who is very friendly and the size of a small horse. I saw how attached he and the dog are to each other.

We left Bea and David took off down another back road to a ferry crossing on the Connecticut River. This was no ordinary crossing, as the tiny ferryboat held only two cars. The wait was not very long because the crossing takes five minutes from shore to shore. A sign stated that this ferry began in the 1690s and was the oldest continuously operating ferry in the country. I can't get over how much history I see everywhere I go.

David drove back to his apartment and shop, and then we went out looking for what he called a tag sale, which we would call a garage sale. Poking through old things most people call junk is something David and I have in common. We had fun comparing notes about the stuff scattered about the yards where we stopped. After we got tired of looking at junk, we went to see Frances. She is pleased that David and I are getting along so well. Being accepted by Janice and David will make things easier for her now that I have become part of her life.

One of the reasons we went to his shop was that David wanted me to meet a couple of his friends. They help in his shop while he is working at the hospital. He introduced me to a man about my age named Tony, a recovering drug addict who has known David for a long time. I also met Mrs. Orpha Blackstone. She is 79 years old but not dressed like most women her age. She wore a pair of bib overalls, a plaid shirt, and a man's straw hat from the 1950s. Mrs. Blackstone could have come in from the farm by the looks of the worn boots on her feet. David had told her the story of my sudden reappearance into his mother's life. She wasn't the least bit surprised when he introduced me as "my brother from California." Mrs. Blackstone greeted me like she had known me for years and said that she was glad to hear that David had a brother.

She lives alone in a large house in the Elmwood section of West Hartford. She has no children and her husband died many years ago. David met Mrs. Blackstone through an uncle who lived next door to her.

I did not understand their relationship at first. David treats her with more respect and patience than I have seen him exhibit with Frances or Janice. I wondered if despite her appearance, Mrs. Blackstone had a lot of money and that was the basis of their friendship. She helps run the store when he is at his other job. I noticed that he is very attentive to her. She told me that David goes to her house and helps her with odd jobs. In return she dotes on him like a grandmother. Once I observed them closely, I saw that David's friendship is more sincere than I had originally thought. In addition to helping with chores, he also provides an otherwise lonely old woman with purpose and companionship. She is his friend and they have a lot in common and enjoy each other's company.

Frances doesn't understand why David is willing to do so much for Mrs. Blackstone. One reason why David likes her is that she doesn't get too bothered by anything he does. He lit up a joint in front of her and she didn't blink an eye. He told me sometimes he uses her phone when he is working for Uncle Albert. Surely Mrs. Blackstone must know.

These errands for Uncle Albert still make me uncomfortable. Either David is earning money at it or he feels a family obligation to his Uncle Albert. How stereotypical it sounds—running numbers for your Italian uncle, the bookie. I don't understand that part of his life.

[Many years passed before I learned more about Uncle Albert. All I knew was that David had worked for him and Frances always told me he was her favorite brother. But the family never revealed details about him or his business activities. He was so well known that when he passed away in his 80s, it was front-page news in Hartford. The lengthy newspaper profile of his life told of a "genial bookie with a big heart."

He had run his penny ante numbers racket for 50 years from his office in the rear of his locksmith shop in a rundown section of the city. Vice detectives hounded him for years because of his numbers business. The FBI also had interest in him as he was reputed to have been an associate of an organized crime family. But the article spoke of his frequent generosity and good works. Locals knew that his financial help kept the neighborhood soup kitchen open for years. He bought clothes for homeless shelters and organized inner city boxing programs for youth. He gave away candy and sodas, and at Thanksgiving, free turkeys to his poor neighbors. He rescued abandoned dogs and many of them came to live with David.

One time, he purchased a stolen organ after he learned it had been taken from a local church, and hired five men to return it to the priests. The news article reported that the State of Connecticut sent relief checks to his store for distribution to several disabled people who had no address. Some were so badly affected by their alcoholism they could not manage their money. Uncle Albert kept a ledger of their checks and became their banker. He cashed the checks and doled out their money a bit at a time. It was well known by many who knew of this arrangement that he disbursed more money than he ever received from the state.

Times changed and when casinos came to Connecticut, Uncle Albert's numbers business suffered. Faced with financial problems, he reputedly got a loan from the mob. This lead to a federal grand jury subpoena and Uncle Albert ended up in jail as an old man, where he sat for months unwilling to reveal his connections.

I regret that I never got to know this colorful relative. If only he had written as many letters to me as Frances.]

Later in the afternoon David dropped me at the hotel, where

I waited for Janice and Frances to come by. Frances wants to talk to me alone. I know what she is going to ask and I am ready.

*** 

7:15 p.m.: Janice dropped Frances and me off at the hotel mid-afternoon. Frances' mood turned serious when we reached my room. She wasted no time getting to the point. Frances was very determined when she opened the conversation.

"I have a question that I want you to answer truthfully. I always taught my kids to tell the truth. You are one of my kids now so I expect you to tell me the truth too. I want to know why you are not married."

I had expected this question and wondered how it would go when I finally answered. I recalled my group therapy in Berkeley when we discussed how I would explain to my mother why I am not married. I hoped that I remembered everything. I was anxious but I was ready to answer her. I said, "Frances, I am gay."

"Gay? Yes, I know you are happy but what the hell does that have to do with you not being married?"

"Frances, I don't think you understand. When I say I am gay, I do not mean I am happy. I mean that I am gay. I am homosexual."

She was stunned. She sat silently for a moment and then shrieked, "Oh my God. Oh my God. It's my fault. This is all my fault." She jumped up from the chair and beat on her breasts and walked around the room as she repeated this. Anyone passing in the hallway outside the room would wonder just what it was that she had done.

"No, Frances. I figured it out long before I ever knew about you."

She sat down and began to cry. I waited for my next cue. Eventually, she calmed down and sobbed into her handkerchief. Suddenly her mood shifted to anger as she lectured me. She rose from her chair again and this time moved closer, pointing an outstretched finger at me.

"You have to change. You just have to. You can't be that way. I want you to change now. You can change for me if you want to."

"I am not going to change. Not even for you. I am happy the way I am. I cannot change this no matter how much you want me to. That will not happen."

She took in what I said and sat down. I waited to see what was going to happen next. Frances jumped out of the chair again.

"YOU HAD NORMAL SEX ORGANS WHEN I LEFT YOU WITH THOSE PEOPLE. WHAT DID THEY DO TO YOU?"

I was not prepared for that question, but I did answer as best I could without laughing, "They didn't do anything to me."

"Oh Jim, you have to change. I want you to change for me. You can if you want to."

"Frances, my sexuality is only one part of who I am. And think about this: It isn't anyone's business who I sleep with. Not even yours."

She said nothing and sat staring at me for a few minutes. Then, her eyes narrowed and her head came toward me. In a deep and serious voice she asked, "Do you wear dresses?"

I wanted to say, "Don't worry about me asking to borrow any of yours." But the occasion was not one for a smartass answer and so I said, "No, I never wear a dress and have no plans to start anytime soon."

She seemed relieved that I correctly answered at least one of her questions. Frances continued sobbing and asking why. She did not let up with her demand for me to change. She begged and pleaded and wept. When that did not move me she tried being angry. It was apparent that we had reached an impasse and neither of us was going to give in.

I don't know if I was angry or just tired, but I had to end this conversation that was going nowhere. If my sexuality was the determining factor of her acceptance of me, I needed to know now.

"Frances, you have to accept that I am not going to change. There is more to me than just being gay. It is just one part of who I am. You asked me to be truthful and I am. This is not easy for me. I could have lied and made up excuses, but I didn't. I told you the truth.

"My being gay is not your fault. You have nothing to do with it. This may sound cruel, but either you accept that I'm gay and not changing, or I'm on the next train back to California."

My heart was pounding. I might have thrown the past six months out the door, but I could not lie about who I was to anyone, not even Frances. Neither of us spoke for a long time. Mentally I changed my train tickets and called Rolland with the news that I would be back in San Francisco sooner than I had planned.

Frances broke the long silence and her voice was steady. "You are right. I asked you for the truth and boy did you give it to me. You could have told me anything and I would never know you were lying. That is more important than whether you are gay or not married. I don't understand how you are. Maybe I will someday or maybe not. But I feel better knowing that you were truthful with me. I know it was not easy but it means so much to me that you did. No matter what, you are still my son." She came to the bed where I sat, and we hugged each other in tears.

I was relieved. The drama had ended and we sat there silently grateful. She was glad for my telling the truth, and I was glad that she could accept it.

Frances wanted to know about Rolland. I explained that we had been living together for ten years. She was glad that I was not alone and said that she wanted to meet him someday. I promised to answer any question she might have about my life and friends in San Francisco. All she had to do was ask.

Her mind was spinning as she absorbed what I had said. At one point, she said, "I know someone else who is gay. I never thought about it before." It turned out to be a man she had worked with in a department store years earlier and still saw around town.

She told me about a trip that she had taken with a "bunch of the old ladies" from the senior center. They had gone on a bus tour to Cape Cod. One night after dinner, she and several of the ladies went to a bar across the street from the motel where they were staying. It was comical to watch Frances have a gay revelation as she relived for me what had happened.

"We went into this bar and there were all these nice young men. They were so nice to us. The bar had a jukebox and the young men asked us to dance and we had a wonderful time. We danced and they bought us drinks and we had so much fun. I thought, 'What a nice bunch of young men.' At the time, I didn't notice that we were the only women in the place. Talking to you, I just figured out that we were in a gay bar. I wonder what those ladies would have thought if they had known where we were."

I said, "So the men in the bar were nice and you had a great time. Some of those ladies hadn't danced in years. It might have been the most fun they had in a long time because those guys got them out on the dance floor. What difference does it make if the men were gay? Not one bit. They were nice and treated you very well. So what if they were gay? It doesn't matter."

She smiled. "I guess you are right. It doesn't matter."

I said, "Promise that you won't tell Janice or David. It's not that I don't want them to know. I do, but I want to tell them at the right time. They should hear this from me and no one else."

I didn't mention that I had already told David. She would be hurt that I had told him first. Frances promised she wouldn't tell them. But she didn't sound convincing.

"Frances, you have to promise. It is my job to tell them, not yours. Do you understand?"

"I swear on the graves of my two dead sons. What's wrong with you? You don't think I can keep a secret? Have you forgotten that I kept you a secret?"

With that, I was convinced. Janice came by afterwards to pick her up and take her home. After two hours of answering her questions, I was exhausted.

***

10:45 p.m.: Around 7:30 p.m., David, Frances, and Louise picked me up. They wanted to go to dinner at the jai lai arena. It wasn't a great choice. The food was overpriced and not that good.

Louise became distracted as soon as her new boyfriend showed up. David was distracted by what I don't know. Frances was her usual talkative self, oblivious that Louise and David weren't tuned in at what was happening at our table. Then David said he had to be somewhere and we left at 10. I was curious about where David had to be. I didn't ask and he offered no explanation. I was a little hurt over not knowing the mystery, and also pissed since it was his idea that we all go out tonight. Then he acted like it was inconvenient for him to be with us, and suddenly wanted to leave. I don't like this inconsiderate side of his personality.

After they dropped me at the hotel, I started thinking that I am ready to leave Connecticut. At times, I am such an outsider because their way of life is so different from mine. It gets frustrating trying to make sense of it all. Frances is trying to cram 34 lost years into one week and I am trying to grab those years and absorb them. That is impossible. David disturbs me when I take a good look at him. When we are together, I enjoy the rush. But his non-stop energy bouncing in every direction and landing nowhere bothers me. I expected finding a brother would mean that I would get a close friend. So far all I have found is someone very closed down inside.

Janice is more black and white. At times we are on the same wavelength, more so than I am with Frances or David. I have a firm idea of who she is and how I relate to her. I wish it were that simple with David and Frances.

I have to write postcards and get some sleep. I have come to the end of yet another day in this emotional free-for-all.

# Chapter Twenty-one

Sunday, September 19, 1976

I woke at eight this morning and walked to the shopping center a quarter of a mile from the hotel for some much-needed exercise. I did laundry and bought film for my camera. The sun-filled morning was fresh and clean after a light rain during the night. I walked back to the hotel, showered, and went to the restaurant for a leisurely breakfast with the newspaper.

David bounced in to the hotel at 10:30. I was annoyed about last night but soon got over it. He wanted us to visit his dog in South Glastonbury again. I was so taken with the area the last time that I was glad to return. At Glastonbury, we drove to an empty shack of a house near the farm where the dog is boarded. This was where David lived before moving to the apartment above the pizza parlor. He loved the location because it was in the country and isolated from "the shit in the city," as he put it. David has a dream of owning a place in a rural area where he and Bea can live. We left the shack and drove to the farm where the St. Bernard is boarded. Instead of playing with Bea in the yard, he loaded her into the van. I say load because the dog is so big, it was like watching David load a horse into a trailer.

We drove several miles down a country road and stopped at a place called Cotton Pond. The pond itself is about a quarter mile off the road, surrounded by trees and bushes that gave it seclusion. I was reminded of a Norman Rockwell illustration where kids are skinny-dipping in a pond, although we did not see a soul. David opened the van door and Bea leaped out and ran toward the pond. She knew where she was. Into the water she went with a large splash and swam around. For a large dog, she glided as effortlessly as a swan.

David shampooed her in the small stream that feeds into the pond. We sat on nearby rocks as we waited for Bea to dry. Both of us were very quiet like we did not want to disturb the silence. Bea snoozed in the tall grass as the sun dried her thick fur. She was worn out from her swim and bath. David lit a joint and drifted off alone with his thoughts. I looked into the sky and closed my eyes to capture the peacefulness of the pond. I may need to mentally return here in the future.

The only sounds came from water pouring over the rocks into the small stream and from insects flying near the surface of the pond. A warm breeze rustled through leaves in the surrounding trees and gusts sent a flurry of yellow and red leaves down from above. They floated in the water until they covered the pond like a tablecloth. The spell was broken when Bea decided the dry cycle was over and jumped up. She was ready to leave. David loaded the gentle St. Bernard back into the van and we drove back to the farm.

After dropping off Bea, we went back to Janice's. Frances was there with Mabel, her good friend of 40 years. When Frances told her about me, Mabel called immediately to tell me how happy she was. She wrote many times in the months before I arrived here, and she is as great a woman as Frances said she would be. I liked her immediately. She and Frances are full of stories from their past. Many are about the hardships of their younger days and raising their kids alone, and being poor but very happy. Despite recalling the difficult times, they never stopped laughing as they bounced off of each other's recollections of the old days. Frances told one story that reminded Mabel of another story and on it went. Both women were exuberant and demonstrative as they told their particular tales. I laughed as I watched the two friends relive their history together. They were like a pair of stand-up comics. I wondered how they could laugh while looking back on such times. But laugh they did.

David was not engaged in Frances and Mabel's storytelling like I was. He tuned them out shortly after they began and quickly lost interest. David has heard their stories many times before. His childhood must have been difficult, and he may not see much to laugh about now.

The show moved from the living room to outside where Janice had set the patio table for lunch. We had a picnic with plenty of good food and more laughs. I was annoyed with David when he announced he had to leave. I wanted him to stay, but that is how he is. He was bored with Frances and Mabel's stories. He doesn't pretend to enjoy himself when he isn't having fun. He leaves without guilt or apology. It doesn't seem polite, but I suppose it is more honest.

I understand why Frances is critical of David but there were a number of times today when she and Janice came down on him too hard. They can be very judgmental when they shouldn't be; for example, when they criticize what he wears or what he does. That partly explains why he didn't stay longer and his affection for Mrs. Blackstone. He is an adult and sometimes Frances and Janice treat him like a child. I don't think they are aware of it. It is just the way they see him. His defense is not to fight back, but to retreat. A few times I wanted to say something when they started in on him. I didn't and kept my mouth shut.

As Frances and Mabel relived the old days, my thoughts turned to David and how hard it must have been growing up as Frances' kid. He didn't have as much independence and freedom as I did. Frances had more control over David's life than Cecilia or Ruth had over mine.

The stories continued for the rest of the afternoon. Mabel's son, Ron, had come with her. Janice and Stanley's children, Nicholas, Kevin, and Katie, were there too. I enjoyed the afternoon and took a lot of pictures.

Frances is more settled and not as anxious as when I arrived, and she has stopped talking about how guilty she feels. She told me that she wrote a letter to Rolland yesterday. When I asked her what she wrote, she told me to mind my own business.

It was late afternoon when the party ended. Janice drove Frances home and took me back to the hotel. As she drove, Janice and I had time for a good chat, our first real talk with no one else around. Again, I see how we share a lot of the same traits. Before I came here, I never thought about being like someone else, because there was never anyone else around like me. Now I find more similarities every hour that connect me to the three of them.

I was very tired by the time I got back to the hotel, and then I remembered I had to call Mr. Zaldonapolous about going down to the coast. What a difference on the telephone this time compared to his friendly manner the other afternoon. Jimmy was stiff and almost formal in his speech, not at all friendly. I imagined his wife sitting nearby listening. He was sorry but things had come up and he did not have time to take me to Mystic Seaport. I was surprised and disappointed. It wasn't about missing the coast, but the sudden turnaround in his demeanor. His change of heart caught me off guard and I was at a loss for words. The trip was his idea, not mine.

I was angry. I was looking forward to spending more time with him. I wanted to learn more about him and more of the family history. Jimmy had wanted me to meet his wife and she might be the reason for changing his mind. Her fear could be that if I spent more time with him, their children would find out about me. Once it was determined I was not a threat, his wife may have decided they didn't need to be bothered about me anymore.

I reacted to what he said as if it were okay. Of course, it wasn't. I managed to say I understood even though I didn't. He gave no indication that I would hear from him again. My gut feeling is that I won't. While I felt my anger growing, I managed to keep it in check. I thanked him for spending time with me on Thursday and told him how much I had enjoyed it. I told him that I would not contact him again before I left, or after I was back in California. Even though I was angry and disappointed, I wanted Jimmy to know that he could stop worrying about me. I reminded him that he has my address and phone number in San Francisco if he wants to contact me. Jimmy said nothing. This made me angrier and added to the awkwardness of the call. He sounded like he didn't want to be on the phone with me but he made no attempt to end the conversation, so I ended it with a good-bye and hung up.

It would have been nice to see Jimmy again but I don't believe that will happen. Right now I am too mad to think about it. It was his decision and I don't know why he made it. My head is so full I can't give it any more thought.

I called David and he will pick me up in the morning to go to his shop. It is going to be hard to leave my new family when I get back on the train. They are crazy—except Janice—but under it all, they are good people.

***

Monday, September 20, 1976

3:45 p.m.: David called at 7:00 a.m. "Be ready in half an hour," he said and was off the phone before I could ask any questions. I rushed around and was out front when he arrived. He picked up Tony and Mrs. Blackstone and drove to his shop where I stayed until he brought me back in the afternoon.

Once we were at the shop, David didn't spend much time there. He needed Tony and Mrs. Blackstone to keep the shop open while he went on errands for Uncle Albert. I spent most of the day with them, wondering why he bothered to pick me up when he left again so quickly. When he returned later, he was subdued, not his talkative self. I was ready to leave. Sitting around got boring after a few hours. We drove to the hotel and I asked if there was something bothering him. I was uncomfortable with the sudden change in his personality.

I wondered if David might harbor resentment about the attention that Frances has paid to me. I don't blame him if he feels jealous. He only had to share her attention with Janice before I showed up. It must have been a shock when Frances told him about me, and her relationship with my father. This was a part of her life that he never knew before and it could bother him more than he admits. I don't know what is going on with David, but his mood has changed. Prior to today, I didn't see him as moody.

He assured me that he was fine and had business things on his mind. I let it go and took him at his word.

David has a beard like mine. When I first saw him I thought, "That is cool we both have beards." Mrs. Blackstone told me that he only started growing it when he found out I had one. I wish I knew him better so I could ask him about his beard, or what business has made him so quiet. The reality is that he and I are strangers, despite our similarities. David acts like a loner. I can't figure out if this is how he really is or if it is a role he plays to keep people at a distance.

I unexpectedly met another blood relative yesterday, Aunt Sylvia. She is Frances' younger sister. David and I were leaving his apartment in the morning and walking toward the van. At a nearby bus stop, an older woman stood waiting for a bus. As we approached, she saw David. "What are you doing? Where are you going?" He answered, "Hi, Aunt Sylvia. Just taking Jim over to Glastonbury to see Bea."

None of Frances' relatives, other than David and Janice, know about me or that I am here. That is how Frances wants it. It was very apparent from the woman's looks that she was one of Frances' sisters. David had never mentioned that his Aunt Sylvia only lived a few blocks down the street from his apartment.

Aunt Sylvia took a long, hard look at me. Actually it was a shocked stare. Panic hit me with, "Oh no, the secret is out." She gazed at me like she recognized the face but couldn't remember where she had seen it. She was at a distinct disadvantage.

Puzzled, she asked, "Are you one of the Postigliones from Bridgeport?" I looked over at David for help and sensed that he enjoyed her confusion. He did come to my rescue but not with any clarification that helped. David said, "No, Aunt Sylvia, he's not from Bridgeport." He continued, like she should have known, "This is my brother Jim from California."

Her eyes widened and her mouth dropped. Aunt Sylvia put her hand over her heart as she sat down stunned on the bus stop bench. With no further elaboration, David jumped into the van with me right behind him. He laughed and yelled out the window, "Call Ma. She'll tell you all about it." I looked in the side-view mirror. Aunt Sylvia must have decided that her trip could wait. She was walking hurriedly down the street toward her house. All I could think was how surprised Frances would be when she received a call from this sister asking who I was and what was going on.

Frances hasn't told her brothers and sisters about me. She said she might tell one of her brothers, but she wasn't sure. I understand why she hasn't been more open with them. Frances is not ready for the questions that they will surely ask. Then there is the guilt she still has about losing me. Added to this, she has barely begun to absorb the meaning of my reappearance. It is reasonable that she hasn't said anything to her family about me. She should get ready. If one sister knows in this tight family, word will be out sooner than Frances expects.

I have to start calling Frances "Fanny." That is who she is to everyone who knows her and has been her name since she was a child. She started off as "Frances" in her first letter and that's who she has been from the beginning. My referring to her as Frances must sound strange to David, Janice, Stanley, and Mabel. Fanny she is from now on. I will get used to it.

I was annoyed with David's absence from his shop this morning, but spending time with Mrs. Blackstone gave me a chance to know her a little better. She is a very important person in David's life. She told me that he has a stash of grass in her basement and uses her phone for his bookie business. She's not bothered by any of it. She may find the illegal activity going on around her exciting. Who knows what she was like when she was younger? She could have been a bit of a rebel herself and David is a pleasant reminder of her own past. He is very respectful and concerned about her and in turn Mrs. Blackstone just lets him be.

David has a unique relationship with this 79-year-old woman. By including her in his crazy life, David is a bright spot in hers. He takes her for rides in the van and she putters around his antique shop and keeps him company. In a sweet way David is doing more for this woman than she is for him.

. I wonder if I will stay in touch with David. He doesn't seem to be the type that writes letters. I know Janice and I will phone and write, and I have no doubt about Fanny. She has never been to California and wants to visit me there. She wants to see where I live, meet Rolland and my friends, and see San Francisco. It would be great to have her visit.

I had low expectations when I started my search for Frances and my father. A letter or telephone call was the most I hoped to receive from either of them. All I wanted was answers to the questions I had since I was 16. I expected my curiosity would be satisfied once I heard the reasons why I grew up without her. Then I planned to slip out of her life as if I had never been there. End of story. However, judging from how strongly she has embraced my return, this visit may be the start of a new story.

***

7:00 p.m.: I just got off the phone with a young woman named Andrea Mykonossos. It was her mother, Katarina, who drove Fanny down to

Colchester to visit me as a baby when I was being boarded with the Sutherlands. Katarina wanted to adopt me and was with Fanny the morning they discovered the Sutherlands had disappeared.

Fanny tried to find Katarina so she would confirm to me what had happened regarding my disappearance. Unfortunately, Katarina died eight years ago but Fanny found her daughter, Andrea. Fanny told her the whole story and Andrea said she wanted to talk to me when I arrived in Connecticut. Tonight she called.

We had quite a talk and laughed at how weird it was that we could have been raised as brother and sister had things happened differently. She hoped the next time I came to visit that we could meet. I hadn't thought about the next visit. It is likely that I will be back. I know I definitely want to return.

***

9:30 p.m.: I stayed in tonight and had dinner downstairs at the restaurant. Janice and David are working. Fanny is stuck at her house as she does not drive or own a car. This break is good for us. Anyway, I am exhausted. This hotel in the middle of suburbia is boring but I will survive, and relax and watch TV for a change. I will call Fanny later.

I think about what this trip has meant so far. First, I am overwhelmed by the reception and my acceptance by Fanny, Janice, and David. They have been so warm and full of love that it is hard to believe. I have only been here one week, yet it is like I have always known them. I fit in with Fanny's family in many ways I did not expect. Of course, it will be hard to leave. I wished I lived closer so I could visit more often. With Fanny and Janice, I see where they are coming from, but with David I am still not sure. He is better at keeping his emotions hidden than they are.

I saw a picture of Tommy, his old drug buddy, in his bedroom and I felt a tinge of jealousy because Tommy knows David better than I do. A few days ago David said, "You've only been here a few days. How can you expect to really know me or them already?" True. I am so absorbed in what has happened since I found Fanny that I want to know it all right now. I know this is stupid. I am being like Fanny, wanting to know everything immediately. My heart wants all the answers right now, but my brain knows it will take time. I have so much to think about on the trip back home. I keep thinking about the call from Andrea. It was such a pleasant conversation, considering that we don't know each other.

It just occurred to me that I have two families. After years of wondering who I was and where I came from, today I find myself in the middle of the answers. I am free, because finally there is no more wondering. If a question comes up, I have a place to go for the answer. I can't express how good that makes me feel. What remains is to try to absorb everything that has happened since I arrived.

***

Tuesday, September 21, 1976

7:30 p.m.: Today Janice drove her four-year-old daughter, Katie, Fanny, and me down to Mystic Seaport, a restored whaling town from the mid-nineteenth century. We stayed for five hours and still didn't see all of the exhibits. I enjoyed the tour and the history of the area. It was very thoughtful of Janice to make sure I saw more of Connecticut than the suburbs. She wanted to make up for Jimmy canceling our trip. Fanny was furious when I told her and hasn't stopped talking about him since. Mystic is 50 miles south of Hartford. I got an idea of how small a state Connecticut is. We drove half way across in half an hour.

In between visiting the historic buildings the three of us talked non-stop. We returned to the hotel at 4:30 p.m. I was pooped from all the walking. Getting up early every morning and in bed late every evening is starting to catch up with me.

I hit the bed for a nap and woke when Mabel telephoned. She told me how happy she was that I have come back into Fanny's life. Mabel was supposed to go with us, but her car was stolen last night and she spent the day dealing with the police. The poor dear. It turned out the car was repossessed and she had no idea why. Then her husband, Tony, was carted away to a dry-out farm in Vermont this afternoon. Mabel didn't say how long Tony would stay in Vermont. He has been there before for the same reason. When he isn't drunk he is good to her, but she never knows when the next bender is coming.

Mabel said that Fanny has started to cry about my leaving tomorrow. Knowing that will not make my departure easier. Fanny promised that she would not carry on, but she is as good at forgetting her promises as she is at making them. But this is just how she is. She speaks without thinking and rarely looks ahead to the possible consequences. Jimmy's memories of her confirm this.

But I have to return home and Fanny must understand. I know it is going to be hard for her, and it will be for me too. Who knew that I would be so involved with Fanny and her family? Now they are my family, too.

*** 

10:00 p.m.: I just got off the phone with Fanny. She is very down about my leaving. I explained we both have to be realistic about the situation, but nothing I said reached her. Finally, I gave up. She has to work this out it in her own way. She said that she could not bear to see me off at the train station and was going to stay home. I talked her out of that for now, but who knows what she decides in the morning.

This is my last night in Connecticut for a while. So much has gone on here starting from the first day right up to the call from Fanny a few moments ago. Without a doubt, I have a better understanding as to where my emotional makeup originates—the Postiglione side for sure. I am sad about leaving.

Despite the doubts I had in the beginning about whether or not I should find my mother, one thing is very clear to me as a result of this visit. I know I did the right thing by searching for Fanny. Having me back in her life will gradually free Fanny from the guilt that she has carried around. It won't happen in the week I was here. But as we know each other better her shame will disappear and she will forgive herself.

I am very lucky. Most people grow up knowing their parents. They know when they were born, why they have their name, whom they are related to, and where they fit into the family history. I never had that information. I had only questions and no answers. Now that I have met my real mother, there are no more unanswered questions about who I am. I have an unfamiliar sense of completeness. It's hard to explain this new feeling. Janice and David have only added to my joy of the whole experience.

I do not mean to negate the father who raised me, Hollis Sutherland. I wasn't really ever his responsibility. Fanny left me with Cecilia. She never met Hollis. Then Cecilia was gone. Thank God that Hollis took over the responsibility of bringing me up. He and Ruth will not disappear from my life because I have found Fanny.

Yet there is relief (satisfaction?) to know that I am related by blood to someone. Here is the proof. Look at them and look at me. Watch them and watch me. I was aware of the similarities even before I got off the bus. I will always remember Janice waiting on the bus platform and my shock of seeing someone who looked like me for the first time in my life. As time passes, more unknowns about myself are bound to surface and I will be surprised again and again.

As I look back at this last week, I wonder who will have a harder time tomorrow when I leave, Fanny or me.

It is impossible to summarize the feelings I have about this week. I don't have enough words, and I don't have enough energy. This will have to do. I am tired and don't want to write anymore. I need to get to bed. Tomorrow looks like a long, long day.

# Chapter Twenty-Two

Wednesday, September 22, 1976

8:45 a.m.: My packed bags are by the door and I am waiting for David. Last night he said he would take me to the train. I have been on the phone with Fanny since I got up. As I expected, she feels bad about my leaving. There is nothing I can do to make her feel better. If she carries on about me after I have left, Fanny is going to be a handful for David and Janice.

How strange it will be to stop in Denver and see Hollis, Ruth, and Bev. It is always weird to visit the part of my past that remains in Colorado. Since leaving and being on my own, my life is so much different. Their lives are on Decatur Street and mine is on 14th Street. We have little to hold us together except a thread to that past. I am not sure how Hollis will react when I tell him about meeting Fanny. I told him over the phone before I left San Francisco that I would meet her but in his typical fashion, he said very little. So I expect he will not have much to say. And that is okay. Ruth showed more interest when I told her.

As a result of this trip, I am no longer angry with Hollis. I had always blamed him for what happened and the emotional distance between us didn't help matters. Now I see that it wasn't his fault. Hollis is an honest man. Honesty was one of the values he instilled in me as a child. I never appreciated all that he did for me. I should be more grateful.

Leaving Colchester like they did was likely Cecilia's idea. She had to know the difficulty Fanny was in and she chose to take advantage of it. I believe Cecilia told Hollis that Fanny had given me up to raise as their own and that it was okay to move away.

Two things stand out now from the talk I had with Hollis when I was 16. First, I remember he told me that he didn't ask any questions when I showed up because Cecilia had stopped drinking. He told me he never met Fanny and she confirmed to me that she never met him.

Then there was the story about the two policemen coming to

their house with Leslie's mother three years after she disappeared and how they forcibly took the little boy away from Cecilia. That experience was probably motivation for Cecilia's decision to leave Connecticut with me.

It is all history now and I see no point condemning Cecilia for what she did. I have to believe she loved and cared for me the best she could until she was no longer able.

I don't know if I am better or worse off because of what happened. In the end, it doesn't make any difference. I can't change the history and I doubt the history I have learned is going to change who I am.

By the time I finish my visit to Denver, I will be glad to get home to San Francisco. I miss Rolland a lot, and the cats, too. I dread going back to work. Actually, the bank and all that crap seem light years away. Let it stay that way for a while longer.

I will be glad to get away from the blandness of the Ramada Inn. Even though I am anxious to get home, I am also sad about leaving. I never guessed that I would be feeling like this a week ago. I wish I didn't live so far away.

But I am ready to leave. I regret that I didn't see much of Hartford or other parts of the state. Except for trips to Glastonbury with David and the day in Mystic with Janice and Fanny, I saw little else. But then playing tourist was not the purpose of my trip. It was about solving the big mystery of my life. In that respect this was very productive and successful.

I regret what happened with Mr. Zaldonapolous. I am angry about how it turned out, and disappointed because I still have unanswered questions about my connection to him. He made the choice to back off and I respect that. I wish I knew why, but I don't. He is a closed book unless he chooses to contact me later. I doubt he will.

My time with Fanny more than made up for my disappointment with Mr. Zaldonapolous. I have the satisfaction that I met him. I am glad that we were able to spend a few hours together. I can't say whether I like him or not. I am neutral at this point. That has to do for now. Who knows?

***

9:30 a.m.: I am still at the Ramada Inn. Fanny calls every five minutes. "Is David there?"

He said he would be here by now.

***

10:30 a.m.: David finally called and said, "Sorry, I got tied up." That pisses me off. It's like he doesn't have a clue about what would happen if I missed my train. He promised to meet me at the station. At this point, I don't care. Despite the good things about him, there is a side of David that is inconsiderate and irresponsible. Unless something is important to him, he refuses to give it much thought. If I had to deal with him every day, this behavior would get to me. This may be the source of the frustration and criticism Fanny and Janice have with him.

***

11:45 a.m.: I am on the train and headed home. Janice and Fanny came by and drove me to the train station in the suburb of Berlin. When we got there, I had problems with my ticket and that wasted 20 minutes at the ticket window. David finally did arrive. I was surprised to see he was dressed up, no cut offs, t-shirt, or dirty sneakers. Fanny held it together better than I expected. Her eyes were red from crying before she arrived, but she didn't cry at the station.

The four of us sat on a hard bench in the station waiting for the train. Mostly it was small talk, which kept us occupied so no one broke down. We discussed plans to visit each other. Everyone promised to write in the meantime.

Then over the loudspeaker, "Southbound Springfield Amtrak train for Meriden, Wallingford, and New Haven arrives in three minutes. Change in New Haven for New York and Boston." I gathered up my bags and they walked me to the platform. We had a final round of goodbyes and I hugged each of them. I expected Janice and Fanny to cry, but they didn't. I didn't expect to see David crying, but he did. I held it together and didn't start crying until I

241

started up the train-car stairs and was out of their view. From my seat I watched them on the platform waving good-bye. In an instant the train pulled out of the station.

One week ago they were strangers. Today they are my other family. My head is spinning from the unexpected connection I made with Fanny, Janice, and David. Becoming part of this family was something I never expected.

I am beginning the long trek home in a day coach that may have been new in the 1920s. Whatever springs or suspension the car once had are gone and the ride is awful. At New Haven I change to the train for New York.

David asked me to call his friend, Tommy, when I reached New York. I was surprised when he also asked me to write when I got home. He didn't strike me as someone who would write letters. Fanny shoved an oversized chocolate bar into my hand as I was getting on the train. Once I was seated I saw the attached note: *"Don't give this away. There is a $20 bill under the wrapper. Use it for film. I love you very much. Fanny."* A Chinese restaurant just passed by my window. The red pagoda looked so out of place in the green hills of New England.

\*\*\*

1:30 p.m.: In New York's Penn Station I put my bags into a coin locker and called Tommy without getting an answer. I left the station and walked over to Broadway, but I didn't stay out long. I wasn't in the mood to be pushed along by the Manhattan crowds. After walking three blocks, I decided to trade the excitement of the sidewalks for the security of the train station. I am sorry I didn't make plans to stay here for a couple of days. How often do I get to New York? But right now I am too tired and what I really want to do is get back on the train and head home. Riding can get boring sometimes, but after this last week I could use some boredom.

\*\*\*

6:30 p.m.: The train slowly leaves Philadelphia. I got on the Broadway Limited a couple of hours ago. We will arrive in Chicago late tomorrow morning. I wrote short letters to Janice, Fanny, and David to thank them for all that they did for me.

*\*\**

8:00 p.m.: At the Harrisburg stop, I dashed off the train, ran down a long flight of stairs into the station, out the front door and to the mailbox to mail my letters. Then it was a mad run in reverse back through the station to the train. All the while the thought raced through my mind, "What if the train leaves without me? There goes my suitcase to Chicago and here I am in Harrisburg."

I am in the slumber coach. It is not very clean or comfortable. The only people I imagine who could slumber in this refrigerator-sized compartment would be the dead. I went to the dining car for dinner a while ago. The staff was rude and the food was terrible.

*\*\**

With lots of time to think about this past week, I have so many feelings it is hard to get a handle on any of them for very long. I am drained emotionally and physically. There is a feeling of being in limbo, not at home, not in Connecticut. I am sitting very still while the train is speeding westward.

This trip was a real "trip." I feel like I took a drug, got high, experienced a previously unknown place, and now I am coming down. I am having flashbacks and am really tired.

*\*\**

Thursday, September 23, 1976

9:00 a.m.: The train just pulled into Ft. Wayne, Indiana. Despite not sleeping well, my body is rested but mentally I am still washed out. A quiet week in Denver is welcome. Usually when I go back to visit I end up bored out of my mind in a day or two. I don't know anyone there anymore, like the kids I went to school with, but I enjoy visiting Bev and her children. Since my life in San Francisco doesn't involve kids, I am not used to their continual commotion and there is always plenty of it at her house with her three running around. I usually feel isolated and trapped there because they live out in the suburbs. I am used to walking out my front door and into the middle of a city. Ruth always tells me I am free to take her car. Even if I did, where would I go?

I noticed how much Ruth and Hollis have aged in these past few years. I don't tell anyone this, not even Bev. I am not sure if she is conscious of the changes that I see each time I visit. Ruth and Hollis follow the daily routines that I remember when I was living there. The white house in College View on South Decatur Street looks so much smaller. I don't know how the four of us lived in such a cramped space.

It is hard to believe how much has changed for me in the 13 years since I left to strike out on my own. Sometimes it feels like it's been twice that long. For sure, I am no longer the same 21-year-old who impulsively took off in an old car headed west. I recall my great need to get away. I had no idea where I was going. I know I learned a few things along the way and I had a good time getting there. Looking back, I see that it all turned out the way it was supposed to.

\*\*\*

9:45 a.m.: Looking out the train window, I see apple trees, giant sunflowers, a road repair crew, a swamp, an old asphalt road along the tracks, cornfields, an old cemetery, barns on the horizon, trash and litter along the roadway, a church spire in the distance, all topped off by white puffy clouds in a blue sky. "Welcome to the Mid-West" banners should be posted across the landscape as we pass farms, grain silos, dirt roads, and cows. This dreamy sequence is interrupted when the train speeds over a bridge that spans the chaos of a freeway rushing toward Chicago.

\*\*\*

11:30 a.m.: What a depressing, ugly area around Gary, Indiana. Giant steel mills with tall stacks spew out dark smoke. Immense towers of rusted scrap iron everywhere. Large mountain ranges made of coal spread in every direction. The oppressive industrial picture soon changes to a collection of run-down houses and apartments. This area is as desolate as any of the barren lands in Wyoming and Nevada. But the western desolation is clean and unpolluted.

A metallic smell boarded the train uninvited. Oddly, off in the distance I see one small splotch of bright blue green—the southern shore of Lake Michigan. The color is so out of place here but it offers a glimpse of beauty beyond the gritty and depressing view from the train window.

***

Friday, September 24, 1976

I stayed in Denver for five days. I visited with Hollis and Ruth, and Bev, who lives a few blocks away with her family. After I left home, my relationship with Ruth and Bev greatly improved. Being on my own and becoming an adult had a lot do with this change. However, my relationship with Hollis stayed pretty much the same. He was still the non-talkative man that I remembered. Nevertheless I made a point to go back to Colorado every other year, as they were still my family. As the years passed and they got older, I become more accepting and less critical of them.

I told them about Hartford and what I found there. Ruth seemed more engaged than my father. She asked a lot of thoughtful questions. My father listened quietly but said very little. I wondered if it was because of his age—he was 73. When I saw that Hollis didn't react to what I was telling him, I was not surprised. After our initial conversation, I did not bring up the subject again. I shared more details about my trip with Ruth when Hollis was not present.

My father had never been a very expressive man. Now I saw how shut down emotionally he was. I didn't understand this when I was growing up. Sadly, I know little about the man or his past.

I saw no need to upset him. I had questions that I wanted to ask him but I didn't. Hollis did not do me an injustice when he left Hartford with Cecilia and me. Admittedly, I was angry when I found out he was not my father. But after I was reunited with Fanny, it didn't matter anymore. Remaining angry with him accomplished nothing. What happened is just history.

Before we met, Fanny resented Hollis for leaving Colchester and taking me. She and I had a number of arguments over the phone when she talked bad about him. Of course, I defended him. He was the only father I knew and Fanny was a stranger to me. After our reunion in Hartford she was able to let go of her anger against Hollis. She called Hollis after I was back in San Francisco and thanked him for taking care of me. Despite what he had done, she realized what a fine job he did raising her son. They had several more conversations and she also talked with Ruth. Hollis invited her to Colorado and said that he would like to meet her. Unfortunately, they never met. He died two years later. Fanny told me many times that she regretted putting off the trip.

***

While working on the final revisions to this book, my editor raised a point I had never considered. He was concerned about the legal implications for Hollis, Cecilia, and Fanny in their roles in my disappearance.

In 1932, ten years before I was born, the kidnapping of Charles Lindberg's infant son was a sensational news event. Congress passed the Federal Kidnapping Act ("Lindberg Law") as a result of the tragic outcome, which made transporting a kidnap victim across state lines a federal offense.

When Hollis and Cecilia disappeared from Colchester with Fanny's baby, technically what they did was a federal crime. They took me from Connecticut to Florida. Then after living in Missouri for a short time, they finally settled in Colorado when I was four years old.

Were Hollis and Cecilia aware of the Lindberg Law and how serious a crime they had committed? Even their possible ignorance of the law did not exempt them from it. The Lindberg case was still in the news six years before I was born, when Bruno Hauptmann was executed in 1936 for the kidnapping.

Hollis was never comfortable talking about the past and he seldom did. I always felt awkward asking him personal questions and I avoided doing so. As a result I grew up knowing little about Hollis's past. I learned much more about him from Ruth after his death in 1978.

I now wonder if one of the reasons Hollis had avoided telling me I was not his son was because he was aware he and Cecilia had committed a crime. Surely he must have feared that I would learn the truth about how they had left Connecticut with someone else's baby.

If Fanny was aware that my disappearance might implicate the Sutherlands in a federal crime, she never mentioned anything like this. She wrote in one of her letters that Katarina and Nikos Mykonossos wanted to call the state police when it was clear the Sutherlands had left Colchester. She specifically wrote "state police." It is possible that the Mykonossos' were making the connection with my kidnapping and the Lindberg Law. Fanny begged them not to involve the authorities and in the end they didn't.

Fanny not wanting the police involved had nothing to do with the Lindberg Law. She was afraid of her family and what they would do if they found out about the baby she had been hiding from them. They had threatened in the past to take her three children away from her. Whether or not this could have happened, she still lived in terror of the threat. She may have known about the Lindberg Law but I believe she was too scared to see it having any connection with my disappearance.

After Cecilia disappeared, Hollis shouldered the challenging responsibility of raising me alone, without questioning his role. He wasn't the perfect father but he was the only father I had. I have no doubt that he did the best he could do for me. Whatever good values I have, I learned from him as a child. It is difficult for me to stand in judgment of him for what he and Cecilia did. It is sad to think how much he must have suffered keeping the same secret as Fanny.

In the end it doesn't matter that Hollis and Cecilia may have committed a federal crime. It is an interesting footnote, but it changes nothing in my story or my life today.

# Chapter Twenty-three

[The following was written while I was still in Connecticut. Fanny wrote this letter two days after we had our talk about why I was not married.]

*September 20, 1976*

*My dear Rolland,*

*Even though we have not met, I want to write to you about how I under-stand my son now that I have met him. Many years ago I got married to the first boy that I thought I loved. I was much too young, and like all young people, no one could tell me anything. Looking back at my life with the eyes and experience of an old lady, I understand much more. That is the advantage God gives you for getting old—some smarts for a change.*

*My husband liked to drink and he washed very little. I mean to take a bath. I lived with him for four years like this. My sisters would visit me and see my children and they would say, "How can you live with him?" As soon as my daughter was born, I left my husband. This was in November 1938. I was only 25 and had three kids.*

*In those days, everyone looked down on women with children not liv-ing with their husbands. Even my family considered me a disgrace. But I wanted to be away from him and his drinking so bad that I didn't care what people might think.*

*I knew that no one was going to take care of me and support my children so I went out and got a job. While it may sound sad, I was very happy because I had my children, a job, and a clean, fresh house that did not smell like beer. Just to live in a clean house made me happy. It still does.*

*In the summer of 1940, I met a young man named Jimmy. I found him to be annoying and didn't like him because I thought he was very ugly. He had a rented room in the same apartment house where I lived. Jimmy worked at his brother's diner down the street. I used to see him go to work because when I was out on the porch he had to walk by me. When I saw him coming I ran away. He always tried to talk to me and ask too many questions about my children and where was my husband.*

One day, my good friend Mabel was with me when he left the apartment house for work. She started talking to him. I noticed his clean hands and fingernails. His hair was clean and his teeth were as white as the freshly laundered shirt he wore. He even smelled clean. That was what first attracted me to Jim's father. Jimmy was the only man I ever wanted to marry. When the summer was over, he did not return to New York. I was so happy.

His family hated me and my family hated him. In their eyes I was still married with three children. His friends and family spat at me and called me bad names. But I walked by and held my head up high. Jimmy and I were happy, but I was the disgrace to his family and mine.

Despite the disapproval by our families, those were two of the happiest years of my life. Jimmy was different. He was quiet sometimes, almost like he was sad. I was always happy. One day, my older sister's husband came to my apartment and grabbed me and gave me a beating. I had to stay in bed for two days at Mabel's. That beating made me more afraid of my family. But I thought that as long as I worked and took good care of my children, I could do what I wanted and they could go to hell.

When I told Jimmy that I was going to have a baby, he panicked. He didn't know what to do. Because of my big mouth we started fighting. The last time I saw him was when I kicked him out of my apartment and told him never to come back. This was a perfect opening for him to get out of this mess. Jimmy must have gone through hell because of me.

In the months that I carried Jim, I worked. He was born and then I ran from place to place trying to hide him from my father and sisters. There is such pain in my heart when I think back to the time after Jim was born.

When I saw Jim for the first time, I recognized him immediately. I did not have to look at any pictures to know that this young man was my son. I walked over to his table and my heart was pounding so hard I thought I might faint. I stood in front of his table. He jumped up and said, "Frances?" I nodded my head as tears poured out of my eyes. He put his arms around me and I think he began to cry also.

In those few seconds, the years of wondering what had happened to my fat baby vanished. Here was a young man that I did not know, but he belonged to me. I wish I could make you understand how I felt at that moment.

In the few days that I have been with Jim, it is like I have known him all my life. It is like I was never away from him. It is so odd to have my son back and there is so much about him I do not know. There is much about *me that he does not know. I can't explain how confusing this is for me. I know Janice and David like a book. But Jim, who is my flesh and blood, is like someone I don't know. Yet I see his face and know he is my son. I watch him and listen to him and I think back to his father. I wish there was some way to tell you how I feel, but I don't think I can make anyone understand what is going through my mind.*

*Jim answered my many questions about his life and how he grew up, but I was bothered by something. One night I called him at the hotel and I told him that I wanted to ask him a question and that we should be alone when I did. Jim didn't seem to be bothered with my request and said, "Whenever you want, we will sit here in my room and you can ask your question."*

*The next day Janice took me to the hotel. I was shaking as I went to his room. He came to the door, smiling his smile that reminded me of his father. I was trembling and his smile disappeared.*

*Rolland, this is very difficult because I do not know you. But I must tell you about this talk. "Why aren't you married?" I blurted out. Jim did not hesitate, "I am gay." At first I didn't know what the hell he was talking about. I am an old lady and never heard someone say "gay" and mean what Jim meant. I was shocked when he told me what he meant. It was then that he told me about you and how important you are in his life.*

*I was not happy about what he told me. Of course, I had many questions for him and he answered every one without apologizing or making excuses. I told him that I wanted him to change and I cried a lot.*

*At some point, Jim got tired of me crying and he said, "Frances, I am not going to change. I am happy with who I am and how I live."*

*He looked at me with big, brown sad eyes that I know so well. I think I was crying but it did not move Jim. He just sat there quietly.*

*Rolland, as I think about what Jim told me, I realize that even if I had brought him up he wouldn't be any different. Who knows? I want him to be happy. He is the only one who knows how he wants to live. If he is happy, then I am happy. I cry because he does not live near me and I missed so much not raising him. He has missed a lot by not being here, but he does not feel that way. He wants to get back to his home with you in California.*

*Jim is more like me than my other children. I can hardly believe it sometimes. Not only because he doesn't give a damn about what other people say, but also because of his eyes. His eyes are like mine. The rest of his face is like Jimmy, but there is no mistaking the eyes. When he talks he rolls them around like I do and they look like they will pop out of his head, just like mine. Jim's father said to him when they met the other afternoon, "You have eyes like your mother." I am glad Jim told me because it made me feel good to think that there was at least one thing that his father remembered about me.*

*Rolland, I hope this letter has brought you some understanding about me. I am sure Jim will tell you a lot of things about me. But I wanted you to hear about me from me. I also want you to know that even though I do not know you, I feel like I love you like another son. If my oldest son had lived, he would be your age. I know how important you are in Jim's life and you are just as important to me. I feel very good inside now that I have written this letter to you.*

*Love,*
*Frances*

\*\*\*

[Fanny wrote this second letter to Rolland a few days later when I was visiting Hollis and Ruth.]

*September 24, 1976*

*Dear Rolland,*

*I don't know when Jim will be home but I want you to give him these lottery tickets. He bought them as we were leaving a jai alai game. He didn't win any money but he had the right color so he will be entered into a drawing for a new car. I don't buy lottery tickets because I have such rotten luck. If I do buy one, I give it to my son-in-law Stanley. I would rather see a young person win the money. I don't give them to David, only to Stanley. He is a wonderful son-in-law and appreciates me when I do little things for him.*

*I finally figured out that Jim fits in between Janice and David. He talks with his hands just like Janice. He can be quiet and foxy like David when he doesn't want to tell you something.*

*I promised Jim that I would not cry at the train station and I didn't. I was happy to see him go because I could tell he was anxious to get home. He looked at me like I would cry because he was leaving. But I am a lot tougher than he thinks. However, I don't think he noticed that when David turned away, his eyes filled with tears. This surprised me. When we left the station, David went straight to his car and never said good-bye to Janice and me. Once we were in the car, Janice started to cry. All my children are sensitive.*

*I feel better since I met Jim. I am no longer afraid like I was when I received that first letter. I do miss him already, but what can I do? He has his life and it is clear the hell out on the other side of the country. How did my fat baby end up out there, I will never understand. He talks about his family in Colorado and wants me to meet them. I don't want to. In fact, when he talks about them, I like him less.*

*I am jealous because they raised him and I didn't. But whose fault was that? I should be thankful that they took care of him and he grew up to be a fine man. But I can't. It was my fault and I am paying for it by not having him with me. I am selfish to feel this way but it is just the way I am. I don't care how many mothers Jim has he is still mine. I cried so much when I thought about him and wondered what happened. Now we have met and I am still crying. His visit did not make the tears go away.*

*He must be freezing in Colorado. I am glad that I bought him a wool sweater while he was here. If only that boy could fly.*

*I wish you could meet my daughter. You cannot believe how good she is to me. Janice is wonderful to everyone. However, she has a habit of being late when she says she will pick me up. Sometimes this drives me crazy. The morning Jim was leaving, she was supposed to pick him up at the hotel, but as usual she was late. We drove in and Jim was pacing outside the front door. She laughed and said, "See, Mother? He walks back and forth like you do when you have to wait." I tell you, Rolland, when she is late I go out of my mind. I get so angry that I think my eyes are going to pop out of my head.*

*When they were younger, Janice and David had red eyes from dust and pollen at certain times of the year. They rubbed their eyes until I took them to the doctor. I did not go with Janice and Stanley when they picked Jim up at the station because I was so nervous. After they dropped him at the hotel, Janice called me. "Mother, his eyes are red and bloodshot like mine and David's." That was the first thing Janice noticed about how he looked like her—bloodshot eyes. She also said that he moves quickly, just like me.*

*When Mabel met him, she made me mad because she kept saying to Jim, "You have to leave California and move to Connecticut. You have to be near your mother in her old age." She kept talking like that to him. I wanted her to shut up but nothing would make me happier than to have him close. But who am I to tell him what to do with his life or where to live? He will never leave the West Coast. He loves it there.*

*Mabel also told him about the bad times that we had when she and I were young girls. Rolland, I did not like that one bit. But Jim listened to everything she said. She is a wonderful person and I am so glad that she accepted Jim. But I wish she would not tell him everything.*

*Well, Rolland, Jim is going to have plenty to tell you about when he gets home. You will probably think we are crazy as hell, running around and fighting and yelling at each other all the time, but we love one another no matter how it might look to the outside. Despite what Jim tells you, believe that we are happy.*

*I cannot tell you how happy I am. I feel like someone gave me a million dollars. No one will know how I felt when Jim put his arms around me. It was like a big unhappy pressure I had bottled up inside was released. If I died tomorrow, I would be happy and at peace.*

*Good night, Rolland. Even though we have never met, if my son loves you, I love you too.*

> *Love,*
> *Fanny*

***

[I received this letter a few days after I got back to San Francisco.]

*September 28, 1976*

*Dear Jim,*

*I am glad that you enjoyed your week here with your new family. Janice was disappointed because we didn't show you much of Connecticut. I told her next time you come we won't talk so much and show you around. We did spend a lot of time learning about each other and that was more important to me than looking at some old buildings.*

*Thank you for the necklace with the jasper stone. It's hard for me to remember the name of the stone. You probably thought I was a dumbbell because I kept asking what kind of stone it was. I wrote it down and that's how I remember. I wore it to the wedding and a lot of people asked me about it. I wore a low cut dress and the necklace looked nice. Janice had a fit every time someone tried to touch it.*

*And thank you for the soapstone jewelry box. I had no place to put my earrings and now I have a place to keep them. The box is on my dresser and the necklace in there too.*

*Jim, don't worry about me getting down about you returning to your home. I feel differently about you since we have met. I was disappointed at how your father acted with you. I spent many years hating Jimmy and I'm lucky that we never married because I could never live with a man so cold. He must have no feelings to have treated you so badly.*

*When I saw you, I finally forgave Jimmy in my heart. Now let God forgive him. You must know that he cannot forget you after he has seen you. He may have tried in the past but now he will carry your image to his grave. I see a bit of him in you, so he isn't that bad. Jimmy will remember your meeting no matter how short it was. Who knows why he changed his mind about taking you to Mystic. Maybe when he saw that you did not come here to hurt him, he did not need to see you again. Who knows?*

*I will call the Sutherlands and talk to Ruth and Hollis someday. I know this is important to you but I need time. I was jealous when you spoke about your family in Colorado. But I was wrong to feel that way. It was not Ruth's fault that she raised you, but I do not forgive Cecilia. In the end I have only myself to blame. If I had not left you with her, she would not have taken you away.*

*As for accepting you as you are and the other things you told me, all I can say is that you are my son. How can I not accept you? As long as you are happy, I do not worry. What counts is that you are a fine young man and I love you.*

*Janice and David call me every day wanting to know if I am okay. They suspect what you told me, but like I promised I said nothing. I have to admit that I don't understand everything about your choice. People talked about this when I was working and I never paid any attention. I was young once and did what I damn well pleased and if someone didn't like it, I said, "Go to hell." The afternoon that we talked, I knew that you were my son. You are lucky that you don't have to answer to anyone about how you live.*

*I am sad that you are not living closer so that I could see you more often. In a way, God has played a cruel trick on me. He gave my son back but only for once in a while. You would not be happy here because you have lived out west for too long. I have spent half of my life in tears over you. Sometimes it seems like nothing went my way. Did I deserve the bad things that happened? Was I that bad?*

*Jim, I want you to be happy in whatever you do. Know that I love you and Rolland even though I never met him. He must be a wonderful man or you would not be living with him. I am happy that you have someone to share your life with. I wish David were not alone.*

*About that $20 bill I put in the candy wrapper. I wanted to put in a $50 bill but I was afraid you might not see it and throw it away. Anyway, I am glad I kept the $50 because I bought you a present instead. Don't get mad. I promise, no more presents. Besides, it was on sale. Nothing gives me more joy than to buy for my children and my grandchildren. I always give them something and it doesn't have to be Christmas.*

*I buy for David because he has no one for him like Janice, who has Stanley. David calls and tells me he is freezing, so I went out and bought him an electric blanket. No one knows, but if I think he is broke, I slip him $20. And when I am broke, he gives me $10. I have been thinking about who I love more, you or David. I can't make up my mind. I know David would like to get away from me sometimes because I can be so hard on him. I wish he went away and figured out what the hell he is doing. He does not want to hurt me or Janice and I know that is why he says, "Yes, Ma. Yes, Janice."*

*Actually, David should marry Mrs. Blackstone. He spends all his time with that old lady anyway. He likes her and would do anything for her. When I tell Janice he should marry Mrs. Blackstone, she says, "Mother, have you lost your mind?" If he did I would laugh and laugh because I think he would be happy.*

*Well, I need to get off my rump and clean this house and iron the clothes. I love you, I love your beard, I love your big feet, I love your hands, and I love the way you talk to me, and how concerned you are about how I feel. I hope you had a good time with your family in Colorado. When you get home to San Francisco, I want you to rest because you are going to need it.*

> *Love to you and Rolland,*
> *Mother (take it or leave it!)*

*P.S. I hate Christmas because I get very depressed. My birthday is December 31 and I remember that horrible night when Jimmy walked out of my apartment. I was very angry because of the baby I was carrying. When I played ball games at school, I could never hit anything. But that night I hit him with the birthday cake perfectly on the back of his head. He never looked back, just walked out with cake falling off of his head and down his black coat.*

*I spent years hating him but things are different since you are back in my life. I still don't like Christmas but maybe this year I won't be so sad. I might go away.*

***

*October 4, 1976*

*Dear Jim,*

*Last night when you called, I was happy to know you are back home. I was relieved because I wondered where you were. I could not get over how concerned you were about me. You kept asking if I was okay.*

*I am very happy about the week you were here and how you looked and how nicely you were dressed. You were so clean—just like your no-good Greek father. I was glad to know you aren't a lush either. You drank wine but not very much. I like that you spoke what was on your mind. And most of all, I was glad that you are a gentleman. I could tell that Mr. Sutherland brought you up in a very good way.*

*I could go on about the things that pleased me. I will never forget seeing you for the first time at the hotel. I thought I was going to die right then and there. Then I thought, "No, I can't die yet. I haven't had a chance to talk to him." I think you were in shock too.*

*I made an appointment with a psychiatrist for next week. Don't get upset. Janice said not to tell you or you will wonder what is wrong. Why shouldn't you know how I feel?*

*After you left, I thought back to Ash Street and the times that I spent with Jimmy. I cannot get him out of my mind. He is there all the time. I can see that damn skinny Greek staring at me. I hope he is haunted for the rest of his life for not being nicer when you were here. I have so much anger toward him. I want to see a doctor and talk about how I feel. I want to forget that man. That may be impossible because every time I see you or your picture, I see him too.*

*Mabel says when I get the bill from the psychiatrist, I will go into such shock that it will make me forget your father. She's nuts. She has never been* to a psychiatrist so what the hell does she know. Neither have I. The appointment is next week so I will think about it until then. I may change my mind if I feel better.

I am happy you are home and I am sure Rolland is glad that you are back. He has been on my mind. He was quiet when I spoke to him on the phone and I love the way he listens when I talk. He doesn't interrupt me like you. Even though I have never met him, I feel like he is my son too. I want to meet him someday. Because Rolland is a big part of your life, it is like he came along with you. Neither of you could replace Billy or Doug, but you fill up the lonely place that has been with me since they died. I am afraid to tell anyone this or they will think I have lost my mind. When I see the psychiatrist, I will tell him.

When you told me you were coming to see me, I thought that it would be like Billy had come back to life. I don't know why but I did for a long time. But when I saw you and listened to you and touched your hand I knew you weren't Billy. You were a different boy. I will tell the doctor these thoughts too.

Your coming back to me has brought up a lot of memories. Not all of them are bad. Some are very good and I like them. Regardless, I am happy that you returned.

I am going to come out to California to see you and Rolland sometime next year. Boy, will my sisters flip out when they hear. They don't know about you and I am not sure I will tell them. They always watched me when I was young. Now that I am old they still have their hawk eyes on me all the time. Fanny in California will drive them crazy because they won't know why I went there.

None of my family has been that far out west. We usually vacation in Florida, so we never get off the East Coast. Janice wants to come with me when I visit you. The only thing is she doesn't like to fly. But I cannot see me taking a train because I would be worn out by the time we got there. Don't forget, I am an old lady. Let Janice take the train. I have to fly. Next year is a long ways off. I will think about it then.

It was a breeze talking to Mr. Sutherland. He may be old but he still has all of his marbles. I am not on the ball like I used to be but somehow I manage. I had a lot of questions about what kind of a boy you were. But he wanted to know about me. Maybe he took me for some kind of bum because I left you with Cecilia. I never met him on those trips I made to Colchester. After a while he seemed to change his attitude toward me and asked what

*I looked like and if you looked like me. He wanted to know the color of my eyes and my hair and how tall I was. I told him I looked like a toothless old hag and he laughed. He said that I sounded like you. I can't remember everything we talked about but we talked for about an hour. He told me to call him back and I will. Maybe I will go to Colorado so I can thank him for raising you to be such a fine young man.*

*Now I am tangled up in something else I didn't tell you about. I have this friend in Virginia named Steve. He is my age and we have known each other for many years. He used to live in Connecticut but he moved to Virginia some time ago. He calls and asks me to come visit him. I hadn't heard from him in a long time. To get my mind on something else, I called Steve. What a mistake. He is a pest because he kept saying, "When are you coming to visit?" If I could get Mabel to go with me I might go. But I have to pay her way because she doesn't have any money.*

*He knows Mabel and thinks she is a dimwit for staying married to Tony. He said, "Why do you want to bring Mabel?" I told him she is a lonely person and she never gets to go on vacation. He said, "Bring her here and I will fix her up with Rip Van Winkle." What the hell is he talking about?*

*I might go at Christmas. He is very fresh and told me that I had better not have gotten fat. I haven't seen him in 30 years. Boy will he be surprised. I told him that I looked like a witch with no teeth. He said, "Then stay home." I love fighting with him. Anyway, I am sorry I called because he will pester me about when I am going to Virginia. I should keep my mouth shut.*

*Tell Rolland that I send him my love. And again, it was so good to talk to you.*

*Love,*
*Fanny*


*P.S. Here is $5 for you to*
*buy your cats some cat candy.*


This was not the last letter from Fanny. It is letter number 54 of the 968 letters I received over the next 22 years. The rest of the letters chronicle our developing mother/son relationship. Fanny traveled to San Francisco with Janice to see Rolland and me in the spring of 1977. The visit was followed by many more Fanny made over the years until her death in 1998. David came to San Francisco a few years later. Remarkably he drove out west and then back to Hartford in his beat up van. He threw a large mattress and blankets in the back, and Bea, his St. Bernard, made the trip with him.

# Epilogue

The April morning I pushed David in his wheelchair into the woods was the first day I began reading this book to him. Thirty years had passed since my first visit to Connecticut when I met Fanny, Janice, and David.

One of David's crazy dreams had been to get out of the city and live in the country someday. Thanks to an inheritance from his friend, Mrs. Blackstone, this dream came true. She passed away a few years after my visit. With the money she left him, he purchased 14 acres of woods near Lebanon, Connecticut and built a house at the edge of the trees. It was always a struggle financially to hang on but he managed. He lived there quite happily for over 25 years, but not alone. During that time he rescued countless numbers of homeless cats and dogs. These neglected and sometimes abused animals found a loving and permanent home with him in the woods. At one time, he even took in an abandoned llama he named Penny.

The stone foundation in the woods where we sat that day was one of his favorite spots. It was a peaceful setting where I could read to him. I could not read the entire manuscript to him in one day. In the weeks that followed, whenever I came to visit I brought the three-ring binder. If he was up to it, we went into the woods and I read another chapter or two.

David never said much after I finished reading a chapter. Usually, he smiled and said, "That's very nice." He never asked questions like I expected. I glanced at him a number of times while I was reading to see his reaction. Sometimes he was gazing out into space as he listened, often with a smile on his face. Did he visualize what I was reading? Did a passage bring back some of his own memories of our mother?

Later, I went with him to the hospital while he received his chemo treatments and read to him while he had tubes in his arms waiting for the medicine to drip into his veins. It was a slow process. I hoped the reading would help get his mind off what he had to endure.

By the time I came to the end of the manuscript, David was

confined to his house because he was very ill. I read the last chapter to him a week before he went into the hospital for the last time. I still did not know what he thought because he had not offered any opinion. When I closed the binder for the last time, I asked, "Well, what do you think? Is there anything I should change?" He looked at me from where he sat in the living room. He smiled and softly said, "Don't change one thing. It is perfect, just the way you read it."

David made an important contribution to this story. His illness motivated me to leave Oregon and move to Connecticut. We spent a great deal of time together. We talked about how different our lives had been because we grew up apart. We wondered about what might have been and the opportunities we had missed. David told me what it was like to grow up as Fanny's child, and I shared with him what it was like to become Fanny's child at age 34.

We were half-brothers who met when he was 32 and I was 34, and we remained connected for the next 30 years. We made visits back and forth across the country and kept in touch by telephone and letters. I began writing my story as a result of the conversations I had with David during his illness and re-visiting Fanny's letters. I could never have written this without both experiences.

After David passed away, I returned to the West Coast. The manuscript was packed up and put away. A year and a half went by before I looked at it again. When I re-read the pages, I realized that writing this story about finding my birth family was a form of therapy for me. Writing helped me cope with the pain and helplessness I felt as I dealt with my brother's illness.

I have many memories of David during his last year. Some of those are difficult to relive now that he is gone. Others are easier. The memories I value most are of the quiet times I spent reading to him from this book about our mother.

# *Acknowledgements*

While I wrote the story, I cannot claim all the credit for turning *Love, Your Mother—Like It or Not* into a book. I had help and I am happy to acknowledge it here.

Thank you to my friend Corbett Gordon, who on seeing the first draft offered encouragement and convinced me that I could turn my manuscript into a book.

Thank you to my friend Sittrea Friberg for her immediate grasp of what I was trying to write and for spending many hours reading countless drafts. Her invaluable suggestions and sense of humor are greatly appreciated.

Thank you to another friend, Trina Robbins. Seeing a later version, she said, "Great start but you really need an editor. Get a copy of *The Dog Walked Down the Street: An Outspoken Guide for Writers Who Want to Publish* by Sal Glynn." I did, and later contacted the author.

Thank you to Sal Glynn, my editor. Sal's patience and editing skills helped me turn a bulky and unruly manuscript into a real book. I learned much about writing and editing from him in the process.

Thank you to my trusted readers, Paul Iarrobino, Corbett Gordon, Jim Friberg, and my sister Janice, for critiquing the final manuscript. Your feedback helped me with the finishing touches.

Finally, thank you to all my friends and family who waited patiently. I hope *Love, Your Mother—Like It or Not* is worth the wait.